Geo. W. Armstrong

The Zionists

&

The third Zionist War

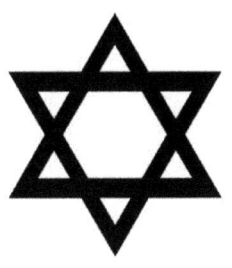

OMNIA VERITAS

Geo. W. Armstrong

The Zionists
&
The third Zionist war

1950

Published by
Omnia Veritas Ltd

OmniaVeritas

www.omnia-veritas.com

THE ZIONISTS 15

PETITION 17

PREFACE 19
1. 21

THE JEWS 21

KHAZAR JEWS 22
ASHKENAZI JEWS 23
INTERNATIONAL BANKER JEWS 24
ZIONISM 28
MARTIN LUTHER 30
BARUCH AND FRANKFURTER 34
THE CONVICTION OF THE ELEVEN COMMUNIST TRAITORS 37

2. 41

THE TALMUD 41

TALMUD SUPPRESSED 42
TALMUD IS VICIOUS 44
JEWISH INTOLERANCE AND HATE 44
TALMUD SHOULD BE DISCARDED 45
TALMUD CONDEMNED BY CATHOLIC CHURCH 46

3. 49

PROTOCOLS 49
THE ZIONIST PLAN 54

Extract from Protocol 1 54

The zionist system bribery, deceit, ... 56
murder and terror 56
Extract from Protocol 3 57
Extract from protocol 5 58
Extract from Protocol 10 59
Zionist power 61
extract from protocol 1 61
Extract from Protocol 2 62
Extract from Protocol 7 63
Extract from Protocol 8 63
Extract from Protocol 12 64
Extract from Protocol 20 64
Zionist "brotherhood" 65
extract from protocol 9 65
Extract from Protocol 11 66
THE DESTRUCTION OF 67
THE CHRISTIAN RELIGION 67
Extract from Protocol 17 67
"ZIONIST POPE OF THE UNIVERSE" 67
ZIONIST ACHIEVEMENT 68

4 .... **69**

WOODROW WILSON 69

PRESIDENT WILSON WAS A JEW 70
PERSONAL NOTE 72
LEAGUE OF NATIONS 75
FEDERAL RESERVE SYSTEM 76

5 .... **79**

FIRST WORLD WAR 79

J. P. MORGAN & CO. 84
ARE BRITISH AGENTS 84
BRITISH DUPLICITY 85
LEAGUE OF NATIONS 87
PRESIDENT WILSON'S PECULIARITIES 90
PROPAGANDA 91
BRITISH-AMERICAN UNION URGED 93

6. 95

PALESTINE AND THEODOR HERZL 95

MINERAL WEALTH OF DEAD SEA 95
A GIGANTIC STEAL 98
TEODOR HERZL 99
KAISER WILHELM INTERESTED 101
NEGOTIATES WITH SULTAN OF TURKEY 103
HERZL INTERVIEWS CHAMBERLIN AND ROTHSCHILD . 107
BARON ROTHSCHILD OF PARIS WAS ORIGINAL ZIONIST
PROMOTER 111
HERZL'S DIFFICULTIES 112
HERZL'S SUCCESS 114
WEALTH OF PALESTINE 116
DOES NOT BELONG TO ZIONISTS 116

7. 117

AUTOBIOGRAPHY OF RABBI STEPHEN S. WISE 117

RABBI WISE WAS A COMMUNIST TRAITOR 118
ZIONISTS DISSATISFIED WITH BRITISH MANDATE 120
ZIONISTS INITIATED SECOND WORLD WAR FOR
PALESTINE 121
RABBI WISE URGED PACKING SUPREME COURT 122

BRANDEIS' HOME PEOPLE REGARDED HIM AS SHYSTER
AND CHARLATAN 125
LLOYD GEORGE ALSO "SHYSTER, CHARLATAN," AND
ZIONIST STOOGE 126
PRESIDENT WILSON AUTHOR OF BALFOUR
DECLARATION 128
COMMUNISTS SHOULD BE LIQUIDATED 129

8. 131

FRANKLIN D. ROOSEVELT WAS A TRAITOR 131

PACKING THE SUPREME COURT 132
BANKING ACT OF 1935 133
CORRUPTION OF THE COURTS 134
"NO BIBLE TEACHING HERE" 135
THE CORRUPTION OF CONGRESS 136
HILLMAN WAS A ZIONIST COMMUNIST 138
FDR RESPONSIBLE FOR 138
PEARL HARBOR DEBACLE 138
INSTIGATED WAR 140
TO ESTABLISH COMMUNISM 140
COMMUNISM 140
RESTORE CONSTITUTIONAL GOVERNMENT 141
THE IDEAL ZIONIST "RULER" 142
REVERSE THE ROOSEVELT-TRUMAN PROGRAM 144

9. 145

IS HARRY SOLOMON TRUMAN ALSO A TRAITOR? 145

THE WELFARE STATE 149
RECONSTRUCTION FINANCE CORPORATION 149

VICE-PRESIDENT BARKLEY ENDORSES THE ROOSEVELT-TRUMAN PROGRAM 150
ATOMIC BOMB AND H BOMB 151
DISPLACED PERSONS 152
THE CRUCIAL TEST OF LOYALTY OF YOUR SENATORS 154
GERMAN EXPELLEES 155
TRAITORS 158
WE ARE ENTITLED TO "THE TRUTH, THE WHOLE TRUTH AND NOTHING BUT THE TRUTH". 160
ADDENDUM APRIL 26, 1950 162
WAR 162
THE ARABS 163
HOLY LAND CHRISTIAN COMMITTEE 163

10. 167

ZIONIST VICTORY AND THE NUREMBERG TRIAL 167

CHURCHILL PROPHECIES WORLD BOLESHEVISM 169
CHURCHILL'S PROPHECY VERIFIED 169
PROPOSED CABINET OF WORLDEMPEROR 170
BOLSHEVIK BRUTALITY 171
VINDICTIVE PEACE SETTLEMENT 173
PRISONERS 174
REPORT OF TRIAL 175
MALMEDY TRIAL 177

11. 179

WAR CRIMINALS 179

HANG THE CONSPIRATORS AND BANISH THE TRAITORS 179

ROOSEVELT BROUGHT ABOUT PEARL HARBOR DISASTER 180
NUREMBERG TRIAL 182
MORGENTHAU-ZIONIST HATE PROGRAM 184
REPORT OF HERTER INVESTIGATING COMMITTEE 185
HANG THE TRAITORS AND BANISH THE COMMUNISTS 189
APPROPRIATE THE MINERALS OF THE DEAD SEA 191

12. 195

MARSHALL & LEVITSKY PLAN 195

BRITISH LOAN 196
JOKERS 198

13. 201

UNITED NATIONS 201

ATLANTIC PACT 202
GENOCIDE CONVENTION 203
WORLD FEDERALIST UNION, INC. 204
COMMUNIST ENDORSEMENT 207
ISRAELI 207

THIRD ZIONIST WAR 209

PETITION 211

BRIEF AND ARGUMENT 213
1. 215

THIRD ZIONIST WAR 215

THE ZIONISTS OF NEW YORK AND MOSCOW
INSTIGATED THE WAR 215
WHY THIS WAR? 216
CHINESE NATIONALISTS 217

2. 219

THE PRESIDENT'S MESSAGE OF JULY, 19, 1950 219

"POLICE ACTION" 221
IT IS IN FACT A THIRD WAR TO PROMOTE A ZIONIST
EMPIRE 222
WAS OUR DEFEAT PLANNED BY TRAITORS? 225
UNDECLARED WAR 225
COMMUNISM OR FREEDOM 227

3. 231

UNITED NATIONS A SHAM AND A FRAUD 231

GENOCIDE CONVENTION 232
THE CELEBRATION 234
"AMBASSADOR" DULLES 236

4. 239

THE FIRST TRAP 239

5. 243

DOUGLAS MacARTHUR, SOLDIER AND PATRIOT 243

THE TRUMAN-MacARTHUR WAKE ISLAND CONFERENCE
.... 247

6 .... **249**

   POLITICS 249

      ISOLATIONISTS *250*
      ELECTION RESULTS *251*
      THE TRUMAN PROGRAM *252*

7 .... **257**

   SABOTAGE 257

      OR WAS IT "PLANNED THAT WAY"? *257*
      GERMANY *259*
      LEHMAN *261*
      DUAL CITIZENSHIP *263*
      GEORGE C. MARSHALL *264*
      Secretary of Defense *264*

8 .... **265**

   VETO OF INTERNAL SECURITY ACT 265

      PERVERSION OF INTERNAL SECURITY ACT *268*

9 .... **271**

   THE SECOND TRAP 271

      GENERAL IKE EISENHOWER *272*
      EISENHOWER'S REPORT TO CONGRESS *273*
      AMERICAN TROOPS TO EUROPE *274*
      STALIN'S THREAT *276*
      BOMB RUSSIA *276*

THE WELFARE STATE 277

10. .... **279**

DICTATORSHIP 279

PRICE AND WAGE CONTROL 279
MOBILIZATION PLAN 282
USURPATION OF POWER 283
IMPEACHMENT AND PROSECUTION 284
INDICTMENT 285

11. .... **289**

ZIONISTS 289

ZIONIST DEPRESSIONS 290
IMPORTANCE OF VOLUME OF MONEY IN CIRCULATION 291
BANISH THE ZIONISTS 292
INDICTMENT 293
THE ANTI-NAZI LEAGUE 295
LIARS AND TRAITORS 301
TRY THE ZIONISTS 302
TREASON AND TRAITORS 303
THE ROTHSCHILDS AND THEIR AGENTS SHOULD BE EXECUTED AND THEIR ILL-GOTTEN GAINS CONFISCATED 304
WAKE UP! 305

12. .... **307**

ISOLATIONISM 307

WASHINGTON' S FAREWELL ADDRESS *311*

THE ZIONISTS

GEORGE W. ARMSTRONG

PETITION

To the President and Congress of the United States
Gentlemen:

I respectfully represent:

1. That the Zionists seek to destroy our republican form of government and to establish a socialist government in place of it; (2) that they have involved us in two world wars in pursuance of this plan; (3) that they seek to acquire the fabulous wealth of the Dead Sea estimated at five trillion dollars, and of the Arabian oil fields estimated at six hundred billion dollars; (4) that this wealth belongs to us and the British Empire by right of conquest; (5) that the Zionists are traitors and should be punished as such.

(a) I allege that a majority of the immigrants who have entered our country since the First World War are socialists and communists; (b) I allege upon information and belief that Herbert H. Lehman, Felix Frankfurter and several Congressmen and other officials are Zionist communists and citizens of the State of Israeli.

Geo. W. Armstrong.

April 29, 1950.

GEORGE W. ARMSTRONG

PREFACE

The first part of this book was published several months ago under the title of "Zionist Wall Street." It was intended only as a preview. These chapters will not be repeated but only supplemented. The Zionists of Wall Street are the financial backers of the Zionists of the world and of the Zionist state of Israeli. They are the head and front of the Zionist political organizations. They created the state of Israeli and they brought about two wars for that purpose.

The Zionists are anti-Christ and have been since His crucifixion. They are as much so now as they were then. They are communists. They would crucify our Savior Jesus Christ today if he stood in the way of their schemes. They attempt to deceive us by assuming Christian names, e.g. Winchell for Lipschitz, and by their so-called "brotherhood" campaign: a rabbi, a protestant preacher, and a Catholic priest working jointly. They proclaim a brotherhood week. They preach tolerance but they practice intolerance.

Their motives are greed and power. They seek to acquire the wealth of the world and to enslave the gentiles. They claim that they are "God's chosen people" and that He promised them that they should rule the world. They are taught this falsehood by their Talmud and their rabbis. They seek to destroy all gentiles and all governments that interfere with their plans. Wars and depressions are necessary to accomplish these purposes and so we have wars and depressions. They always win and the gentiles (goi) always lose.

The Zionist Jews will denounce this booklet as anti-Semitic and me as an intolerant anti-Semite. I am anti-Semitic only to the extent that the Jews are anti-Christ and anti-American. I am no more antiSemitic than was our Lord and Saviour Jesus Christ who denounced the Zionists as idolaters, liars, thieves, and murderers.

I know their history and understand their purposes. I have tried to tell the truth about them without bias or prejudice, and without fear. They are intolerant and vindictive. I realize that I may be persecuted, but if this booklet is of service to my country, I will cheerfully accept the punishment.

There are a few tolerably good Jews but they are mostly of Sephardic origin, as were Benjamin Disraeli and Woodrow Wilson, and not of the Khazar tribe who are of Mongolian origin, as are the Rothschilds. It is estimated that 85% of the American Jews are of Khazar or Ashkenazi origin and that only 15% of all Jews are of Sephardic origin, which is about the percentage of good Jews.

The purposes of this book are two-fold: (1) to bring about the trial and conviction of the traitors who have involved us in four depressions and two wars, and to thereby restore our solvency; (2) the repeal of section one of the 14th and 15th amendments to our National Constitution and the limitation of the 16th, and to thereby preserve constitutional government. I intend to devote my fortune, which I hope may be a considerable one, to the accomplishment of these purposes.

Geo. W. Armstrong

April 29, 1950.

1.

THE JEWS

The problem of the Jew has faced every nation throughout all history. In the settlement of that problem the Jew has been driven out of every Christian country in which he has been domiciled. It is now the turn of the United States to face that problem, for the Jews are determined, not only to make their last stand here, but they hope to take us over, —lock, stock and barrel. The fact is that Zionism is the No. 1 problem before the world today. Solve that problem, eliminate the Zionists from politics — local, national and international — and civilization will take a long step forward and the problem of establishing world peace can be undertaken with every hope of success.

There are three tribes of Jews, viz: the Ashkenazim, Sephardim, and Khazars. The Ashkenazim and Khazars are of northern Europe and southern Russia, and the Sephardim are of southern Europe and Asia, and northern Africa. The three tribes have the same religion, tribal customs and general characteristics; all of them are governed by their rabbis and their Talmud. In every country and in every age they have been money lenders and traders.

The orthodox Jews or Zionists are ambitious for dominance over the Christians and they have obtained it through the power of their money. Generally speaking, they control and from early times have controlled the banking systems, the transportation systems, news agencies and press of the world. They are exceedingly clannish and are always a cell within the nation in which they reside; they do not assimilate. Originally the Sephardims were the richest and most cultured tribe; many of them married Christians and became Christians (Marranos). (A Christian Jew is called a "Marrano.") With the rise of the Rothschild power, the Ashkenazim and Khazars became the dominant tribes.

KHAZAR JEWS

The Jews that govern Russia and seek to govern the world are of Ashkenazim or Khazar origin. Palestine was never their home: it is doubtful if the Khazars are in fact Jews. The Encyclopedia Britannica[1] states that,

"They (the Khazars) are assigned to the Turkish stock by Latham and Haworth, to the Ugrian by Klaprath and have even been claimed as Jews on account of their use of the Hebrew character and the profession of Hebrew faith among them."

It further states that,

"The Khazars were an historic figure on the borderland between Europe and Asia for at least 900 years (190-1100 A.D.) ... Their home was in the spurs of the Caucasus and along the shores of the Caspian, and their cities, all of them populous and civilized commercial centers, were upon the delta of the Volga, the river of the Khazars."

They were overrun by the Mohammedans who claim to be the descendants of Ishmael. They are probably hybrid Ishmael-ites and to that extent only are they the "seed of Abraham." They are communists and the most backward of

---

[1] Vol. 14, page 39.

the three tribes. It is reported that the Jews that have recently settled in Palestine are atheists and communists. The Bolsheviks have been transporting them to Palestine and secretly supplying them with arms, and directing their war against the Arabs and British.

All Jews are divided into two classes, viz: the Orthodox (or Zionist Jews) and the reformed Jews. It is estimated that about 85% of them are Orthodox and Zionist. They are governed by their rabbis and Talmud, and are socialists and communists. This is not true of the reformed Jews, who are good citizens in the country in which they reside; they accept the laws and customs of such country and are loyal to its government. The Zionists maintain their B'nai B'rith and antiDefamation and anti-Nazi Leagues with their numerous spies. They are our secret enemies.

ASHKENAZI JEWS

The author of "Unity in Dispersion," a history of the Zionist organization published in 1948, says on page 377:

"The Sephardic world comprises a million Jews, the majority of whom live in Moslem countries. The Ashkenazi world in East Europe forms the bulk of world Jewry. Eastern European Jews are reported descendants from Khazarites who formed an ancient kingdom in the Caucasus composed largely of Mongolian stock and who were early converted to Judaism. It has been stated that these Ashkenazi are not racial or true Jews, like the Sephardic, which were dispersed west along the northern shores of Africa."

This book's 381 pages evidence great research on the part of the author, A. L. Kubowitzki, a Jew. He and his book were endorsed by Rabbi Wise, who boasted of his association with him. It is true, that the Jews of Europe, as well as Russia, are not the descendants of Jacob, and that Palestine is not their ancient home, and that they are principally converts of Mongol an origin. It is true also that they now constitute the great majority of the race and dominate it. The Rothschilds are Ashkenazi Jews of Mongolian descent and by reason of their great wealth and service to world Jewry are the rulers of the race.

INTERNATIONAL BANKER JEWS

This is a supplement to the chapter Rothschild Money Trust, page 7-13, Zionist Wall Street.

The international banker Jews are Zionists and dominated by the Zionist Rothschild money trust. The Rothschild firm was first organized by the Zionist Rabbi Mayer Amschel Rothschild of Frankfurt, Germany, as M. A. Rothschild & Sons as a perpetual partnership, prior to the French Revolution. Later a similar firm WPS organized by his son Nathan Rothschild as N. M. Rothschild & Son of London.

The two Rothschild partnerships have dominated the economic and political fortunes of the people of the world since their organization. They are largely responsible for all of the financial panics and depressions and of the major wars since the French Revolution and including it. The first and second World Wars were initiated by Zionist Jews against the Christians for the purpose of promoting their Zionist world empire. They established the League of Nations which was a failure. The United Nations is also a failure and therefore a third war will be necessary for their purposes, and it appears inevitable.

It will likely come about through deflation and strikes. Our weakness is the fact that New York Communist Jews control both our industries and labor organizations. They can tie up our railroads and industries and starve us into submission. The Zionist Wall Street international bankers Jews are our enemies; they are more dangerous than the Politburo of Russia. If they again betray us into war, we may be defeated. We have hybrid Jew Mark Clark as Commander in Chief of our army; our Atomic Commission is pro-Jewish. Both political parties have declared for deflation; President Truman is actively seeking to bring it about, and therefore deflation and war are serious threats. They aspire to restore the gold standard and to deflate the world. Our money is out of balance with the monies of all other countries, so much so that many of them cannot buy our goods.

The international Jew bankers not only control our railroads and industries but they control our banking system and the executive department of our government. The Austrian Jew Felix Frankfurter is the dominating member of our Supreme Court. Tom McCabe, president of the Scott Paper Company, a Morgan firm, is Chairman of the Board of our Federal Reserve System. Paul Hoffman, E. R. A. Administrator, is president of the Stude-baker Corporation which is controlled by the Zionist Jewish international banking firm of Lehman & Company.[2]

The Marshall Plan was the concoction of Wall Street Zionist Jews. It was written by the Russian Jew Leon Levitsky. The purpose was to finance socialism and communism in Europe and to bankrupt America. Wall Street Zionist Jews organized a committee headed by Henry L. Stimson, erstwhile Secretary of War and attorney for Kuhn, Loeb & Co., which raised a huge fund to promote its adoption by Congress.

---

[2] Lehman gave the UNRRA relief funds entrusted to him, to Communist rulers who used them to promote socialism and communism.

The socialist United Nations is also a product of these same Wall Street Zionist Jews. Its charter was prepared by the Russian Communist Jew Leo Pasvolsky and the communist Alger Hiss, then of our State Department, who piloted its adoption by the San Francisco conference. (Hiss was a protege of Justice Felix Frankfurter). It was designed as the initial charter of the Zionist World Empire to be later expanded by usurpation and amendment. We American taxpayers are practically supporting it, paying 90% of its expenses, and it is costing us in excess of one hundred million dollars annually. The special session of the 80th Congress appropriated $65,000,000 for the erection of its capitol in New York City by a bipartisan vote.

It is estimated that there are thirteen million Jews in the United States, about three million of them being in the city of New York, and that they own about 80% of our wealth. They dominate Tammany Hall and New York City. We now have approximately one-half of the Jews of the world.

I repeat that the Zionist Jews control our economy and the executive department of our government, and have considerable influence in the legislative and judicial departments. They control not only our transportation and banking systems but the cinema, the radio, the advertising and news agencies and with a few exceptions, the metropolitan press and publishing houses. They dominate the steel, tobacco, liquor and clothing industries and the chain and department stores. They finance the democratic and republican parties and through them elect our officers.

Their program is to destroy the Christian governments of the world, including our own, and to establish a Zionist Empire with a Zionist emperor; to confiscate the property of the Christians and to enslave them. They have made great progress; they have established the Russian Soviet Empire, and with our help, the state of Israeli; they are dominant in

China and seriously threaten England, France, Italy, and the United States. They have brought about four serious depressions in the United States and threaten another, and they have involved us in two disastrous wars in pursuance of this purpose.

The Orthodox Zionist Jews have been a disturbing element in every country in which they have lived. It is due to their racial characteristics and their rabbinical training. They are greedy, antiChristian, and worshippers of gold. They are intolerant, bigoted and self assertive; a Jew in any committee or bureau is a majority; as witness our U. S. Supreme Court. We can criticize an Englishman or an Irishman or any other race, but not a Jew which is forbidden as anti-Semitism; as witness the Nuremberg trials and the indictment and trial of 31 alleged seditionists in Washington and the conviction of William Dudley Pelley.

It is estimated that the Rothschild Morgan firm controls corporations with net assets of thirty billion dollars and that eight Jewish controlled corporations have net assets of eighty billion dollars; about one-half of our national wealth measured by dollars of their present value. Their conviction for their treachery and the resultant cancellation of their bonds would restore our solvency and our freedom from debt slavery. In fact, there is no other way to do so except by inflation, which they will not permit. President Truman asserts the republican party is controlled by monopolies but he has not the courage to say that these monopolies are controlled by Zionist Jews, nor the frankness to say that they also control the national democratic party and his government. Be it remembered that Zionism means communism; all Zionists are either socialists or communists. That is the creed of the Talmud and the Protocols.

ZIONISM

The fundamental ideology or philosophy of Zionism is that the Jews are the "chosen people" and that God promised them that they should possess and rule the world. It is based on the first five chapters of the Old Testament as interpreted by their rabbis and their Talmud. The Zionists have been taught this false doctrine and they believe it and are attempting to bring it about through a world government. The Protocols represent their method of establishing their kingdom. Zionism is a political cult and the rabbis are its teachers and politicians; its objective is a world Jewish empire as projected by Theodore Herzl in their Protocols.

We cannot know much about Zionism for their organizations, conventions, and proceedings are racial and secret. We can only get an occasional glimpse of their plans and operations and such information about them as they are willing for us to have, for they control the press, radio, and cinema. The great majority of the Jews (an estimated 85% of them) including the international banker Jews are Zionists and thereby have the mighty-power of ostracism.

Zionism existed prior to the Christian Era. Its leaders then, as now, were rabbis, scribes, pharisees, elders and hypocrites. They were the gentry who crucified Christ. They are just as murderous and as merciless and as cruel now as they were then. Christ said of them, "Woe unto you scribes, pharisees, hypocrites for ye are like unto whited sepulchres which indeed appear beautiful outward, but are within full of dead mens bones, and of all uncleanness."—St. Matthew 23:27.

This is just as true now, as it was then. They will murder any man who opposes their schemes if they can safely do so. They have been the murderers of our Presidents and courageous statesmen. They were the murderers of the Czars and rulers of Europe; Count Bernadotte and the Shah of Persia are their two latest prominent victims.

They are determined to suppress and destroy Christianity for it is necessary in order to establish their communist Judaic Empire. Mrs. Eleanor Roosevelt was no doubt correct in saying that Cardinal Midzinsky was an anti-Semite. That was the real offense of the Bulgarian protestant group. That was the offense of the victims if the Nuremberg kangaroo court for which some of them were murdered and others imprisoned. That was the offense of Pelley and the 31 alleged seditionists. That is a part of the plan to suppress and destroy Christianity, viz: murder, bribery, deception and intimidation.

They deceive us by their "brotherhood" weeks and "Protestant, Catholic and Jew" campaigns, financed by the B'nai B'rith, and their change of names from "berg" and "isky" to Christian names. They are anti-Christ by teaching and tradition and have always been so. Our greatest protection against them is the Catholic Church and not the Protestant, I regret to say.

The Zionist system of government is state socialism ruled by a dictator and commissars and spies. It is the "welfare state," which must have a dictator and spies to make it work. None of us loves to work until we develop the "work habit." We must be induced to work by the hope of reward or compelled to work by the fear of punishment. We won't work for the pleasure to be derived out of it. God made us that way; it is His plan.

The Zionists have established their system in Russia and her satellite states, in the state of Israeli and in the Eastern Zone of Germany. They are rapidly developing it in England through the labor party and they seek to establish it in America through the A.F. of L. and C.I.O. William Green, president of A.F. of L., in an interview said he "preferred the welfare state to a Wall Street State." The poor man apparently does not know that the Wall Street Zionists seek to convert our government into a welfare state which they will rule.

The Zionist welfare state is "anti-Christ" because Zionism is antiChrist. Gone will be our fundamentals of Christianity, viz: faith, hope and charity and repentance and forgiveness of sin, gone will be our freedom and independence. Gone will be our home and family life. Gone will be the chastity of our wives and daughters. Our lives will be subject to the will of our Zionist masters. It will be a government of commissars and spies with a dictator, and woe to the man who encounters the displeasure of a commisar or a spy.

MARTIN LUTHER

Martin Luther said of the Jews and their Talmud:

"Therefore know, my dear Christian, that next to the devil you have no more bitter, more poisonous, more vehement an enemy than a real Jew who earnestly desires to be a Jew (an orthodox Jew) ...

"Since childhood they have devoured such poisonous hatred against the Goyim (gentiles) from their parents and Rabbis, and still devour such without ceasing, that according to Psalm 109 it has gone over into their flesh and blood, bone and marrow, and has become their life and being. And as little as they can alter flesh and blood, bone and marrow, so little can they change such pride and envy. They just have to stay that way and be ruined, if God does not perform a special miracle." He further said:

"They do not work, do not earn anything from us, neither do we donate or give it to them. Yet they have our money and goods and are lords in our land where they are in exile...

"Do not their Talmud and Rabbis write that it is no sin to kill if a Jew kills a heathen (Gentile), but it is sin if he kills a brother in Israel! It is no sin if he does not keep his oath to a heathen. Therefore, to steal and rob (as they do with their usury) from a heathen, is a divine service. For they hold that they cannot be too hard on us nor sin against us, because they are the noble blood and circumcized saints; we however, are the cursed Goyim. And they are the master of the world and we are their servants, yea, their cattle!"

Martin Luther said further:

"They hold us Christians in captivity in our own country; they let us work in the sweat of our noses, while they appropriate money and goods, sitting behind the stove, are lazy, gluttlers and guzzlers, live well and easy on goods for which we have worked, keep us and our goods in captivity through their cursed usury, mock us and spit on us, because we must labor and permit them to be noblemen at our expense. Thus they are our lords and masters, we their servants with our own property, sweat and labor! and to thank us and reward us, they curse our Lord!"[3]

Our Lord Jesus Christ denounced them in still more forceful and direct language. He said to the Jews a short time before they crucified him:

"Ye are of YOUR father the devil, and the lusts of your father ye will do. He was a murderer from the beginning, and abode not in the truth, because there is no truth in him. When he speaketh a lie, he speaketh of his own: for he is a liar and the father of it." St. John 8:44.

---

[3] "The Jews and Their Lies" by Martin Luther, pages 28, 30, 31. 37.

And so they were and are today and always will be so long as they are governed by their rabbis, their scribes, pharisees, hypocrites, and their Talmud; their "tradition" as Christ called it. They haven't changed and they can't change and they don't want to change. Their tradition (Talmud) is their religion. They are taught it by their mothers in their infancy, their schools during their adolescence and their rabbis in their maturity. They are born that way and are educated and trained that way. They are a stubborn, "stiff necked," vain, self assertive, purse proud, gold worshipping people. Our Lord and Savior Jesus Christ did not reform them, nor can we do so.

George Washington, the father of our country, said of the Jews:

"They work more effectively against us, than the enemy's armies. They are a hundred times more dangerous to our liberties and the great cause we are engaged in ... It is much to be lamented that each state, long ago, has not hunted them down as pests to society and the greatest enemies we have to the happiness of America."[4]

Benjamin Franklin said of them:

"There is a great danger for the United States of America; this great danger is the Jew. Gentlemen, in every land which the Jews have settled, they have depressed the normal level and lowered the degree of commercial honesty. They have remained apart and unassimilated, — they have created a state within a state; and when they are oppressed they attempt to strangle the nation financially as in the case of Portugal and Spain. For more than 1700 years they have lamented their

---

[4] Maxius of George Washington by A. A. Appletan & Company, page 125-6, copyright 1894.

sorrowful fate, — namely, they were driven out of their motherland, but gentlemen, if the civilized world today should give them back Palestine and their property, they would immediately find pressing reasons for not returning there. Why? because they are vampires, and vampires cannot live on other vampires — they cannot live among themselves; they can only live among Christians and others who do not belong to their race.

"If they are not excluded from the United States, by the Constitution, within less than 100 years, they will stream into this country in such numbers they will rule and destroy us and change our form of government for which we Americans shed our blood and sacrificed life, property and personal freedom. If the Jews are not excluded within 200 years, our children will be working in the fields to feed the Jews while they remain in the Counting House gleefully rubbing their hands.

"I warn you, gentlemen, if you do not exclude the Jews forever, your children's children will curse you in your graves. Their ideas are not those of Americans even when they have lived among us for ten generations. The leopard cannot change its spots. The Jews are a danger to this land and if they are allowed to enter they will imperil our institutions; — they should be excluded by the Constitution."[5]

Our Lord and Saviour Jesus Christ, Martin Luther, George Washington and Benjamin Franklin would now be regarded as antiSemites and criminals by the Zionists. They would all have been convicted by the Nuremberg court and probably assessed the death penalty. They boast that Haym Soloman helped finance the Revolutionary War. It is true. He was the representative of N. M. Rothschild & Son. The Rothschilds have financed both sides of every war including our

---

[5] This is precisely the situation today.

Revolutionary War and the War Between the States. That is their system, for they profit by war. No matter which side loses, they win. Mrs. Ludendorf, the wife of the German General Ludendorf, testified at her trial for anti-Semitism that Jas. P. Warburg of Kuhn, Loeb & Co., loaned Hitler $34,000,000.

The Zionists are mean and vindictive. This statement is based on personal experience. They are cruel and merciless and relentless; this statement is based on observation. They have no mercy for a fallen foe. They are responsible for the murderous governments of Russia, Hungary, and other countries, and the Nuremberg trial. They are indeed "like unto whited sepulchres, that are beautiful outwardly but within are full of dead men's bones."

They are fair and attractive in their promises, which are made only to deceive. They are masters of intrigue and deception. They have cowed the press and politicians, the press by their advertising and the politicians by their control of press, radio and cinema; and both by their B'nai-B'rith, A.D.L., anti-Nazi League and spy systems.

BARUCH AND FRANKFURTER

Bernard Baruch, who is reputed to be at the head of the Jewish Sanhedrin, and Justice Felix Frankfurter of our Supreme Court, are the political leaders of the Jewish race. Baruch finances political parties and congressional candidates and advises presidents and congressional committees; and Frankfurter nominates Communist appointees for important government positions.

The late Senator Long likened the wily Baruch to a watchful old crow. In a speech in Congress he said:

"I remember one time when I tried to shoot an old crow. I was riding along and saw the crow on a log in a field, so I just rode up behind a thicket so the crow could not see me and reached into my buggy to get my gun. Thick as that thicket was, the minute my hand got near the gun the old crow flew away ... He (Baruch) stood with the Hoover Administration until it was wrecked inside out ... Then old brother Baruch came right on back down to the White House and got hold of another President (Roosevelt). We have presidents and presidents but Baruch goes on forever."[6]

Nobody knows whether this wily old crow is a democrat or a republican or a communist. He thought Dewey would be elected and had his picture taken with him. He correctly appraised Truman as "uncouth, ignorant and incompetent."

General Hugh Johnson, formerly N.R.A. chief, gave us an accurate picture of the activities of Justice Felix Frankfurter in an article published in the Saturday Evening Post, October 25, 1935:

"His 'boys' have been insinuated into obscure but key positions in every vital department — warders of the marches, inconspicious but powerful. Wherever to know, check, influence or control what goes on in government it would be a good thing for a Big Happy Dog to have a Little Happy Hot Dog planted there is one there, alert and quietly active ... Two or three infest Henry Wallace. The area in and about the Federal Trades Commission literally writhes with them. The Justice, Interior, Labor, and Treasury Departments harbor their quotas. Other hosts for them are PWA, AAA, FERA, TVA, and SEC. They have had a guiding hand in the drafting of nearly all legislation ... To them the constitution is just a foil for clever fencing — an antedeluvian joke to be respected in

---

[6] Congressional Record, 75th Congress, page 7592.

public like a Sacred Cow and regarded in private somewhat as Gertrude Stein probably regards the poet Tennyson or any other Victor-lan."[7]

And his "hot dog boys" are Jew Communists and many of them said to be homosexuals. They are not accidents, they are selected and placed for the purpose of destroying our system of government.

These two (Baruch and Frankfurter) together with Henry Morgenthau and Sam Rosenman are directly responsible for the Roosevelt and Truman maladministrations and they are responsible for our present unfortunate condition. They were and are the agents of the Zionist Politburo of Wall Street. It was through them that Henry

L. Stimson, erstwhile attorney for Kuhn, Loeb & Co., obtained his appointment as Secretary of War, Frank Knox as Secretary of the Navy, and Edward Stettinius, partner of Morgan & Co., as Secretary of State.

It was through Frankfurter that the head of the spy ring J. Peters (true name Isidore Boornstein), Alger Hiss and other communists obtained their jobs in our State Department. Most of the spies that have been revealed by the Committee on Un-American Activities have been Jews and got their jobs through Justice Frankfurter or Bernard Baruch. Every bribetaker, with the exception of Congressman May, so far as revealed, has been a Jew; the Garson Brothers, Bennie Myers, etc. The war was a great picnic for the Jews. They flocked to the bureaus and took them over. The Zionist Jews initiated the war, ran it, and at its conclusion bought the wreckage at a fraction of its cost, and created the United Nations for the alleged purpose of preventing future wars.

---

[7] Roosevelt Red Record, pages 81-83.

The F.B.I. revealed that a Jew professor in the Minnesota State University named Weiberg, who assisted in the Atomic Bomb laboratory, disclosed the secret of the atomic bomb to the Russian Communist Politburo. He has not been prosecuted as a traitor, and probably will not be, but if he is and is convicted, the punishment will be a mere "slap on the wrist" as in the case of the eleven communists who were convicted of treason in Judge Medina's court in New York and the spy Gubitschev. It appears that this secret and also the H bomb secret were given to Russia by the British Zionist Dr. Fuch and by Harry Hopkins, President Roosevelt's assistant.

The Truman administration usually selects New York for the trial of traitors, where most of the judges and jury men are Zionists, instead of elsewhere in America where the judges and jury men are loyal Americans. The conviction of the arch traitor Alger Hiss, Roosevelt's companion and advisor, was a disappointment to our Secretary of State and probably also to our President.

THE CONVICTION OF THE ELEVEN COMMUNIST TRAITORS

The eleven months trial of the eleven communists had the appearance of a Zionist publicity stunt but it should be said to the credit of the Judge and jury that the defendants were all convicted.

Here is a list of them:[8] Eugene Dennis, alias Frank Waldron, an ex-convict;

Jacob Abram Storbel, an Austrian Jew and immigrant from Galicia;

---

[8] Congressional Record November 18, 1949, pages 15, 161-2.

Irving Potash, an ex-convict and Jewish immigrant from Kieve, Russia;

Jno. Williamson, alias Jno. Miller, an immigrant from Scotland;

Gus Hall, true name Gus Halberg, a Jew and ex-convict whose parents were immigrants from Finland;

Carl Winter, true name Carl Weiberg, whose parents were immigrants from Russia and Jews;

Robert Thompson, alias Bob Condon, an ex-convict, whose punishment was assessed at three years instead of five;

Gilbert Green, true name Gilbert Greenberg, a Jew;

Jno. Gates, true name Paul Roganstrief, a Jew. He is editor of the communist paper "Daily Worker";

Harry Winston and Benjamin J. Davis, negroes, the only two whose names were not assumed names. Six Jews, two negroes and three race unknown.

The foreman of the jury was a mulatto negro woman. The punishment to all except Thompson was five years imprisonment instead of death, as provided by our common law. Pending the trial of this case, a bi-partisan Congress reduced the penalty for conspiring to overthrow our government from ten years to five years.

The trial Judge was, therefore, justified in imposing a light penalty for the most serious offense that can be committed against our government. The fault lies with our "fair deal" President and his "fair deal" bi-partisan Congress. They now seek to admit more Zionists through their alleged Displaced Persons bill, introduced and sponsored by the New York Jew

Congressman Celler, chairman of the House Judiciary Committee. The obvious purpose is to win elections and to communize America.

It was reported by the Associated Press, November 3, 1949 that Judge Medina refused to allow bond for the eleven convicted Communists and that the New York Circuit Court of Appeals granted them bond in the sum of $260,000 which means that they are free pending their appeal and will probably escape as did Eisler. The eleven months' trial of the eleven convicted communist traitors was a spectacular farce. It is reported to have cost us $700,000 and now they are loose to continue their operation. It is a safe prediction that not one of them will ever be seriously punished.

What a reflection upon the Roosevelt-Truman "New Deal" and "Fair Deal" alleged democratic administrations, and the New York Circuit Court of Appeals. I venture the assertion that a majority of the judges of this court are socialists and communists and are of the same race as Justice Felix Frankfurter, who was a character witness for the traitor Hiss, and of Judge Kaufman who tried him. It is not a coincidence that these traitor trials are held in New York and alleged sedition trials in Washington. They were planned that way. What a tragedy that there is no longer any safety in our courts, which are the final arbiters of our rights. No orthodox Jew Judge can render a just decision between a Christian and a Jew without violating the law of his Talmud.

It was revealed by Major Geo. R. Jordan that Harry Hopkins[9] supplied the bolsheviks with our atomic bomb blue prints and secrets, and with material for making them. Harry Hopkins (Raschid) was then a member of Roosevelt's "kitchen cabinet" and lived with him in the White House.

---

[9] Said to have been a Zionist Jew whose real name was Harry L. Raschid.

Major Jordan was the officer in charge of the transportation of the material from Alaska to Russia. The secret was obviously given to Russia with Roosevelt's permission. Later one Weiberg, a Zionist Jew professor in Minnesota State University who was employed by the government as a scientist in the manufacture of the bomb, was alleged to have supplied additional information. These revelations appear to be authentic. If true, they are conclusive evidence that Roosevelt was a traitor and that he sought to communize America.

Klaus Fuchs, the British scientist, who confessed that he gave the bomb secrets to the Russians, was a refugee from Germany during the Hitler regime and was obviously a Zionist Jew. These traitors are no worse than other Zionists. They are all traitors; they are taught treachery by their Talmud and Protocols. All of them are our enemies, who seek to destroy our govenment and to enslave us and appropriate our property.

2.

THE TALMUD

> "It (the Talmud) contains every kind of vileness and blasphemy against Christian Truth."
>
> —Pope Gregory IX

There are three versions of the Talmud, viz: the Mishnah, containing the essence of the oral law; and the Palestinian, first published in 1522-3, and the Babylonian.[10] The Jewish Encyclopedia, page 161, states that the only complete manuscript of the Babylonian is in Leyden, Holland. It says that "during the Middle Ages the Talmud was frequently attacked since it formed the voice teaching of the Jewish religion and was regarded as the core of Jewish resistance to Christianity."

The Mishnah consists of dissertations by Jewish rabbis while they were in captivity in Babylon. I have seen the 40 volumes of the Babylonian by Radkinson in the Chicago Public Library, but it is not to be found in the smaller libraries.

---

[10] Jewish Encyclopedia, Vol. 10, page 166.

TALMUD SUPPRESSED

The Babylonian interpretations and amendments were written during the period from 200 to 500 A.D.[11] The first printed edition in Hebrew "of the whole Talmud containing all of its blasphemies against the Christian religion was published in Venice in the year 1520 ... The Jews fearing for themselves began to expunge parts of it openly inimical to Christians and published a revised edition of it at Basle in A.D. 1578." It appears to have been further modified at a Synod of Jewish rabbis in Poland in the year A.D. 1631 where it was decided that nothing should be printed "that would annoy Christians and cause persecution of Israel." The final edition was published in Spain in A.D. 1648.[12]

Thus it appears that the Jewish rabbis out of consideration of expediency have not published their entire Talmud and that at least a part of it is transmitted orally through their rabbis.

The Emperor Justinian prohibited the distribution of "Talmudic books in A.D. 553." Popes Gregory IX and Innocent IV condemned them as "containing every kind of vileness and blasphemy against Christian Truth." They have been condemned by many other Roman Pontiffs.[13]

Father B. Pranaitis of Russia, a Roman Catholic theologian and Hebraist of the Roman Catholic College of the Imperial Academy of St. Petersburg, published in 1892 in Latin and Hebrew many quotations from the Talmud revealing their intolerant anti-Christian spirit. This booklet was translated and copyrighted and published in 1939 by Col. E. N. Sanctuary,

---

[11] "The Talmud Unmasked," page 12.

[12] "The Talmud Unmasked," page 21.

[13] "The Talmud Unmasked," page 22, 23.

156 Fifth Ave., New York, a learned American biblical scholar and a veteran of World War I.

In his epilogue to this book Father Pranaitis said that he was warned by his friends not to publish it, that if he did so he "would perish at the hands of the Jews"; that his friends reminded him of Professor Charini who "was suddenly killed after he had undertaken to translate the Talmud into the vernacular"; and of the monk Didacus of Vilna and "others who had been persecuted for having revealed secrets of the Jewish religion." He concluded by saying:

"The book you now hold in your hand is the best proof that I did not heed these warnings of my friends. I consider it unworthy of me to keep silent just for the sake of my own personal safety while the conflict rages between the two camps of 'Semites' and 'Anti-Semites,' both of which claim they are fighting for the truth, while I know that the whole truth is not to be found in either camp. But whatever befalls me because of what I have done, I shall gladly suffer it. I am prepared to lay down my life THAT I MAY BEAR WITNESS TO THE TRUTH."[14]

And Father Pranaitis was murdered by the bolsheviks.

Colonel Sanctuary was one of the defendants in the Washington trial of the thirty alleged seditionists. No evidence of any character was introduced against him during the 7 1/2 months of this trial. His only offense was the translation and publication of the book, "The Talmud Unmasked."

---

[14] "The Talmud Unmasked," page 22, 23.

TALMUD IS VICIOUS

The Talmud is not only the Bible of the Zionists but it is also their legal and moral code; and the rabbis are not only priests but they are also Jewish teachers and lawyers and judges for Jewish courts. Rabbi Browne says of the Talmud:

"And the fact that in bulk the chaff far exceeds the wheat should not be at all surprising. After all the Talmud is the product of an age when a peculiar type of mind alone could thrive. Israel was exhausted."

This is the judgment of an intelligent Zionist rabbi, a former associate of the Zionist Rabbi Wise, most prominent American rabbi. Only a Jew can say such things about the Talmud. If a gentile (goi) should even intimate that it is a book of hate and resentment from ancient injuries and that "the bulk of it is chaff" he would be denounced as an intolerant anti-Semite. In the case of Father Pranaitis he was killed; and in Colonel Sanctuary's prosecuted as an anti-Semite for the offense of translating and publishing the Talmud in part. It is worse than "chaff." It is malicious and vicious and is not entitled to be classed as a re-ligious book.

JEWISH INTOLERANCE AND HATE

The Talmud denounces Christ as a bastard and gloats over his crucifixion. It glorifies the Jew and characterizes the goi (Gentiles) as idolaters and as beasts. It asserts "that the Jew alone is a man, that the whole world is his and all things should serve him, especially animals that have the form of men." (Talmud Unmasked, p. 68.) It tells the Jews not to "eat with the idolaters, make no covenant with them, and show them no mercy, and turn them away from their idols or kill them." (Talmud Unmasked, p. 83.) They are taught to hate the goi (Gentiles), to cheat them and to spurn them as inferiors.

This is the Jewish religion as revealed in the Talmud, and that Americans are called upon to recognize and tolerate as religious freedom.

"The Jews lifted it (the Talmud) to a place of importance above the very Bible, and they studied it far more diligently. They memorized it from end to end — every one of its sixtythree enormous divisions."[15]

That may be true of the rabbis but it is rather an extravagant statement regarding the Jewish people as a whole.

Rabbi Browne argues in defense of the Talmud, or apology for it,

that

"There are in it myths and vagaries, idiotic superstitions and

unhappy thoughts, things that are not merely irrational but sometimes even quite offensive ... It is like life — a higgledypiggledy mingling of both good and bad, of both wisdom and folly. For it came directly out of life, directly out of the hateful, exciting, hopeful, despairing heroic life of the Jewish people ... It contains very nearly everything."[16]

TALMUD SHOULD BE DISCARDED

It is high time that this obsolete "idiotic and superstitious" religion of pride and intolerance and hate be discarded. If it is

---

[15] "Stranger Than Fiction," page 197. Rabbi Browne was associate rabbi with the Zionist leader, Dr. Stephen S. Wise of the Free Synagogue of Greater New York, for a period of two years.

[16] page 186.

true, as Rabbi Browne argues, that the purpose of the Talmud was to preserve the Jewish race as a separate race and to prevent its assimilation with other races, it has accomplished that purpose. It has been responsible for much of the alleged persecution of the Jewish race, for people who hate are usually hated.

It is significant that Rabbi Browne does not mention Ishmael in his interesting book. He discusses the history of the Israelites, an extinct race as shown by his own writing. The elaborate "History of the Jewish People" by Margolis and Marx (822 pages, published by "The Jewish Publication Society of America" in 1941) is also a history of the extinct race of Israelites. The Jews cannot be blamed for desiring to escape the odium of the curse of God upon the race of Ishmael, or of being classed as hybrids. It is but natural for them to seek to adopt the history of another tribe even if it is extinct and not a very glorious one.

TALMUD CONDEMNED BY CATHOLIC CHURCH

Formal accusations were made against the Talmud in 1242 before Pope Gregory IX, charging that it "contained blasphemies against God, against Jesus, and against Christianity." The Pope appointed a commission to hear the charges, the Jews were represented by "Jehiel son of Joseph of Paris" and three others; evidence was introduced and a trial was had. The commission sustained the charges and ordered the Talmud burned, and accordingly

"Twenty-four cart-loads of Hebrew books were committed to the flames in Paris ... In 1247, at the solicitations of the

Jews, the case was reopened and the Talmud condemned a second time."[17]

The Talmud was proscribed in Spain in 1415, and it was ordered burned in Italy in 1559.[18]

It is difficult for the Christian mind to conceive the depravity of the Talmud and the Protocols; the one is just as bad as the other. We can hardly realize that people with whom we mix and mingle daily and who are intelligent and of good appearance, believe in the false teaching of the Talmud, and that they plan to enslave us as set out in the Protocols. It is true. They have always been that way. We can, therefore, understand why the Jews have been driven from every Christian country in which they have resided.

The Zionists are our enemies and they must be driven from our country. Our Lord and Saviour Jesus Christ warned us against them. He likened them to "whited sepulchers that within are full of dead men's bones." He said that they are liars, thieves and murderers. They have not changed from that day to the present time. We must remember that they are anti-Christ and violently opposed to His teachings. Some of our mushy brained, mealy mouthed, milk and water theologians do not appear to understand the Scriptures.

---

[17] "History of the Jewish People," page 378.
[18] Id., 445 and 507.

GEORGE W. ARMSTRONG

3.

PROTOCOLS

> "And it was said by the prophets of old that we were chosen by God himself to rule over the whole earth ... And the weapons in our hands are limitless ambitions, burning greediness, merciless vengeance, hatreds and malice."
>
> —From Protocol 9.

This chapter is a supplement to the Protocol chapter in Zionist Wall Street. There are 24 Protocols. They set forth in detail the Zionist plan for subjugating the goi (gentile "cattle") and establishing their Zionist Empire. A Russian bugaboo is necessary to stampede us into another war and it may be necessary for them to create another Pearl Harbor to do so.

The Talmud and Protocols are closely related; the one represents the philosophy of the Zionists; the other their plan of action. They are both founded on the false assumption that the Jews are the "chosen people" of God, that they are entitled to rule the gentiles whom they call "goi" (meaning cattle), and to possess their wealth, and that it is no offense to lie to them, to cheat them and to murder them.

They are both based on the moral and political principles of the Talmud. They are in substance the political principles of the Florentine statesman, Niccolo Machiavelli, as set forth in his book, The Prince, which was published about 400 years ago. He prescribed the rules for a diplomat, which are, (1) that promises must be made only to deceive and mislead others to sacrifice their own interest; (2) that friends or allies must be betrayed as a matter of course as soon as they have served their purpose; (3) that there must be kept up a spurious aspect of benevolence and benefit for the common man; (4) that enmity and class war must be promoted.

These are the basic principles of the Protocols and of the Marxists and their Talmud. They are the principles that now govern the world and have governed it since the adoption of the Protocols in 1897. They are the principles employed by "Zionist Wall Street" and the Zionist administrations of the Russian Politburo, of the Churchill, Atlee, Cripps administrations of the British Empire, and of the Wilson, Roosevelt, Truman administrations of America. Truman is not such an accomplished diplomat as were Wilson and Roosevelt; not for lack of will but for want of ability.

The Zionists deny the authenticity of the protocols but they themselves have established their authenticity by judicial decree in the Swiss Court of Appeals. It is true, as they claim, that the trial judge, a Zionist by the name of Levy, held that the protocols are spurious, but the case was appealed and reversed by the Appellate Court. The Zionists cite the Levy decision and not the final judgment. The issue in the case was whether or not the protocols are a forgery and a slanderous reflection upon the Jews. The Swiss Court of Appeals held that this charge was not established and dismissed the case.

The protocols have been verified by the history of the world since their adoption. The Zionist historians admit that they organized politically at their world conference in Bazle, Switzerland in 1897, and that Theodore Herzl was their leader. They then created a secret "inner action committee" to direct their operations. They then knew the fabulous mineral wealth of Palestine and surrounding country and determined to acquire it.

The protocols represent their plan of campaign and they have created wars and depressions in pursuance of them. The administrations of Wilson, Roosevelt and Truman in America, of Lenin and Stalin in Russia, and of Churchill and Atlee in England have all been Zionist administrations and have all promoted a Zionist Empire. The Zionists have governed the people of America, Russia and the British Empire by lies and deception.

The authenticity of the protocols has recently been confirmed by the Zionist A. L. Jubowitsky in his history of the World Jewish Congress entitled "Unity in Dispersion" (diaspora) published in 1948. He shows that the World Jewish Congress really took shape in 1840 when the Jewish Board of Deputies in Britain and France became politically powerful and thereafter when the B'nai B'rith was established "for the purpose of uniting the Jews of the world into one body." He boasts that Jewish power became absolute in the United States with the formation of the American Jewish Committee, the New York Kilhillah and the establishment of the American branch of the B'nai B'rith.

It was about 1840 that Benjamin Disraeli, a Sephardic Christian Jew, was Prime Minister of the British Empire and when the British Jews were permitted to vote and hold office. But the Jews were well established in power throughout Europe even before they were enfranchised, as a result of their money and bribery. Mr. Disraeli graphically describes their station in his book "Sidonia", a fictional history of Lionel Rothschild published in 1844. Disraeli says of the Jewish power of that period:

> "You never observe a great intellectual movement in Europe in which the Jews do not greatly participate. The first Jesuits were Jews: that mysterious Russian diplomacy which so alarms Western Europe is organized and principally carried on by Jews; that

mighty revolution which is at this moment-preparing in Germany, and which will he in fact a second and greater Reformation, and of which so little is yet known in England, is entirely developing under the auspices of Jews, who almost monopolize the professorial chairs of Germany. Neander, the founder of Spiritual Christianity, and who is Regius Professor of Divinity in the University of Berlin, is a Jew. Benary, equally famous, and in the same university, is a Jew. Wehl, the Arabic Professor of Heidlberg, is a Jew.

"I resolved to go myself to St. Petersburg. I had on my arrival an interview with the Russian Minister of Finance, Count Cancrin; I beheld the son of a Lithuanian Jew. The loan was connected with the affairs of Spain; 1 resolved on repairing to Spain from Russia. I travelled without intermission. I had an audience immediately on my arrival with the Spanish minister, Senor Mendizabel; I beheld one like myself, the son of a Nuovo Christiano, a Jew of Arragon. In consequence of what transpired at Madrid, I went straight to Paris to consult the President of the French Council; I beheld the son of a French Jew, a hero, an imperial marshal, and very properly so, for who should be military heroes if not those who worship the Lord of Hosts?

"We fixed on Prussia, and the President of the Council made application to the Prussian minister, who attended a few days after our conference. Count Arnim entered the cabinet, and I beheld a Prussian Jew. So you see, my dear Coningsby, that the world is governed by very different personages to what is imagined by those who are not behind the scenes."

Disraeli says of Rothchild ("Sidonia") :

"No minister of state has such communication with secret agents and political spies as Sidonia. He held relations with all the clever outcasts of the world. The catalogue of his acquaintance in the shape of Greeks, Armenians, Moors, secret Jews, Tartars, gypsies, wandering Poles and Carbonari, would throw a curious light on those subterranean agencies of which the world in general knows so little, but which exercise so great an influence on public events."

That was substantially the station of the Jew in 1914 when Kaiser Wilhelm of Germany initiated the first world war. It was not the Kaiser who declared war; it was his premier Bethman Holweg, a descendant of Amschel Rothschild, and his Jewish cabinet. The Kaiser was only a conceited figurehead. The first World War was for the wealth of Palestine and the creation of a Zionist Empire.

The Kaiser gave the Lenin-Trotsky party permission to cross Germany and as a result he eliminated Russia and substituted America as an ally, and lost the war. The war was not begun to avenge the murder of an Austrian duke; that was but a flimsy excuse. It was begun for the establishment of a Jewish Empire in pursuance of the plan of the Protocols. The League of Nations was only an intermediate step in that direction which has now been supplanted by the United Nations.

Nor did we enter the war for the purpose of preserving the freedom of the seas; that was also only a flimsy excuse. We entered it for Zionist purposes, viz: the establishment of a Zionist empire with the wealth of Palestine. The Zionists double-crossed the Kaiser and they have double-crossed us. Bear in mind also that the double-cross is a part of the code of the Zionist: "words should not agree with the deeds of the diplomat." It should be remembered also that the Rothschilds and their agents are the head and front of Zionism.

THE ZIONIST PLAN

EXTRACT FROM PROTOCOL 1

"What I am about to set forth, then, is our system from the two points of view, that of ourselves and that of the GOYIM (i. e., gentiles).

"It must be noted that men with bad instincts are more in number than the good, and therefore the best results in governing them are attained by violence and terroriza-tion, and not by academic discussions. Every man aims at power, everyone would like to become a dictator if only he could, and rare indeed are the men who would not be willing to sacrifice the welfare of all for the sake of securing their own welfare...

Honesty and Frankness Are Vices

"The political has nothing in common with the moral. The ruler who is governed by the moral is not a skilled politician, and is therefore unstable on his throne. He who wishes to rule must have recourse both to cunning and to make believe. Great national qualities, like frankness and honesty, are vices in politics, for they bring down rulers from their thrones more effectively and more certainly than the most powerful enemy. Such qualities must be the attributes of the kingdoms of the GOYIM, but we must in no wise be guided by them ...

Plan Is to Lead the Mob

"Before us is a plan in which is laid down strategically the line from which we cannot deviate without running the risk of seeing the labour of many centuries brought to naught.

"In order to elaborate satisfactory forms of action it is necessary to have regard to the rascality, the slackness, the instability of the mob, its lack of capacity to understand and respect the conditions of its own life, or its own welfare. It must be understood that the might of a mob is blind, senseless and unreasoning force ever at the mercy of a suggestions from any side. The blind cannot lead the blind without bringing them into the abyss; consequently, members of the mob, upstarts from the people even though they should be a genuis of wisdom, yet having no understanding of the political, cannot come forward as leaders of the mob without bringing the whole nation to ruin.

"Only one trained from childhood for independent rules can have understanding of the words that can be made up of the political alphabet.

"A people left to itself, i. e., to upstarts from its midst brings itself to ruin by party dissensions excited by the pursuit of power and honors and disorders arising there from. Is it possible for the masses of the people calmly and without petty jealousies to form judgments, to deal with the affairs of the country, which cannot be mixed up with personal interest? Can they defend themselves from an external foe? It is unthinkable, for a plan broken up into as many parts as there are heads in the mob, loses all homogeneity, and thereby becomes unintelligible and impossible of execution.

.Despotic Ruler Is Necessary

"It is only with a despotic ruler that plans can be elaborated extensively and clearly in such a way as to distribute the whole properly among the several parts of the machinery of the State; from this the conclusion is inevitable that a satisfactory form of government for any country is one that concentrates in the hands of one responsible person. Without an absolute despotism there can be no existence for civilization which is carried on not by the masses but by their guide, whosoever that person may be. The mob is a savage and displays its savagery at every opportunity. The moment the mob seizes freedom in its hands it quickly turns to anarchy, which in itself is the highest degree of savagery.

"Behold the alcoholized animals, bemused with drink, the right to an immoderate use of which comes along with freedom. It is not for us and ours to walk that road. The peoples of the goyim are bemused with alcoholic liquors; their youth has grown stupid on classicism and from early immorality, into which it has been inducted by our special agents — by tutors, lackeys, governesses in the homes of the wealthy, by clerks and others, by our women in the places of dissipation frequented by the goyim. In the number of these last I count also the so-called "society ladies" voluntary followers of the other in corruption and luxury.

THE ZIONIST SYSTEM BRIBERY, DECEIT, MURDER AND TERROR

"Our countersign is — force and make-believe. Only force conquers in political affairs, especially if it be concealed in the talents essential to statesmen. Violence must be the principle, and cunning and make-believe the rule for governments which do not want to lay down their crowns at the feet of agents of some new power. This evil is the one and only means to attain the end, the good. Therefore we must not stop at bribery, deceit and treachery when they should serve towards the attainment of our end. In politics one must know how to seize the property of others without hesitation if by it we secure submission and sovereignty.

"Our State, marching along the path of peaceful conquest, has the right to replace the terrors of war by less noticeable and more satisfactory sentences of death, necessary to maintain the terror which tends to produce blind submission. Just but merciless severity is the greatest factor of strength in the State; not only for the sake of gain but also in the name of duty, for the sake of victory, we must keep to the programme of violence and make-belief. The doctrine of squaring accounts is precisely as strong as the means of which it makes use. Therefore it is not so much by the means themselves as by the doctrine of severity that we shall triumph and bring all governments into subjection to our super-government. It is enough for them to know that we are merciless for all disobedience to cease."

EXTRACT FROM PROTOCOL 3

"The aristocracy, which enjoyed by law the labour of the workers, was interested in seeing that the workers were well fed, healthy and strong. We are interested in just the opposite — in the diminution, the killing out of the GOYIM. Our power is in the chronic shortness of food and physical weakness of the worker because by all that this implies he is made the slave of our will, and he will not find in his own authorities either strength or energy to set against our will. Hunger creates the right of capital to rule the worker more surely than it was given to the aristocracy by the legal authority of kings.

"By want and the envy and hatred which it engenders we shall move the mobs and with their hands we shall wipe out all those who hinder us on our way.

"When the hour strikes for our Sovereign of all the World to be crowned it is these same hands which will sweep away everything that might be a hindrance thereto.

"This hatred will be still further magnified by the effects of an economic crisis, which will stop dealings on the exchanges and bring industry to a standstill. We shall create by all the secret subterranean methods known to us and with the aid of gold, which is all in our hands, a universal economic crisis whereby we shall throw upon the streets whole mobs of workers simultaneously in all the countries of Europe. These mobs will rush delightedly to shed the blood of those whom, in the simplicity of their ignorance, they have envied from their cradles, and whose property they will then be able to loot...

"Ever since that time we have been leading the people from one disenchantment to another, so that in the end they should turn also from us in favour of the King-Despot of the blood of Zion, whom we are preparing for the world."

EXTRACT FROM PROTOCOL 5

"What form of rule is to be given to these communities if not that despotism which I shall describe to you later? We shall create an intensified centralization of government in order to grip in our hands all the forces of the community. We shall regulate mechanically all the actions of the political life of our subjects by new laws. These laws will withdraw one by one all the indulgences and liberties which have been permitted by the goyim, and our kingdom will be distinguished by a despotism of such magnificent proportions as to be at any moment and in every place in a position to wipe out any goyim who oppose us by deed or word...

"However, it is probably all the same to the world who is its sovereign lord, whether the head of Catholicism or our despot of the blood of Zion! But to us, the Chosen people, it is very far from being a matter of indifference ...

"For every one of them must bear in mind that any agreement against us would be unprofitable to itself. We are too strong—there is no evading our power. The nations can not come to even an inconsiderable private agreement without our secretly having a hand in it.

"Per Me Reges Regnant. 'It is through me that Kings reign.' And it was said by the prophets that we were chosen by God himself to rule over the whole earth. God has endowed us with genius that we may be equal to our task...

"In order to put public opinion into our hands we must bring it into a state of bewilderment by giving expression from all sides to so many contradictory opinions and for such length of time as will suffice to make the GOYIM lose their heads in the labyrinth and come to see that the best thing is to have no opinion of any kind in matters political, which it is not given to the public to understand, because they are understood only by him who guides the public. This is the first secret ...

"By all these means we shall so wear down the GOYIM that they will be compelled to offer us international power of a nature that by its position will enable us without any violence gradually to absorb all the State forces of the world and to form a Super-Government. In place of the rulers of today we shall set up a bogey which will be called the Super-Government Administration. Its hands will reach out in all directions like nippers and its organization will be of such colossal dimensions that it cannot fail to subdue all the nations of the world."

EXTRACT FROM PROTOCOL 10

"The mob cherishes a special affection and respect for the geniuses of political power and accepts all their deeds of violence with the admiring response: 'rascally, well, yes, it is rascally, but it's clever! ... a trick, if you like, but how craftily played, how magnificently done, what impudent audacity! ...

"We count upon attracting all nations to the task of erecting the new fundamental structure, the project for which has been drawn up by us. This is why, before everything, it is indispensable for us to arm ourselves and to store up in ourselves that absolutely reckless audacity and irresistible might of the spirit which in the person of our active workers will break down all hindrances on our way.

"When we have accomplished our coup d'etat we shall say then to the various peoples: 'Everything has gone terribly badly, all have been worn out with sufferings. We are destroying the causes of your torment—nationalities, frontiers, differences of coinages. You are at liberty, of course, to pronounce sentence upon us, but can it possibly be a just one if it is confirmed by you before you make any trial of what we are offering you.' ... Then will the mob exalt us and bear us up in their hands in a unanimous triumph of hopes and expectations. Voting, which we have made the instrument which will set us on the throne of the world by teaching even the very smallest units of members of the human race to vote by means of meetings and agreements by groups, will then have served its purposes and will play its part then for the last time by a unanimity of desire to make close acquaintance with us before condemning us.

"To secure this we must have everybody vote without distinction of classes and qualifications, in order to establish an absolute majority, which can not be got from the educated propertied classes. In this way, by inculcating in all a sense of self-importance, we shall destroy among the goyim the importance of the family... .

"In order that our scheme may produce this result we shall arrange elections in favor of such presidents as have in their past some dark, undiscovered stain, some 'Panama' or other—then they will be trustworthy agents for the accomplishment of our plans out of fear of revelations and from natural desire of everyone who has attained power, namely, the retention of the privileges, advantages and honor connected with the office of president... .

"The president will, at our discretion, interpret the sense of such of the existing laws as admit of various interpretations; he will further annul them when we indicate to him the necessity to do so, besides this, he will have the right to propose temporary laws, and even new departures in the government constitutional working, the pretext both for the one and the other being the requirements for the supreme welfare of the State.

"By such measures we shall obtain the power of destroying little by little, step by step, all that at the outset when we enter on our rights, we are compelled to introduce into the constitutions of States to prepare for the transition to an imperceptible abolition of every kind of constitution, and then the time is come to turn every form of government into our despotism."

Zionist Power

Extract from Protocol 1

"In our day the power which has replaced that of the rulers who were liberal is the power of Gold. Time was when Faith ruled. The idea of freedom is impossible of realization because no one knows how to use it with moderation. It is enough to hand over a people to self-government for a certain length of time for that people to be turned into a disorganized mob. From that moment on we get internecine strife which soon develops into battles between classes in the midst of which

States burn down and their importance is reduced to that of a heap of ashes.

"Whether a State exhausts itself in its own convulsions, whether its internal discord brings it under the power of external foes—in any case it can be accounted irretrievably lost; it is in our power. The despotism of Capital, which is entirely in our hands, reaches out to it a straw that the State, willy nilly, must take hold of; if not— it goes to the bottom...

"Out of the temporary evil we are now compelled to commit will emerge the good of an unshakable rule, which will restore the regular course of the machinery of the national life, brought to nought by liberalism. The result justifies the means. Let us, however, in our plans, direct our attention not so much to what is good and moral as to what is necessary and useful...

"Our power in the present tottering condition of all forms of power will be more invincible than any other because it will remain invisible until the moment when it has gained such strength that no cunning can any longer undermine it."

EXTRACT FROM PROTOCOL 2

"In the hands of the States of today there is a great force that creates the movement of thought in the people, and that is the Press. The part played by the Press is to keep pointing out requirements supposed to be indispensable, to give voice to the complaints of the people, to express and to create discontent. It is in the Press that the triumph of freedom of speech finds its incarnation. But the goyim States have not known how to make use of this force; and it has fallen into our hands. Through the Press we have gained the power to influence while remaining ourselves in the shade; thanks to the Press we have got the gold in our hands, notwithstanding that we have had to gather it out of oceans of blood and tears. But it has paid us, though we have sacrificed many of our people. Each victim on our side is worth in the sight of God a thousand goyim."

EXTRACT FROM PROTOCOL 7

"We must be in a position to respond to every act of opposition by war with the neighbours of that country which dares to oppose us; but if these neighbours should also venture to stand collectively together against us, then we must offer resistance by a universal war.

"The principal factor of success in the political is the secrecy of its undertakings; the word should not agree with the deeds of the diplomat...

"We must compel the governments of the goyim to take action in the direction favoured by our widely-conceived plan, already approaching the desired consummation, by what we shall represent as public opinion, secretly prompted by us through the means of that socalled "Great Power"—the Press, which, with a few exceptions that may be disregarded, is already entirely in our hands.

"In a word, to sum up our system of keeping the governments of the goyim in Europe in check, we shall show our strength to one of them by terrorist attempts and to all, if we allow the possibility of a general rising against us, we shall respond with the guns of America or China or Japan."

EXTRACT FROM PROTOCOL 8

"We shall surround our government with a whole world of economists. That is the reason why economic science forms the principal subject of the teaching given to the Jews. Around us again will be a whole constellation of bankers, industrialists, capitalists and—the main thing— millionaires, because in substance everything will be settled by the question of figures.

"For a time, until there will no longer be any risk in entrusting responsible posts in our States to our brother-Jews, we shall put them in the hands of persons whose past and reputation are such that between them and the people lies an abyss, persons who, in case of disobedience to our instructions, must face criminal charges or disappear—this in order to make them defend our interests to their last gasp."

EXTRACT FROM PROTOCOL 12

"Not a single announcement will reach the public without our control. Even now this is already being attained by us inasmuch as all news items are received by a few agencies, in whose offices they are focussed from all parts of the world. These agencies will then be already entirely ours and will give publicity only to what we dictate to them.

"If already now we have contrived to possess ourselves of the minds of the goy communities to such an extent that they all come near looking upon the events of the world through the coloured glasses of those spectacles we are setting astride their noses; if already now there is not a single State where there exist for us any barriers to admittance into what goy stupidity calls State secrets; what will our position be then, when we shall be acknowledged supreme lords of the world in the person of our king of all the world."

EXTRACT FROM PROTOCOL 20

"Huge capitals have stagnated, withdrawing money from the States, which were constantly obliged to apply to those same stagnant capitals for loans. These loans burdened the finances of the State with the payment of interest and made them the bond slaves of these capitals. The concentration of industry in the hands of capitalists out of the hands of small masters has drained away all the juices of the peoples and with them also the States.

"The present issue of money in general does not correspond with the requirements per head, and cannot therefore satisfy all the needs of the workers. The issue of money ought to correspond with the growth of population and thereby children also must absolutely be reckoned as consumers of currency from the day of their birth. The revision of issue is a material question for the whole world.

"You are aware that the gold standard has been the ruin of the States which adopted it, for it has not been able to satisfy the demands for money, the more so that we have removed gold from circulation as far as possible."

ZIONIST "BROTHERHOOD"
EXTRACT FROM PROTOCOL 9

"And the weapons in our hands are limitless ambitions, and malice."

"It is from us that the all-engulfing terror proceeds. We have in our service persons of all opinions, of all doctrines, restorating monarchists, demagogues, socialists, communists, and Utopian dreamers of every kind. We have harnessed them all to the task: each one of them on his own account is boring away at the last remnants of authority, is striving to overthrow all established form of order. By these acts all States are in torture; they exhort to tranquility, are ready to sacrifice everything for peace: but we will not give them peace until they openly acknowledge our international Super-Government, and with sub-missiveness.

"The people have raised a howl about the necessity of settling the question of Socialism by way of an international agreement. Division into fractional parties has given them into our hands, for, in order to carry on a contested struggle one must have money, and the money is all in our hands...

'We have got our hands into the administration of the law, into the conduct of elections, into the press, into liberty of the person, but principally into education and training as being the corner-stones of a free existence.

"We have fooled, bemused and corrupted the youth of the goyim by rearing them in principles and theories which are known to us to be false although it is by us that they have been inculcated."

EXTRACT FROM PROTOCOL 11

"The goyim are a flock of sheep, and we are their wolves. And you know what happens when the wolves get hold of the flock?...

"For what purpose then have we invented this whole policy and insinuated it into the minds of the goys without giving them any chance to examine its underlying meaning? For what, indeed, if not in order to obtain in a roundabout way what is for our scattered tribe unattainable by the direct road? It is this which has served as the basis for our organization of secret masonry which is not known to, and aims which are not even so much as suspected by, these goy cattle, attracted by us into the "show" army of masonic lodges in order to throw dust in the eyes of their fellows."

THE DESTRUCTION OF THE CHRISTIAN RELIGION
EXTRACT FROM PROTOCOL 17

"We have long past taken care to discredit the priesthood of the goyim, and thereby to ruin their mission on earth which in these days might still be a great hindrance to us. Day by day its influence on the peoples of the world is falling lower. Freedom of conscience has been declared everywhere, so that now only years divide us from the moment of the complete wrecking of that Christian religion; as to other religions we shall have still less difficulty in dealing with them, but it would be premature to speak of this now. We shall set clericalism and clericals into such narrow frames as to make their influence move in retrogressive proportion to its former progress.

"When the time comes finally to destroy the papal court the finger of an invisible hand will point the nations towards this court. When, however, the nations fling themselves upon it, we shall come forward in the guise of its defenders as if to save excessive bloodshed. By this diversion we shall penetrate to its very bowels and be sure we shall never come out again until we have gnawed through the entire strength of this place.

"ZIONIST POPE OF THE UNIVERSE"

"The King of the Jews will be the real Pope of the Universe, the patriarch of an international Church.

"But, in the meantime, while we are re-educating youth in new traditional religions and afterwards in ours, we shall not overtly lay a finger on existing churches, but we shall fight against them by criticism calculated to produce schism."[19]

ZIONIST ACHIEVEMENT

They govern the world and have temporarily acquired the wealth of Palestine. They have overthrown several of the governments of Europe and have established communistic dictatorships in place of them:

The Khazar Jew, Joseph Stalin,[20] is dictator of Russia; the Jew, Manuilsky, is dictator of the Ukraine;

the Jew, Jacob Berman, is dictator of Poland;

the Jewess, Anna Pauker, is dictator of Rumania; the Jew, Rakosi, is dictator of Hungary;

the Jew, Ilya Ehrenburg, is editor of the official organ, "Pravda;" the Jew, Judin, is editor of the official "Cominform Fortnightly."

---

[19] Copies of The Protocols may be secured from Gerald L. K. Smith, P. O. Box D-4, St. Louis 1, Mo. E. M. Biggers, Houston, Texas. Pioneer News Service, P. 0. Box 435, Chicago 90, Ill.

[20] His face indicates his Mongolian origin.

4.

WOODROW WILSON[21]

"The political has nothing in common with the moral. The ruler who is governed by the moral is not a skilled politician, and is therefore unstable on his throne. He who wishes to rule must have recourse both to cunning and to make believe. Great national qualities, like frankness and honesty, are vices in politics, for they bring down rulers from their thrones more effectively and more certainly than the most powerful enemy. Such qualities must be the attributes of the kingdoms of the GOYIM, but we must in no wise be guided by them."

—from Protocol 1.

There has never been a more artistic liar than Woodrow Wilson. He was even more plausible than Franklin D. Roosevelt, and he had as pleasing and ingratiating appearance and speech as Roosevelt. As pious and unctious and hyocritical as was Roosevelt, Wilson was more so. Roosevelt had the candour to admit that he was a hybrid Jew, but Wilson never conceded that he was a pure bred Jew. The fact is we are an unsuspecting, gullible people.

---

[21] This chapter is a supplement to "Zionist Wall Street , " Chapter 4, "Woodrow Wilson and the Federal Reserve System". The statement that he was a "Jewish Marrano" was based on a newspaper report and I therefore had some misgiving about it, and sought confirmation in the Universal Jewish Encyclopedia, which contains a history of only prominent Jews. President Wilson had the appearance of a Gentile and in that respect was different from President Truman.

PRESIDENT WILSON WAS A JEW

The Universal Jewish Encyclopedia, page 426, confirms President Wilson's Jewish descent and the fact that the Jews elected him. It states that,

"The period of his (Wilson's) presidency 1913 to 1921 was marked by the application of idealism in both domestic and international affairs, by the participation of the United States in the First World War, by the summoning of Jews to high position in which they rendered important services in connection with these significant events. His association with individual Jews began in 1928 when Henry Morgenthau, Sr., inspired by his idealism, invited him to speak at the dinner celebrating the 4th anniversary of the free Synagogue in New York. Morgenthau took an active part in Wilson's campaign for the Democratic nomination and was chairman of the Democratic finance committee ...

"He appointed Morgenthau ambassador to Turkey in order to serve the welfare of the Jews in Palestine, Bran-deis as judge of the Supreme Court, Eugene Meyer, chairman of the War Finance Corporation.

"In 1918 at the urging of a delegation of Zionist leaders headed by Stephen S. Wise he endorsed the plan for the establishment of a national Jewish home in Palestine. During the peace conferences at the close of the war he consistently championed the cause of the Jewish minorities and aided in having protective clauses written into the treaties. He reached back into the Hebrew Bible to select the word "Covenant" to describe the agreement constituting his favorite dream of a League of Nations ...

"He appointed the following Jews to important offices: Abram Elcus, Lewis Einstein, Ira Nelson Morris, Paul

Warburg, Frank W. Taussig (author of a text book on political economy), Leo S. Rowe, Morton Vogel and Milton Straussburg."

The Jewish Encyclopedia also confirms the fact that Wilson was deeply interested in giving Palestine to the Jews. It confirms the claim that he brought about the "Balfour Declaration" and that we entered the war to establish the League of Nations and Palestine as a Jewish home. It was the plan of the Kaiser to acquire Palestine and its mineral wealth for the German Empire. He was informed of the wealth of the Dead Sea and surrounding country for he contemplated building a railroad to Palestine. He was evidently doublecrossed by some one, probably his Prime Minister, Bethmann Hollweg, a Rothschild descendant, for he gave his permission, with his blessing, for Lenin and Trotsky to cross Germany into Russia. He thus obtained the conquest of Russia, one of our allies.

This crooked deal obviously meant that we were inveigled into the First World War to establish a Jewish world empire through the League of Nations and to give the Rothschilds the wealth of Palestine. The first war failed to accomplish this purpose and so we had a second one. Franklin Roosevelt truly said that "things don't just happen—they are planned that way." The Zionists now have, according to plan, the wealth of Palestine and their United Nations, and a $65,000,000 capitol building in New York City that we, the gullible Christian "goyim cattle" have paid for with "sweat and blood and tears."

I am entitled to credit for first revealing the duplicity of president Wilson in appointing Paul Warburg Vice-Governor of the Federal Reserve System and in approving the Warburg amendment, thereby converting the system into a central bank with authority to fix and regulate our economy, as set forth in my first book, "The Crime of '20."

PERSONAL NOTE

This was my maiden effort in book writing. I knew nothing about the money and Jew problems prior thereto. My bankruptcy provoked me to study the history of money and our banking system which led to a study of its authors, the Rothschilds.

Mr. William J. Cameron was the editor of Mr. Ford's Dearborn Independent and the reputed author of "The International Jew." He was an authority on the gold standard and also understood the Jewish problem. He wrote me after reading the manuscript of my "Crime of '20," as follows:

> Mr. Armstrong:
>
> I think that yours is the most vivid and compelling of all the writings on finance that have come here. In book form it ought to go well.
>
> W.J. Cameron

The late great Thomas A. Edison was a student of the money problem and wrote me regarding it as follows:

From the Laboratory of Thomas A. Edison, Orange, N.J.

March 7, 1922.

Mr. George W. Armstrong,
G.W.Armstrong & Co. Inc.,
Fort Worth, Texas.

Dear Sir:-

        I want to thank you for your letter of February 27 and also for the complimentary copy of your book, "The Crime of '20". The book is immensely interesting.

        Something is bound to come out of this agitation on the subject of money. It seems to me there is something wrong somewhere. It is a very complex subject, but I feel sure it can be analyzed and made clear.

Yours very truly,

Thos A Edison

PS get Carter Glass speech in Senate defending the Reserve J. Bank, He sent me one

Mr. Edison said of the gold standard:

"Gold makes pretty jewelry and picture frames and is used effectively for filling teeth. Otherwise, it is an almost wholly useless substance. Yet we hold it as the standard of all values.

"The gold standard system is largely fiction. Banks have a gold reserve of, say, fifty percent of their note issue. This is fifty percent alleged real reserve and fifty percent pure gamble, the banks taking the gambling chance that the note holders will not call on them all at one time. Finally, if things go wrong, and the note holders begin to demand the fifty percent gold, the banks fall back upon the credit of the government and the merchants' notes through the Federal Reserve.

"It seems absurd to me that all our values should be based on boxes of metal in any treasury. It is an absurdity, but everyone has been educated to believe that absurdity is common sense...

"Under the present system our government certifies to the amount of gold in disks and bars of metallic alloy. Then they are packed into boxes and kept traveling continuously all over the world—New York to London, London to Bombay, back to New York, and so on."[22]

LEAGUE OF NATIONS

President Wilson made his second race for the presidency on the platform that he "kept us out of the war." The Zionists brought about the sinking of the Lusitania and put the blame on the Germans. President Wilson declared war for the alleged purpose of "preserving the freedom of the seas", a doctrine that is now obsolete. The British secret report No.

---

[22] *The Diary and Sundry Observations of Thomas A Edison*, edited by Dagobert D. Runes, page 192-3.

1919 (discussed later) sheds a flood of light upon the criminals who brought about the war, and their motives.

Upon the conclusion of the war, President Wilson met with Lloyd George of England and Clemenceau of France to write a peace treaty and the League of Nations. President Wilson was guided by Bernard Baruch who rented a house in Paris and was his intimate adviser and companion. Lloyd George was accompanied by Phillip Sassoon of the Rothschild family and a member of the British Privy Council; Georges Clemenceau had as his adviser Georges Mandell whose true name was Jereboam Rothschild and who was then the ruling head of the Rothschild family and a member of the French Cabinet. It was a Rothschild peace treaty and a Rothschild League of Nations. It was in violation of every promise that President Wilson made the Kaiser which induced him to surrender. The Kaiser was shamelessly double-crossed and the seeds of the second world war were then planted.

FEDERAL RESERVE SYSTEM

Our Congressmen have been deceived by Zionist lies and cowed by Zionist power. The Federal Reserve Banking System which was originally intended as a decentralized system, responsive to the demands of industry and commerce, has been perverted into a central bureau with despotic power over the welfare of the people. Despite the fact that it has brought about three depressions, 1920, 1930 and 1937, Congress granted an indefinite extension of its Charter by the "Banking Act of 1935."

President Wilson and Senator Glass are not entitled to credit for the original act but they are both responsible for the Warburg amendment changing the system to a central bank controlled by the Federal Reserve Board. The author of the original act was Senator Robert L. Owen of Oklahoma, then chairman of the Senate Banking Committee. He had the powerful support of William J. Bryan and William G. McAdoo.

GEORGE W. ARMSTRONG

5.

FIRST WORLD WAR

The British Secret Service Report No. 1919, called the "Col. E. M. House letter," contains an official and authentic report of the first world war, the agency that brought it about and the purpose of it. This report in its entirety is highly interesting but the discussion here will be limited to "Imperial Unity," J. P. Morgan & Company, British Duplicity, and the League of Nations.

This report, or letter, was presented to the House of Representatives by Congressman Thorkelson of Montana, and is published in the Congressional Record of October 11, 1939, p. 598-604 inclusive. Its authenticity was discussed by members of the House and an effort was made to strike it from the Record, which failed. See Congressional Record, October 13, 1939, p. 714 et seq.; also of September 9, 1940, p. 17835; and September 11, 1940, p. 18311.

The letter or report is not published in the bound volumes of the Congressional Record of October 11, 1939, or the appendix of that date. Evidently some interested person prevented its publication, despite the refusal of the House of Representatives to strike it from the Record. The text as here set forth can be easily verified by reference to an original unbound copy of the Congressional Record of October 11, 1939. It will be published in full in the next edition of this booklet.

It was called the "Col. E. M. House letter," but it is not a letter. It is an official report made by an important officer of the British Secret Service, on stationery of the British Consulate. It reveals its official character and its verity upon its face.

No minor official would dare write such a letter to the British Prime Minister, or dare discuss the important subjects contained in it, except in the line of duty. Moreover, it was written by a man who KNEW and whose duty it was to know.

It was not written by Col. E. M. House. This name was merely an adopted name; a nom de plume. It is the custom of secret agents to disguise themselves under a number or an assumed name. The letter is known as the British Secret Service Report No. 1919. See Congressional Record, October 13, 1939, p. 714.

It discloses that it was probably written by Lord Northcliffe, who was at that time the head of the British Propaganda Department in enemy countries. He sustained toward Lloyd George the same intimate relationship that once existed between Woodrow Wilson and Colonel House, and this fact may explain the name he assumed.

This document should be considered in connection with the drive by the Fair Dealers, the press, the radio, and the uplifters, for the Atlantic Pact, "Union Now," "Federal Union, Inc.," etc., for it will enable us to determine the true meaning of it all.

The immensely wealthy private bank of N. M. Rothschild & Son, and the Zionists, controlled the British Empire then as well as now. Then they controlled the Bank of England, the press, the railroads, and the industries with minor exceptions. Lord Northcliffe was the publisher of the Daily Mail and other papers.

The report follows:

Imperial Unity

"The Right Honorable David Lloyd George, Sir:

British Consulate New York City June 10, 1919

I was highly honored by your personal letter of May 24 last, and wish to thank you for the cordial expression of approval of my work which it contained. You were very good enough to require from me a frank and confidential account of the campaign conducted under my direction in this country, together with such suggestions as might further help to lead it speedily to a successful conclusion. As the campaign had been under way for a considerable time before you were called to direct the destinies of England, I shall review it from its commencement, and, emboldened by your sanction, I shall freely make whatever suggestions seem to me good.

Prom the moment of my arrival here, it was evident to me that such an Anglo-American alliance as would ultimately result in the peaceful return of the American Colonies to the dominion of the Crown could be brought about only with the consent of the dominant group of the controlling clans.

For those who can afford the universities, we are, as I have already mentioned, plentifully supplying British-born or trained professors, lecturers, and presidents. A Canadian-born admiral now heads the United States Naval College. We are arranging for a greater interchange of professors between the two countries. The student interchange could be much improved. The Rhodes scholarships are inadequate in number. I would suggest that the Carnegie trustees be approached to extend to American students the benefits of the scheme by which Scottish students are subsidized at Scottish universities. If necessary, a grant from the treasury should be obtained for this excellent work, which, however, should remain for the present—at least outwardly—a private enterprise ...

Through the Red Cross, the Scout movement, the Y M.C.A., the church, and other humane, religious, and quasi-religious organizations, we have created an atmosphere of international effort which strengthens the idea of unity of the English-speaking world. In the co-ordination of this work, Mr. Raymond Fosdick, formerly of the Rockefeller Foundation, has been especially conspicuous. I would also like to mention President Nicholas Murray Butler of Columbia University, who has eloquently advocated this form of internationalism and carefully emphasized its distinction from the false internationalism which is infecting the proletariat.

The Overseas Club in this country now contains nearly a hundred thousand pledged members with a journal of their own. Our thanks are due to Lord St. George's, St. David's, St. Andrew's, and Pilgrim Clubs, together with the Daughters of the Empire, the Prince of Wales Fund, and the other associations and guilds connected with our multitudinous war charities, enable us to pervade all sections and classes of the country, and provide us with a force of empire builders whose loyalty and services are both invaluable to us and highly appreciated by the native colonists...

The censorship, together with our monopoly of cables and our passport control of passengers, enables us to hold all American newspapers as isolated from the non-American world as if they had been in another planet instead of in another hemisphere. The realization of this by the Associated Press and the other universal news gatherers—except Hearst—was most helpful in bringing only our point of view to the papers they served.

British-born editors and reporters now create imperial sentiment in most American newspapers. As their identity and origins are not usually known, they can talk and write for us as Americans to Americans...

Below that level, imperial unity cannot be securely established upon the debris of the Constitution here. We will not passively permit this unity to be now menaced when it is all but perfect. Has not America, while still maintaining an outward show of independence, yielded to our wishes in the Panama Canal tolls and Canadian fisheries' disputes, as was fitting and filial? Was not America happy to fight our war in Europe? Was not America, like Canada, willing not only to pay her own war expenses but also to loan us money for ours ? Was not America, like Canada, content to seek nothing in return for her war duty, so long as the motherland was completely indemnified in Egypt and the rest of Africa, in Persia, Mesopotamia, Syria, and elsewhere? Was not America as proud to be honored by knighthood and lesser titulary distinctions, as Canada was, or, rather, more proud?

Has not President Wilson canceled the big Navy program and dutifully conceded to us the command of the seas, confident that we shall defend America against all future foes that may threaten our supremacy, just as we defended America and Canada against Germany? In matters lingual, legal and financial, fiscal, commercial, social, evangelical, administrative, martial, naval, educational—are not in all these matters the established relations of America to England, in kind—if not precisely in degree—identical with the relations of the other colonies and dominions to the Crown? Indeed, I might justifiably sustain the thesis that soi-distant American Republic is now more happily and more closely bound to the Empire than are, for example, the ungrateful and insolent colonies which lately were the Boer Republics.

As long as President Wilson, with our Canadian-born Secretary of the Interior, Mr. Franklin Lane, with our Scotch-born Secretary of Labor, Mr. W. B. Wilson, and with our

London-born Mr. Samuel Gompers,—now controls the administration, imperial unity will daily grow more intimate and more perfect. But I regret to inform you that our committee on American Elections has reported (Appendix 38) that no matter how lavishly we finance the next election, the Wilson administration will pass, and with it, perchance, that absolute administrative control over the legislature, which has meant so much to us. Willful, wanton, and wicked men will unite in the next election with labor and those industrialists who profit-patriotism ratio has been allowed to fall below the threshold of loyalty to imperial unity. These combined forces of disorder will seek to elect a legislature which will attempt to make the administration responsible to it, instead of to us and our auxiliaries, and will strive to rend the bonds which bind this colony to the motherland, for the sole, selfish, and seditious purpose of erecting a separate, national, economic unit independent of us—and even perhaps, competing with us. We must, therefore, hasten to remove from this legislature, with the aid of our supporters here, such of its powers as could be used against imperial unity.

J. P. MORGAN & CO. ARE BRITISH AGENTS

In the financial world the Anglo-American alliance is a wellestablished fact. And as the consortium for China, and the security company for Mexico show, our brokers and their aids have become the unchallenged financiers of the world. We have been particularly fortunate in our fiscal agents here, Messrs. Pierpont Morgan & Company. The commissions they charged, both as our brokers and purchasing agents no doubt were high enough to warrant their summary treatment at the hands of Mr. Balfour during his visit here. But they advantageously placed our many bond issues and every American holder of these bonds having now a stake in the Empire is a defender of its integrity and a potential supporter of its extension over here. Their services in putting this country into the war way not been altruistic, but they were nonetheless effective. They contributed liberally to our Americanization campaign. They ousted Miss Boardman, and through Messrs. Taft and H. P. Davidson they nationalized and directed the American Red Cross, and then internationalized it under the direction of Mr. H. P. Davidson. Through Mr. Thomas Lamont they purchased Harpers Magazine and the New York Evening Post. Through advertisers they control, they have exerted widespread influence on newspaper policy. Messrs. Lamont and Davidson gave you valuable aid at the peace conference. They loaned $200,000,000 to Japan that our ally might build a fleet to compete with America on the Pacific carrying routes. Their attempts to retain for us control of the international mercantile marine are well known to you. And I would be amiss if I did not remind you that they relieved the government of considerable embarrassment by pensioning worthily the widow of our late Ambassador Sir Cecil Spring-Rice, at a time when the antagonism of Lord Northcliffe made it impossible for us officially to do so. As the greater part of their capital is invested within the Empire, the Government of His Majesty will doubtless have opportunity to appreciate the value of the services of Messrs. Pierpont Morgan & Company.

BRITISH DUPLICITY

Through our fiscal agents here and our aids who act for other Allied countries, as Sir Clifford Sifton acts for Rumania, we have become the world's purchasers. Moreover, the war has made us the custodian of the greater part of the world's raw materials. With moneys lent to us by the American Government for war purposes, we have, acting through quasi-American companies, by the aid of Mr. Connor Guthrie, obtained control of the large oil fields in California and in Costa Rica, And through the nationalization of His Majesty's Government of the Cowdray, Pearson, and Royal Dutch Shell interests in Mexico, we, having become masters of the Mexican, Canadian, Rumanian, Armenian, Persian, and lessor oil fields, now largely control the oil fuel of the world and thereby the world's transportation and industry. We have not yet succeeded in controlling the pipe lines owned by the Standard Oil Company, and its subsidiaries, for those companies have long been established. But, although uncontrolled companies may continue to get their oil to the seaboard, the proposed system of preferential treatment at our universal oiling stations for ships supplied at the port of departures with British oil (Appendix 37) will prevent the use of any oil but ours on the high seas.

This control would enable us to exert such pressure as would make American industrial interests amenable to His Majesty's pleasure. But it would be unwise to make disciplinary use of our fuel power before we secure remission of our $4,000,000,000 debt. Otherwise, the American industrial interests might retaliate by forcing the United States Government to exact from us the agreed interest, to maintain tariff barriers against our merchandise, and to withdraw support from the rate of exchange, which would make our labor and resources for years pay tribute to this country—an unnatural, an unfilial, and unthinkable proceeding. We are conducting a vigorous campaign for the cancellation of this war debt, on the grounds (a) that we fought America's fight for her for 2 years, while she was prospering in cowardice; and (6) that at least the material burdens should be distributed justly, if the world is to be made safe for democracy. Synchronously with this agitation for the remission of our debt, we are agitating for further loans of American money to rebuild our markets in Europe. There is no possibility of these two agitations endangering their mutual success, for we have repeatedly proved beyond question that the American mind cannot synchronously fix and correlate facts, with two cognate items on the statements to be judged each on its merits. Hence, we are able in a cloud of candor to state the merit of the loan—viz, that unless the money be lent to us we cannot pay the interest on it. In these agitations we are receiving valuable, if not wholly disinterested, aid from our financial auxiliaries and fiscal agents (J. P. Morgan & Co.) ...

In Mexico our friends made a tentative adventure with the gallant Blanquet, but it miscarried, perhaps owing to a slight misunderstanding between the bond interests and the industrial interests. However, we are quietly continuing our work in Mexico until the United States Government shall be put in a position to take it over. An American war with Mexico would cost us nothing; it would satisfy certain American industrial interests; it would guarantee our title to the Mexican oil fields; it would humble, by impoverishing, this purse-proud people; it would give us an opportunity to show the American that he—isolated in the world—needs our protection against our ally, Japan; and while America was busy warring we would enjoy a clear field in the European, African, and Asiatic trade, together with the monopoly of the markets of a South America hostile to the Monroe Doc-trinaries of democracy. For these reasons our press is fully reporting Mexican outrages, but a strange apathy seems to have fallen on the people, an apathy from which only border raids or special atrocities will arouse them.

LEAGUE OF NATIONS

In other words, we must quickly act to transfer its dangerous sovereignty from this colony to the custody of the Crown. We must, in short, now bring America within the Empire. God help-ing us, we can do no other. The first visible step in this direction has been taken; President Wilson has accepted and sponsored the plan for a League of Nations which we prepared for him. We have wrapped this plan in the peace treaty so that the world must accept from us the League or a continuance of the war. The League is in substance the

Empire with America admitted on the same basis as our other colonies.

The effectiveness of the League will depend upon the power with which it can be endowed, and that will hinge upon the skill with which the cardinal functions of the American legislature are transferred to the executive Council of the League. Any abrupt change may startle the ignorant American masses and rouse them to action against it. And us. Our best policy, therefore, would be to appoint President Wilson first president of the League. When the fourteen points seemed to our Government twice seven daily sins, I analyzed with care his diverse and numerous notes and discourses and divided them into their two parts: One, the Wilson creed, "I believe in open covenants and in the freedom of the seas," etc.; and two, the Wilson commandments, "Might shall not prevail over right, the strong shall not oppress the weak," etc. From the "too proud to fight" and "he kept us out of war" episodes, I ventured to deduce (September 29, 1918, Appendix 36) that he would a.t the appropriate moment oblige us by transferring the "not" from his commandments to his creed without as much as a "may I not," and in such a way that his people will be none the wiser.

The plain people of this country are inveterate and incurable hero worshipers. They are, however, sincere in sentiment; and for a hero to become established in the public shrine, he must first succeed in getting his name associated with the phrases and slogans that seem to reflect the undefined aspirations of the average inhabitant. When this has been accomplished the allegiance is at once transferred from the sentiment to the sentimentalist, from the ideal to the maker of the longed-for phrase. -No one understands this peculiarity of the native behavior better than Mr. Wilson, which accounts largely for his exceptional usefulness to us. He knows that Americans will not scrutinize any performance too closely, provided their faith in the performer has been adequately established. Mr. Wilson has since made the transfer amid American acclamation. In the same way he will now be able to satisfy them that far from surrendering their independence to the League they are actually extending their sovereignty by it. He alone can satisfy them on this. He alone can father an anti-Bolshevik act which—judicially interpreted—will enable appropriate punitive measures to be applied to any American who may be unwise enough to assert that America must again declare her independence. And he alone, therefore, is qualified to act for us as first president of the League.

I confess I am a little uneasy lest in the exigencies of diplomatic combat, Mr.Wilson may not have found the joy he anticipated from matching his wits against the best brains of Europe. He is easily slighted and remarkably vindictive. It is the highest degree desirable that any traces of resentment his mind may be harboring against us should be radically removed before he returns. I would, therefore, suggest that the work of adulation planned in Appendix 32 should be instructed to consult the inventories I have prepared (appendixes 4583), which show that he is now surfeited with diamond stomachers, brooches, and bracelets, Gobelin tapestries, mosaics, and vases, gold caskets, and plates.

The program we arranged for his visit to England (appendix 33) including a royal reception at Buckingham Palace, with which the President was well pleased. The fruitful visit of the President to the King should be returned as early as possible. I would suggest that as soon as the President is settled once more in the White House, the visit should be returned by His Royal Highness, the Prince of Wales, who would be an admirable representative of His Royal Sire, and would satisfy President Wilson's sense of fitness. It is perhaps unfortunate that there is not a Presidential daughter of the Prince's age, for such a union would have greatly advanced our purpose not only with the American people, but also with a President who feels that lese majeste should be punishable with 20 years' imprisonment, and who acts as if he considered his son-in-law, Mr. McAdoo, as his heir apparent...

PRESIDENT WILSON'S PECULIARITIES

Too great attention cannot be given at this time to the Presidential peculiarities, for his devotion to our purpose will depend upon our ability to pander to them. I would suggest that the new ambassador to Washington should be chosen only after the most careful thought. He should not be too clever, lest Mr. Wilson shun him. He should be able to evince hilarity at the most venerable jest, no matter how often he may have to suffer it. This qualification is vitally important whether Mr. Wilson's "humor" is merely assumed to perpetuate the "human" tradition established for Presidents by Lincoln, or whether it is studied descent from Jovelike isolation to Jovelike jest. The ambassador should be a Wilson worshiper. I enclose (appendix 34) resumes of the methods of worship practiced by various members of his inner circle. The appointee would do well to familiarize himself with them, and my services are at his disposal should be desire more extended information on the method of worship he selects. He should of course be a commoner, that we may not lose democratic favor—preferably a professor—and sufficiently subsidized to be able to entertain regally. If a list were submitted to Mr. Wilson he might be prepared to indicate all of whom he did not approve, and the one against whom he expressed no preju-dices should be appointed. The pressing need of our embassy at Washington is not so much an ambassador as a gentleman in waiting to the President.

I would suggest that his powers as President of the League of Nations be left undefined for the present. He may be trusted to assume what power he can and to use it in the interests of the Crown.

A grant of a privy purse of $100,000,000 would prove most acceptable to him and would be useful for private espionage, private wars, Siberian railroads, etc. His appointment should be for life, and you might definitely promise him that any instructions he may care to convey concerning his successor will receive the most careful attention of His Majesty's Government...

Nevertheless, it would be well quickly to reinforce him in the presidency of the League of Nations by staging the first session of the League in Washington. This will convince these simple people that they are the League and its power resides in them. Their pride in this power should be exalted. Perhaps you, yourself, might condescend to visit this country. Or, if that be impracticable, you might send such noble statesmen, and stately noblemen, as will suffice to make of the first League session a spectacle of unsurpassed brilliance. Indeed, it would be well to commence at an early date a series of spectacles by which the mob may be diverted from any attempt to think too much of matters beyond their province. The success of the Joffre, Vivianti, Balfour, and other missions in amusing the people while the country was quietly put into the war shows that similar missions would likewise amuse the people—while the country was quietly put into the League. I would suggest that missions of thanksgiving to America be organized, and that His Majesty the King of the Belgians, Cardinal Mercier, Field Marshal Foch, Venizelos, and an eminent Italian or two be sent seriatim.

PROPAGANDA

While awaiting these diversions for the vulgar, we art incessantly instructing them in the wonders of the League. Its praises are thundered by our press, decreed by our college presidents, and professed by our professors. Our authors, writers, and lecturers are analyzing its selected virtues for whomsoever will read or listen. As will be seen from appendix 39, circular issued by the League of Nations committee, we have enlisted 8,000 pulpiteers or propagandists for the League. We have organized international and national synods, consistories, committees, conferences, convocations, conventions, councils, congresses, and assemblies, as well as their State, municipal, and district equiv alents, to herald the birth of the League as the dawn of universal peace. A special Sunday will be observed as League Sunday in all churches. In this connection, may I remark that the appointment of Mr. Raymond Fosdick to the Secretariat of the League, has pleased not only the Rockefeller interests but also the less disingenuous uplifters, for it stamps the League as an endowed organization for promiscuous uplifting, under the triple crown of religion, respectability, and finance. Agriculturalists, bankers, brokers, chartered accounts, chemists, and all other functional groups capable of exerting organized professional, business, financial, or social pressure are meeting to endorse the League in the name of peace, progress, and prosperity...

The World's Peace Foundation has issued for us a series of League of Nations pamphlets, which, with our other literature, tax the mails to the limit of their capacity. Our film concerns are preparing an epochmaking picture entitled "The League of Nations." In brief, our entire system of thought control is working ceaselessly, tirelessly, ruthlessly, to insure the adoption of the League. And it will be adopted, for business wants peace, the righteous cannot resist a covenant, and the politicians, after shadow-boxing for patronage purposes, will yield valiantly lest the fate of the wanton and willful pursue them...

By these means we hope smoothly to overcome all effective opposition on the part of our colony, America, to entering the League—that is, the Empire. As soon as the League is functioning properly, His Majesty, in response to loyal and repeated solicitation, might graciously be pleased to consent to restore to this (people their ancient right to petition at the foot of the throne; to confer the ancient rank and style of governor general upon our Ambassador, that this colony may enjoy a status inferior to no other colony's; to establish the primacy of the metropolitan see, with the Right Reverend Dr. Manning as first primate; to appoint Mr. Elihu Root lord chief justice of the colony, and to nominate Messrs. W. H. Taft, Nicholas Murray Butler, J. P. Morgan, Elizabeth Marbury, Adolph Ochs, and Thomas Lamont to the colonial privy council; as a special mark of royal and imperial condescension, to rename the Federal Capital of the Colony Georgetown, and lest section jealousy be thereby excited, to grant royal charters to the cities of Boston and Chicago entitling them thereafter to style themselves, respect-ively, Kingston and Guelf— concisely to bestow in time and in measure such tokens of the bounty of the Crown as the fealty of the colonists merit...

BRITISH-AMERICAN UNION URGED

Since that memorable day, September 19, 1877, on which the late Cecil Rhodes devised by will a fund "to and for the establishment, promotion, and development of a secret society—the true aim of which and object of which shall be the extension of British rule throughout the world, and especially the ultimate recovery of the United States of America as an integral part of the British Empire"— the energy and intelligence of England has not been spent in vain. It would perhaps be presumptuous of me to refer here to the admirable services rendered not only by LORD NORTHCLIFFE (the probable author of the report) and the corps of 12,000 trained workers whom he introduced here during the year as purchasing agents under the direction of Sir Campbell Stuart, but also the Right Honorable Arthur

J. Balfour, and by Lord Reading. But my report would be incomplete without a reference to Mr. Andrew Carnegie, of Skibo Castle, Suthelandshire, and New York City. He unobtrusively assumed the mantle of the late Mr. Cecil Rhodes. Through the Carnegie Foundation, he obtained such control over the professorate of this country that even President Wilson was a suppliant for a Carnegie pension before this people and allied gratitude placed him beyond prospective want.

The Carnegie League to Enforce Peace and its affiliate League of Small Nations are even now leading the van in our fight. In the North American Review, June 1893, Mr. Carnegie wrote: "Let men say what they will, I say that as surely as the sun in the heavens once shone upon Britain and America united, so surely is it one morning to rise, to shine upon, to greet again, the reunited states—the BritishAmerican union."

The object of Cecil Rhodes is almost attained. The day prophesied by Mr. Carnegie is near at hand, the day when the American Colonies will be in all things one with the motherland, one and indivisible. Only the last great battle remains to be, fought—the battle to compel her acceptance of the terms of the League of Nations."

6.

PALESTINE AND THEODOR HERZL

"His Majesty's government view with favor the establishment in Palestine of a national home for the Jewish people and will use their best endeavors to facilitate the achievement of this object, it being clearly understood that nothing shall be done which may prejudice the civil and religious rights of the existing non-Jewish communities in Palestine or the rights and political status enjoyed by Jews in any other country."

—Balfour Declaration.

MINERAL WEALTH OF DEAD SEA

The value of the minerals of the Dead Sea is estimated at five trillion dollars. This estimate appears to be optimistic but it is supported in part by the report of the Crown Agents of the British Colonies entitled "Production of Minerals From the Waters of the Dead Sea" (page 2). It is alleged that all copies of this booklet containing this report have been destroyed except those in the British Museum, Colonial office, and House of Commons. This official report estimates the minerals, except oil, in 1925 as follows: Magnesium Chloride, 22,000 tons, value 600 billion dollars; Potassium Chloride, 20,000 tons, value 75 billion dollars; other minerals valued at

1,200 billion dollars; or a total of about three trillion dollars, exclusive of oil.[23]

This enormous value staggers the imagination. I am unable to appraise the effect on the human race if the Zionists gain undisputed title to it, or if it should be devoted to public use.

This huge concession was first granted by the British Colonial Secretary to the Russian Zionist Moise Novemeysky in 1923 and finally granted on January 1, 1930, by the British House of Lords to "Palestine Potash Limited", a joint stock company. This company, so far as known, is composed wholly of American, British, and Russian Zionist Jews. Mr. H. H. Klein, a patriotic Jew, states that there are 1500 American stockholders and that they organized themselves into a corporation known as "Palestine Associates Inc.," with a capital of $400,000,000 and that this group owns 581,000 shares of the parent company. He states that Moise Novemeysky owns 30,000 shares; that Casenove Nominees Ltd., owns 221,075 shares; that Palestine Economic Corporation, dominated by the Warburgs, owns 45,111 shares, and that the Anglo Palestine Bank Nominees owns 42,935 shares. He says also that Palestine Potash Ltd. has three American directors, viz: Benjamin Brodie, Julius Simons, and Robert Szold, whose brother is a member of the banking firm of Lehman Bros.

Mr. H. H. Klein says of the British concession and the protocols: "The aim of Zionist leaders was to establish a Jewish state in Palestine. Why?

Was it in order to fulfill the plan outlined in the Protocols of the Learned Elders of Zion, for world conquest; or was it to protect the concession for the exploitation of all the

---

[23] The Palestine Mystery, pages 12 and 13.

chemical wealth in the Dead Sea in Palestine, estimated at five thousand billion (five trillion) dollars?

"If it is for the purpose of world conquest, then Jews have been fatally deceived, because Zionist leaders and their financial backers maintain that the Protocols are a forgery. If it is for the purpose of extracting chemical wealth from the Dead Sea, then Jews have been shamefully imposed upon because that purpose has never been mentioned by Zionist leaders.

"If the Protocols are a 'forgery' whatever that may mean, it is the most remarkable 'forgery' ever perpetrated because every step outlined in that amazing document of over 30.000 words, is an accomplished fact. This so-called forgery was published fifty years ago. At that time, the value of the chemicals of the Dead Sea was known to the financial backers of Theodor Herzl who is known as the 'father of Zionism'."

The financial backers of Theodor Herzl were M. A. Rothschild & Son of Paris and N. M. Rothschild & Son of London. Mr. Klein confirms the opinion expressed by Henry Ford in The International Jew, viz: That the protocols explain current history. There can be no reasonable question about the authenticity of the protocols and the fact that they were adopted by World Zionist Jewry and that they represent the plan of the Zionist Jews for creating a World Empire. The first and second World Wars were for that purpose and so, likewise, was the Jewish invasion of Palestine. That was also the purpose of the League of Nations and is the purpose of the United Nations—all Zionist enterprises.

Mr. Klein says further that the "American Group," owners of 51,000 shares of Palestine Potash, Ltd., incorporated in 1930 under the name of "Palestine Associates, Inc.," and that "at least seven of the directors of this corporation are members of the American Jewish Committee." He says that ex-Governor of New York Herbert H. Lehman has been honorary head of Palestine Economic Corporation for many years and that this corporation "owns banks, water companies, land holding companies, hotels, and agricultural corporations in Palestine." He says that these facts have been concealed from the Jews and that they have been used as tools by their Zionist leaders. Henry Morgenthau, Jr. is now at the head of this corporation.

The "Balfour Declaration" was made in a letter from Lord Balfour to Lord Rothschild. This same Lord Rothschild was a member of the Zionist International Conference at Bazle, Switzerland in 1897 that adopted the protocols. This same Lord Rothschild was also a member of the British House of Lords that gave this huge wealth to Palestine Potash Ltd. The Rothschild interests are at the head of political Zionism and they promoted the invasion of Palestine. Their position in our government and financial system is such that they can bring about deflation and a third world war.

A GIGANTIC STEAL

If Palestine has one fourth of its estimated mineral value it will enable the Zionists to control the destiny of the peoples of the world. The Zionist invasion of Palestine is a gigantic steal and an infamous outrage against Christian civilization. Under present circumstances it means a third world war and that the new state of Israeli will line up with the Bolsheviks. The only way to avoid it and to assure permanent peace is to destroy the Rothschild agencies, — alias Zionist Wall Street. It is indeed the best way to restore the solvency of our country and of the world, and to restore constitutional government.

The "Balfour Declaration" to Lord Rothschild and the gift of this fabulous wealth to him and his fellow Zionists is evidence that he and his fellow Zionists then controlled the

British Empire. If the British Government were authorized to give it to the Zionists they had the power to keep it or to give it to us as security for our donations, or to give it to the United Nations for the preservation of world peace. They gave it to the war-promoting Zionists for the obvious purpose of promoting Zionism.

TEODOR HERZL

Theodor Herzl, of Austria, was the founder of Political Zionism. It was established at a secret convention of Zionist leaders August 29th to 31st, 1897, in Bazle, Switzerland. It was at this convention that the "Bazle Programme" — the Protocols were adopted. Herzl presided at the conference and it was due to his untiring energy and zeal that the conference was called. The object of the Bazle Programme was to unite the scattered Jews of the world into a separate and independent nation and a World Empire. The "Protocols of the Learned Elders of Zion" represent their method of accomplishing this end, and evidently Herzl was one of the authors.

The Zionists revere Herzl as their messiah. They transferred his remains from Austria by airplane and reburied them with pomp and ceremony in Jerusalem. They published a very laudatory "Memorial" of him under the auspices of "The New Palestine," official organ of the Zionist Organization of America, edited by Meyer W. Weisgal, and copyrighted in 1929 by "The New Palestine." This Memorial contains many laudatory contributions by prominent Jews. It contains also Theodor Herzl's diary, admitting that it was censored and expurgated by the editors. This diary is an interesting history of Herzl's effort to arouse the Jews to the importance of nationalization, and of his financial difficulties and sacrifices in doing so.

Palestine was not the ancestral home of the Khazar and Ashkenazim Jews. That is only a pretense for obtaining its mineral wealth and the creation of a Zionist Empire. The Jews have always had good homes in America and all other countries in which they have lived. They are the usurers of the world and have always been. They were designated the aristocrats of Europe by the Zionist leader Samuel Untermeyer. They are not farmers. I have never known or heard of a Jew farmer and I have lived a long time and farmed in three states, viz: Texas, Mississippi, and Oklahoma. Some of them OWN farms, but they do not work them. There may be some "displaced" Jews but we support them. If given the best farms in America or Palestine, they would not work them. They don't know how to farm and farming in Palestine or America is not their purpose. They farm the Christians, not the land.

The ancestors of the small Sephardic tribe once lived in Asia but their descendants constitute only about 5% of the present Jewish population. The present day Jews, including the Rothschilds, are either of the Ashkenazi or Khazar tribes. These Jews are and always have been nomadic predatory people. It was a company of these Jews that bought and sold Joseph. They have always been traders and the dealers in slavery and narcotics and usury. The Roosevelt fortune was founded by a Jewish opium smuggler.

A few days after the adjournment of the first Bazle convention, towit, on September 3, 1897, Herzl said of it in his dairy: "If I were to subsume the Bazle Congress in one word which I shall not do openly—it would be this: at Bazle I founded the Jewish State."[24]

---

[24] Diaries of Theodor Herzl, page 149.

They appointed an "inner action committee" at this first Congress and founded the "Jewish Colonial Bank." He says, (page 151):

"The Bazle Congress represents the creation of the Society of Jews for the Jewish State ... The work of the next few years will be the creation of the Jewish Company, temporarily called the Jewish Colonial Bank."

The protocols obviously represent the programme of their secret "Inner Action Committee."

KAISER WILHELM INTERESTED

Herzl first sought the aid of Kaiser Wilhelm. He says of the Kaiser in his diary, October 19, 1898:

"The Kaiser, in the dark uniform of a Hussar, came toward me. I stood still and made a deep bow. He came up to me, almost to the door, and offered me his hand. I believe he said that he was glad to see me, or something like that. I said: 'Your Imperial Majesty, I am happy to be the recipient of this distinction.'...

"He soon took over the lead and explained why he considered the Zionist movement of worth. Unfortunately I was an embarrassed listener, and I had to exert all my strength in preparing the replies, so that I have not been able to retain all the details. He never mentioned the Jews except as my 'Landsleute'—and not in an exactly friendly tone. He had no doubt that we had sufficient money and manpower at our disposal to carry out the colonization of Palestine. Here my attention failed a little, for I was observing my own impression that my three years of work have made of the world 'Zionism,' a terme recu, which the Kaiser used freely in speaking with me.

" 'There are,' he said, 'among your Landsleute certain elements which it would be well to have immigrate into Palestine. I am thinking, for instance, of those cases where there are a number of usurers among the country people. If these were to take their wealth and settle in the colonies, they would make themselves more useful.' These were his words, more or less.

"The Kaiser observed that he believed the Jews would set about the colonization of Palestine if they knew that he would keep them under his protection, and that they really would not be leaving Germany.

"I said: 'Your Excellency, that is purely a matter of money.

As a writer I regret to have to say it.'

"I felt my arguments growing stronger and stronger under the encouragement of the Kaiser's approval."[25]

Herzl later met the Kaiser in Palestine, to-wit, on October 28, 1898. He said of this meeting:

"He laughed, and flashed with his kingly eyes: " 'How are you?'

'I thank Your Majesty. I am seeing the country. How has your Majesty's journey been so far?' "His eyes flashed.

'Very hot. But the land has a future.' " 'At present it is still sick,' I said...

'It needs water, much water,' he said, speaking downward at me.

---

[25] Pages 154-5.

'Yes, Your Majesty. Colonization on a grand scale.' "He repeated: 'It is a land of the future.' "The spectators of Mikveh Israel were utterly dazed. A few of them asked who that had been. The Rothschild administrators looked timid and irritated...

'The settlements which I have seen, the German as well as those of your Landsleute, may serve as a model of what can be done in this country. The land has room for all. Only provide water and shade. For the native population, too, the colonies can serve as models to be imitated. Your movement, with which I am well acquainted, contains a healthy idea.' ...

'Well, you certainly don't lack the money," exclaimed the Kaiser jovially, and slapped his whip against his boots. 'You have more money than all the rest of us.'"

The Kaiser was willing to sponsor the establishment of a Jewish state in Palestine as a colony of the German Empire, but that did not fit in with Herzl's plans. It would have meant that the German government would acquire the mineral wealth of Palestine and Herzl wanted it for the Rothschilds and Zionists and their independent state.

NEGOTIATES WITH SULTAN OF TURKEY

Failing to make a satisfactory deal with the Kaiser, Herzl sought to acquire Palestine from the Sultan of Turkey, first with the Kaiser's support and later by direct negotiation with the Sultan's minister, N. Bey. He first offered Bey 1,000 francs to arrange for an interview with the Sultan. Seeing that was not enough, he offered 20,000 francs. He said of N. Bey in his diary-August 22, 1899:

"At first he was dry, unfriendly, as if he did not know why I had come. Soon I got the truth out — the twenty thousand francs were not enough. He said: 'Considering your position in the Zionist movement, an audience means a great deal to you. Besides, any banker would offer me twice as much as you did for an audience with the Sultan.'

'We won't haggle about this,' I said. 'You will get forty thousand.' ...

'You ought to give this man ten or fifteen thousand francs, to make Stimmung for you.'

"I saw where this was leading to. Money talks. I said to him, almost harshly: 'I shall give you ten thousand francs in advance, and thirty thousand on the day of the audience. How you use that money is your business. I won't ask you what you have done with it.'

"He became as soft as butter and said: 'Done! I'll have to add some money of my own to it, but the speculation is worth it. I believe I can earn a couple of million on this: and that's worth a risk.'"[26]

"Herzl said of his interview with the Sultan (page 170-1): "But this is not enough for me. I told him (the Sultan) through Ibrahim that I was devoted to him because he was good to the Jews. The Jews all over the world were grateful to him. I in particular was ready to serve him in every way possible, naturally not on a small scale — I left that to others — but on a large scale.

"Then the Sultan said: 'I always have been and still am a friend of the Jews. I rely chiefly on Mussulmans and Jews. I haven't as much faith in my other subjects as in them' ...

---

[26] Pages 164-5.

'The Public Debt I consider to be the thorn. If this could be removed then Turkey could once more blossom in her strength, in which I believe' ...

'Well then,' I said, 'I believe I can. But the first and principal condition, a condition precedent, is absolute secrecy.'

"The ruler lifted his eyes to heaven, placed his hand on his bosom and murmured: 'Secret, secret!'

"I said,—as from now on I kept the reins of the conversation in my hand—that I could carry through this operation through my friends on all the Exchanges of Europe, if I had the help of His Majesty. But this help had to consist, at the right time, of a mass measure in favor of the Jews, made public in the proper way.

"Ibrahim sucked in with astounded looks the words of his master and translated them with joy. 'His Majesty has a court jeweler, who is a Jew. He could give anything of a friendly nature to him, to publish in the papers. He also has a Chief Rabbi for the Jews, the Chasham Bashi. He could also tell him.'

"My impression of the Sultan is that he is a weak, cowardly, but thoroughly well-meaning person. I think he is neither treacherous nor cruel, but a deeply unhappy prisoner, in whose name a thieving, infamous and dishonest cam-erllia commit the most shameful acts ...

"The dishonesty and bribery which began at the door of the palace and wind up only at the foot of the throne are probably not the worst. Everything is business, and every official is a thief. At least, I hear this on every side, and from what I know of the way things are done, I do not believe this to be a calumny.. ..

"I still see him before me, this Sultan of the dying robber kingdom. Small, shabby, with his badly dyed beard — which is probably dyed only once in a week, for the Selamlik. The hook-nose of a clown, the long yellow teeth and the big gap in the upper jaw to the right. The fez drawn down deep over his head, which is probably bald — the protruding ears. The strengthless hands in the big white gloves, and the ill-fitting, big, multicolored cuffs. The bleating voice, the limitation in every word. And that rules! As a matter of fact he rules only in appearance and in name."

Herzl proposed to lend the Sultan 1,500,000 pounds (about five million dollars) if the Sultan would grant a charter giving the Zionists Palestine. The Sultan, Herzl says, did not know anything about its vast mineral wealth. It was only known to Herzl and the Rothschilds. The editor of the Memorial says in a footnote:

"Herzl will not budge before he has the charter. The Sultan apparently will not budge before he gets money—if then."[27]

"However, the impasse was partially broken. The Sultan would open his empire to all Jews who wish to become Turkish subjects, but the regions to be settled were to be decided from instances to instances, and Palestine was not to be included. The Company could colonize in Mesopotamia, Syria, Anatolic, but not in Palestine. A Charter without Palestine I refused at once."[28]

It was obviously the plan of Herzl to found a Zionist Empire. That probably was also the purpose of the Rothschilds and other rich Jews, and it was the only basis on which Herzl could interest them in his Zionist Empire

---

[27] Diaries, page 173.
[28] Diaries, page 174.

scheme. This plan was clearly revealed in his diary memo of September 4, 1899, as follows:

"Yesterday, after the opera, I had supper in the Hotel Bristol, with Martin Furth. He told me that the day before he had met

N. Bey at the races. The latter had spoken to him very favorably of Zionism. It was not impossible, he said, to win the Sultan over to the idea, as the latter was a friend of the Jews. BUT THE NEWSPAPERS OUGHT NOT TO WRITE THAT WE WANT TO FOUND A JEWISH EMPIRE. N. Bey, said Furth, has been very serious about it. He asked me if I knew him. "Very faintly," I said."[29]

HERZL INTERVIEWS CHAMBERLIN AND ROTHSCHILD

Herzl approached the British through Lord Rothschild and the British Prime Minister Chamberlin, to-wit: on October 23, 1902. He said in his diary of that date:

"I laid the entire Jewish question before the immobile mask which is Joe Chamberlain. My relations to Turkey,

'I am in negotiation with the Sultan,' I said in English. 'But you know what Turkish negotiations are. If you want to buy a carpet, first you must drink a half dozen cups of coffee and smoke a hundred cigarettes. Then you discuss family stories, and from time to time you speak a few words again about the carpet. Now I have time to negotiate, but my people have not. They are starving in the Pale. I must bring them immediate help.' And so on. The mask smiled at the carpet story. I then

---
[29] Diaries, page 165.

passed on to the subject of the territory which I wanted from England."

Herzl also said:

"I set my hopes on Chamberlain, whom I shall see next week. He stands at a distance from the whole business, sees it from a higher point — AND DOES NOT KNOW THE VALUE OF THE BIG STRETCH OF LAND FOR WHICH I AM ASKING."

But the Rothschilds knew the value of the "big stretch of land" for which he was asking. When he and the Kaiser visited Palestine they found the Rothchild agents there (see supra). Lord Walter Rothschild to whom the Balfour Declaration was made, was not at first very friendly to his colonization scheme. Herzl (p. 176) says of his interview with him:

"In England, said Rothschild, there will never be any antiSemitism, etc. In France, too, it was something else, etc. He does not believe in Zionism. We should never get Palestine, etc. He is an Englishman and wants to remain one. He 'desires' me to say this and that to the Alien Commission, and not to say this and the other.

At this point the business became too stupid for me. I had interrupted him a couple of times. But now I began to overshout him in such a way that he was dazed and kept his mouth shut...

'I shall tell the Commission what I think proper and the truth as I see it. That is my habit, and I shall cling to it now, too.'

It was false, I said, that the powers were against our going to Palestine. I have influenced Germany and Russia in our favor. England, I thought, would have nothing against it. I was PERSONA GRATIA with the Sultan.

'Yes,' he threw in, 'The Sultan is naturally friendly to you because you are Dr. Herzl of the Neue Freie Presse.'

'It would be stupid and arrogant of me,' I said, 'to read the Commission a lecture on the characteristics of the real Englishman. I shall simply say what terrible misery there is in the East, and that these people must either get away or perish. The need in Rumania has been known to us since 1897; the Congress petition received no attention. In Galicia it is perhaps even worse. There are seven hundred thousand people there in misery. They also begin to move.'

My Lord said: 'I hope you are not going to say that to the Commission. Or else we shall have restrictions.'

At this point I became massive: 'Certainly I shall say it. You can count on that.'

Whereupon his jaw dropped, he rang, and called his brother Leopold.

To him he repeated what had been said, and added that in my opinion Jewish charity had merely become a machine for the suppression of the cry of misery...

At the same time I shall make a semi-official attempt to get in touch with Lord R. He is in a furious rage against me — perhaps this is the psychological moment for the conclusion of peace. When he was asked in the Commission why he was opposed to calling me, he said that I was a demagogue, a windbag."

But he sold Rothschild on his plan as being the practical one to obtain what both of them wanted. He said (Diaries, page 177):

"We went into the dining room, where I met Lord Roseberry's son and later Alfred, the third Rothschild, a true spiritual child of his father.

"Later, in my Lord's study, Alfred told me of his very high Austrian and Russian orders. 'Great, what? Krone-noden, first class.' The same Alfred asked me what I wanted to do for the Jews. Colonization? Good. But why in Palestine? It sounded so Jewish.

"After the coffee I went over to the writing desk and asked him:

'Would you like to hear my scheme now?' 'Yes'.

"I shoved my chair closer to his better ear and said: 'I want to get a Charter for Colonization from the English Government.'

'Don't say Charter. The word doesn't sound so good now.' 'Call it what you like. I want to found a Jewish colony in British territory.'

'Take Uganda.'

'No, I can use only this ... ' And as there were several others in the room I wrote on a piece of paper: Sinai Peninsula, Egyptian Palestine. Cyprus. And I added: 'Are you for it?'

"He reflected, grinning, and answered: 'Very much.'

That was victory! I then added on the piece of paper: STOP THE SULTAN FROM GETTING MONEY.

"He answered: 'I prevented Rumania from getting money. But here I can do nothing, as the great powers want it. They want to have the railway built.'

"I said: 'The Sultan offered me Mesopotamia.' He, astounded: 'And you refused?'

'Yes.'"

BARON ROTHSCHILD OF PARIS WAS ORIGINAL ZIONIST PROMOTER

Baron Edmond Rothschild of Paris, the managing partner of the original M. A. Rothschild & Son banking firm was the main support of the Zionist political movement in the beginning. Herzl says in his diary (page 196) :

"For three extraordinarily difficult years they struggled against overwhelming odds, and would surely have been defeated had not a miracle saved them...

"The miracle was this: When one of the colonists of Rishon le Zion went to Paris and there saw Baron Edmond Rothschild and told him of the work of the Jewish settlements, the Baron grew so enthusiastic about the colonists that he immediately sent his representative to Palestine to study conditions and to help the settlers with money and advice. From that day on Baron Rothschild's interest in Jewish colonization has never waned; indeed, this work fame to fill his entire life. He is known, and quite properly, as the father of Jewish colonization in Palestine. There is no doubt that it would have been impossible to preserve the early Jewish settlements and to establish new ones had not the Baron generously assisted the colonists at the beginning. He it was who, when the colonists did not know what branch of agriculture to choose, directed them toward wine-growing, by sending them expert instructors and good French vines, and by building large wine-vaults for them. In the first years, moreover, the Baron bought their grapes at a fixed price, thus assuring them of a definite income."

There can be no doubt about the fact that the principal purpose of Herzl was to nationalize the Zionists and to create a Zionist Empire. The Rothschilds wanted the minerals of Palestine.. They knew about the fabulous mineral wealth of the Dead Sea and they wanted it and had taken steps to acquire it before meeting Herzl. Herzl's "Inner Action Committee" and Jewish Colonial Bank did not supply him with sufficient money for his campaign and he became very much discouraged in the early stages of it.

HERZL'S DIFFICULTIES

In April 1899 he says (Diaries, page 162-3):

"While these gentlemen direct affairs, the worries of getting money for the preliminary work devolve on me. The guarantee fund is exhausted; I believe the money is being badly managed. Now H. writes me that he needs another six hundred to one thousand pounds."

"Never was a greater task undertaken with less adequate means.

"Tomorrow I must again ask pardon of my 'chiefs' for the leave of absence I have taken without their permission. Who knows how long they will let me carry on in this way?

"The movement demands my constant travel; and there is no doubt about it that the Neue Freie Presse can dismiss me for neglect of duty, 'with all the respect in the world for difference of opinion'. This pitiful clash of duties wearies me, unnerves me and wears me out more than anything else."

He says on August 23, 1899 (Diaries, page 163-4):

"Je La Connais Aussi. My work will look much more marvelous when people will get to know with what money worries I had to struggle as a result of my efforts of Zionism.

"I miss at every turn the fifty thousand kronen which I have sunk in the movement: the lack of the money makes me less free than ever in my relations to the Neue Freie Presse."

He appears to have been disillusioned by November 9, 1899. He says (Diaries, page 166):

"This is a good lesson for me. I suppose it would be even worse if I were completely ruined.

'Put not your trust in Princes — They are an eternal delusion' is something I might well say about the 'help' of the German Kaiser.

"But when I think of my followers, so easily prone to rebellion, I can add the end of the verse;

'He that cries Hosannah for you today Tomorrow will cry: Crucify!'

"And, indeed, I put my trust neither in Princes, nor in the people, but in myself."

And on May 1, 1900, he says (Diaries, page 167): "I have a first class epitaph for myself: 'He had too high an opinion of the Jews.' "

HERZL'S SUCCESS

But after obtaining the support of the Rothschilds his spirits were revived. He records on June 13, 1901 (Diaries, page 172):

"Society is interested in me. I am a social curiosity, a dish; people come to meet Dr. Herzl.

"Yesterday Sir Francis Montefiore was here with several ladies and gentlemen. There were Princess Lowen-stein, Lady Jane Taylor, and others whose names I have forgotten. Also Gilbert Farquhar, lord and actor.

"I shall use Princess Lowenstein, in order to reach the King. For they all invited me. Lady Jane was present as spectator at the last Congress and said her daughters envied her because she was lunching with me."

It appears from Herzl's diary that the Rothschilds had agents on the ground in Palestine when he met the Kaiser there on October 29, 1898 for he records the fact that "The Rothschild administrators looked taunt and irritated." They no doubt had other plans for obtaining the mineral wealth of the Dead Sea and feared that the presence of Herzl and the Kaiser would interfere with them. It was necessary for Herzl to sell Lord Rothschild on his colonization scheme as being the surest and best method to reach their goal.

When Herzl sold his plan of conquest to Lord Walter Rothschild, managing partner of N. M. Rothschild & Son and managing director of their Bank of England, his financial troubles were over. There was no longer any need for his colonial bank.

N. M. Rothschild & Son took over the financing and management of Herzl's World Empire scheme and Herzl became their lieutenant. Herzl is now dead but the perpetual Rothschild partnership never dies. The two enormously rich partnerships of M. A. Rothschild & Son of Paris and N. M. Rothschild & Son of London then and now control the gold and press of the world with minor exceptions, and the economy of the people of the world. It was to Lord Rothschild that Lord Balfour wrote his note promising Palestine. It was the agents of the Rothschilds that wrote our Federal Reserve Act. It was the agents of the Rothschilds that inveigled us into two wars and established the Zionist United Nations. The Rothschilds control the economy of the people of the world and seek to enslave them.

The Protocols represent the program of the Zionist "Inner Action Committee" then and now. They are the program of the Rothschilds. As bigoted and cruel and satanic as they are, they are not any more so than the Talmud and the Zionist Politburos of Moscow and Wall Street. They are founded upon the Talmud and breathe its spirit. They were obviously written, at least in part, by Theodor Herzl himself. He was a very adroit and cunning man, a facile writer and a master of intrigue and deception, as revealed by his diaries and other writings. But there is no mention of them in his dairy. The Zionists have sought to suppress them. If Herzl had actually referred to them, his Zionist editors would have omitted the reference.

The rich Zionists do not want Palestine as a "home" but for its mineral wealth, estimated at five trillion dollars. It is reported that they have a few collective farms patterned after the Soviet system and that they live in the cities and employ the Arabs to do the work. Their ancestral home propaganda is only camouflage, a smoke screen, to hide their real purpose. The majority of them are contented to live in the countries in which they reside, and their refugees to remain in idleness at our expense in German homes (given them by President Truman's order) until they can migrate to America.

WEALTH OF PALESTINE DOES NOT BELONG TO ZIONISTS

This enormous mineral wealth belongs to the Allies of World War I by right of conquest. It did not belong to the British — who were only its custodians by virtue of a mandate. The Zionists stole these minerals by the newly created and recognized state of Israeli. Theft is an ugly word but it forcibly expresses the truth. Lord Balfour knew nothing about these minerals when he made his conditional promise. He did not promise a state and the minerals of Palestine, but, based on his restricted promise, the Zionists have created a state which includes the minerals within its boundaries. But Herzl and the Rothschilds knew about these minerals when they sought the "home," and as early as 1897.

We need these minerals for our national defense and we must repudiate this concession and recover them for the use and benefit of ourselves and our Allies of World War I. Morover, their enormous wealth is sufficient to restore the solvency of the British and ourselves and our other Allies. The recovery of these minerals together with the destruction of Zionist Wall Street will establish the peace of the world and it will probably be a permanent peace. There is no other way. The Rothschilds must be banished and their ill gotten wealth confiscated and devoted to the public good.

7.

AUTOBIOGRAPHY OF RABBI STEPHEN S. WISE[30]

The son of Rabbi Wise, James Waterman, described by the Dies Committee as a Communist, and one Justine Wise Polier, published his memoirs under the title "Challenging Years" soon after his death on April 19, 1949. They state that he was born in Budapest, Hungary on March 17, 1874, and that he was the son of Rabbi Aaron Weisz, and that he was an associate and follower of Theodor Herzl; that he founded the first Zionist Federation in New York on July 4, 1947 and journeyed a year later, to the second Zionist Congress in Switzerland "where his personal friendship with Herzl began and his compact with Israel's destiny was sealed."[31]

They publish the following pictures of him as illustrative of the outstanding events of his life, to wit: On page 105, a picture with Nathan Straus, Louis D. Brandeis, and James Waterman Wise. On page 200, a picture with Albert Einstein and Thomas Mann, both Communists. On page 305, a picture with Mrs. Eleanor Roosevelt and on the same page a picture of him opening the second World Jewish Congress in 1948. He says on this page:

---

[30] Published by his son James Waterman Wise and Justine Wise Polier.

[31] "Challenging Years", (XII and XIV.)

"During the period between World Wars I and II, I participated actively in almost every Zionist Congress that was held. Convened every two years, these congresses became a major institution in Jewish life. They provided the tribunal of the Jewish world, above and beyond all others, before which Jewish questions could be dealt with in the spirit of courage and trustfulness, at all costs and at all hazards. It was the platform from which we spoke to the Jewish people and to the world."

RABBI WISE WAS A COMMUNIST TRAITOR

It will be observed that all of these pictures, with one probable exception, were with Zionist Communists. His conduct, as represented by his autobiography reveals that he was an active and vicious communist and very active in promoting Zionist, Communist organizations despite the fact that he pretended to oppose communism. He says,

"Several principles always guided the positions I took on Zionist problems at the congresses and elsewhere. I insisted at all times that there could be no compromise with the fundamental principle of Jewish peoplehood and the reestablishment of a Jewish commonwealth ... A philanthropic, economic, cultural, or spiritual interest in Palestine was laudable and helpful. BUT IT WAS NOT ZIONISM. Accordingly, I was constrained to oppose a development that would, in my view, endanger the character and the heart of the Zionist movement."

He says on page 309 that his colleague, Dr. A. Leon Jubowitzki has published a true history of the World Jewish Congress in his recent volume "Unity in Dispersion." He says that "religion is one of the elements in the life of the Jew, the chief element... but being a religious people does not alter the fact that we are a people," and entitled to a political status and state.

He was the founder of the communist American Jewish Congress and an active promoter of the Jewish World Congress. Obviously he was an active and vicious communist. It was at his insistence that Roosevelt packed the Supreme Court with communists and socialists and it was for the purpose of destroying our constitution and communizing our government and establishing in place of it a "welfare state,"

On page 316 Rabbi Wise says,

"I GO BACK TO THE FIRST SESSION OF THE WORLD JEWISH CONGRESS. TWO HUNDRED AND EIGHTY DELEGATES, REPRESENTING THE JEWS OF THIRTYTWO COUNTRIES FROM ALL PARTS OF THE GLOBE, ATTENDED THE SESSION (Bazle, 1897). For years, my first words to the delegates were those of the ancient benediction of our people, the scheheche-yonu, 'Blessed Art Thou, O Lord, our God, King of the Universe, who hast permitted us to live until and to attain unto this hour.'

Out of that session there finally emerged the World Jewish Congress, uniting in voluntary and democratic association, the Jewish communities of many lands. At the time, I said that its functions would be:

To bring the Jews together of many different lands and many different views who do not meet together in any other way: to bring Jews together on a new plane, not that of giving and receiving, but for an interchange of views touching every manner of Jewish problems with a view to their solution; and to help Jews of one land face the problems of Jews of other lands, to invite their counsel and invoke their experience.

At the same time, I adumbrated the principle that has remained the fixed policy of the World Jewish Congress."

ZIONISTS DISSATISFIED WITH BRITISH MANDATE

The Zionists were very much dissatisfied with the British administration of Palestine. They wanted to establish a state immediately and probably felt entitled to it since through Justice Brandeis and J. P. Morgan & Co., they had gotten us into the war on the promise of it. Rabbi Wise says as to the British administration:

"But as the years passed, I could not but come to the conclusion that British governments were seeking to whittle down the Balfour Declaration and were increasingly violating both its letter and spirit. The Churchill White Paper of 1922 cut off approximately four fifths of the territory in which the Jewish National Home was to be established. There were the persistent attempts to limit if not to eliminate Jewish immigration and land purchase, to foist a permanent minority status on the Jew of Palestine — all culminating finally in the unspeakably tragic White Paper of 1939 and Ernest Bevin's vicious anti-Zionism of the past few years. Indeed, British policy, as I declared at one Zionist congress, has too often appeared as if the Balfour Declaration read, 'The aim of His Majesty's Government is to hinder and to obstruct, to retard and to frustrate, the establishment of the Jewish National Home.' The officials of the Colonial Office habitually treated the Jews as an invasive and troublesome group in Palestine rather than as its rightful rebuilders. Paradoxically enough, the status of the Jews in Palestine, in British eyes, was neither the favored status of a native population nor yet the position of a people with whom a covenant had to be scrupulously observed...

"The conference brought the most grievous hurt to the Jewish settlement in Palestine and to world Jewry. In the end, a plan was disclosed, subsequently known and hated throughout the Jewish world as the MacDonald White Paper. It placated the Arabs in order to appease Hitler's lieutenant, the Mufti. It proposed and later enforced an arrangement that was the complete negation of the Balfour Declaration. The scheme undertook drastically to curtail Jewish immigration into Palestine over a five-year period, to establish an Arab State in Palestine after five years, and to make any subsequent Jewish immigration conditional on Arab consent...

"From April, 1939, until November, 1947, more than eight years, we suffered tragically under the White Paper. As a result of the elections of June, 1945, which placed the Labour party in power, the evil waxed greater and greater. The Labour government ignored and violated every pledge.

"Fortunately, after years of the most lamentable and cruel injustice, the policy of Balfour was gloriously vindicated. But what a sorry, sordid, heartbreaking tale lay between the adoption of the White Paper by the British House of Commons in the spring of 1939, and the approval of partition by the United Nations, the declaration of statehood, the heroic defense of the state of Israel, and the world-wide recognition that has at last triumphantly come to the support of Israel!"

ZIONISTS INITIATED
SECOND WORLD WAR FOR PALESTINE

Obviously the boycott of Germany was intended as the initiation of a war not only to crush Germany but also to establish and enlarge their assumed title to Palestine. Rabbi Wise says of this boycott:

"In Geneva, the World Jewish Conference was convened on September 5. I introduced and urged the unanimous adoption of a resolution calling for a world Jewish boycott of Germany. The resolution was unanimously adopted. I had been urged to call for such a boycott for many months...

"I was firmly convinced that a world Jewish boycott could only be declared by a world assembly of Jews."

"In 1940, the world situation and the problems of America at home called for the re-election of Roosevelt. While supporters of Wendell Willkie stated that he agreed with F.D.R. on International policies but not on his national policies, I did not agree that they could be separated. I felt and said then that antiNew Dealers would undo every plan and method of national self-defense....

"They also failed to recognize that so-called Roosevel-tian 'friendliness to Jews' was not a token of pro-Jewish-ness but of his Americanism.

He had not failed to appoint to high office Jews whom he regarded as extraordinarily fitted for the post — for example, Justice Frankfurter. Frankfurter was not appointed because he was a Jew, or despite his being a Jew, but because the President regarded him as the best man in the country for the Supreme Court at that particular time, irrespective of every other consideration."

RABBI WISE URGED PACKING SUPREME COURT

Rabbi Wise says of the packing of the Supreme Court, "America had twice chosen Franklin D. Roosevelt for the Presidency, the second time by an overwhelming vote in support of a program as well as a person. That program, which was clearly announced in Madison Square Garden on

October 31, 1936, became impossible of attainment because of the composition of the Supreme Court. The Supreme Court was not contemporaneous with the America of that day. Save for a few exceptions, it represented the America of Harding, Coolidge, and Taft, who had named its majority.

When President Roosevelt came to grips with that issue, the real regret of his opponents was not over the 'presidential usurpation', but over the failure of the President to resort to usurpation. Extraconstitutional action on the part of the President had been confidently predicted. Presidential usurpation would have been damned with partisan delight and profit. But the proposal of the President contained every element of unforgivable surprise. ...

"Among those who purported to be shocked by the President's proposal I found no one who had ever expressed one word of surprise or regret over the basically unconstitutional usurpation of legislative function by the Supreme Court in the preceding years — which had in fact negated the will of the people and the decisions of the Congress to correct through the New Deal the evils of the great depression.

"Because the real basis of the proposal and its vehement opposition were not in my eyes a legal or constitutional question, but rather a conflict of forces for and against the program of social justice as presented by Roosevelt, I supported the President, and took issue with the Bar Association, local and national, who led the opposition.

"These are for the most part fearful lest the social dreams and hopes of liberals such as is the President receive the legal warrant of that court, which, in its steadfast and unbending defiance of the nation's will, does most to halt the march of American democracy to the goal of social and economic justice.

"Throughout this period I kept the President informed of the facts concerning Zionism and Palestine."

Thus it appears that this Hungarian born Communist Jew influenced Roosevelt to pack our Supreme Court over the protest of the American Bar Association. (And as a "side-bar" remark: Truman has continued to pack it.) It appears also that Rabbi Wise influenced Roosevelt to ignore the third term tradition that had prevailed since Washington refused the third term. It also appears that he had a hand in betraying us into the second war in the "defense of Palestine" not then established or under attack, for he says:

"On June 9, 1941 the President answered:

'In this particular matter (the Near East campaign) therefore, I can merely call to the attention of the British our deep interest in the defense of Palestine and our concern for the defense of the Jewish population there; and, as best I can, supply the British forces with the material means by which the maximum of protection to Palestine will be afforded.'

"The next day I left for Washington, and after conferences with high government officials felt more confident that the British would be made to understand that there must be adequate equipment — guns, tanks, and planes — for our people in Palestine."

It appears also that it was the Zionist purpose and programme to give Palestine to the poor Jews and the wealth of the Dead Sea to the rich. The probability is that President Wilson did not know about this immense wealth of the Dead Sea but the Rothschilds knew all about it and were scheming to get it.

Rabbi Wise says on page 197:

"When I saw Wilson in Paris, he promised that he would receive a delegation of the American Jewish Congress during his brief stay in Washington between his two Paris trips. We were concerned both with the fulfillment of the Balfour Declaration and the assurance of minority rights for Jews in East European lands. A delegation including Judge Mack, Louis Marshall, Bernard G. Richards, and myself met with the President at the White House. We presented our case and the President made a vigorous affirmation both on behalf of a Jewish Palestine and minority Jewish rights in Central and Eastern Europe. I stayed behind for a moment, after the others had left, in order to tell the President of some of the difficulties we had begun to face in Paris. 'Mr President,' I said, 'World Jewry counts upon you in its hour of need and hope.' Placing his hand on my shoulder, he quietly and firmly said, 'Have no fear, Palestine will be yours.'"

BRANDEIS' HOME PEOPLE REGARDED HIM AS SHYSTER AND CHARLATAN

Rabbi Wise says of Brandeis,

"You know that I respect him as one of the finest servants of the Republic. I thereupon dispatched Norman Hapgood to Boston to ascertain what these charges (against Brandeis) really meant. Norman went to Boston and returned with a most startling report, seeing that he is the warmest of the friends of Brandeis. His investigation showed that the largest number of those interrogated spoke of Brandeis as though he were a shyster and charlatan... .

"The warmth of the President's communication was little more honoring to Louis D. Brandeis than an almost simultaneously issued letter of former President Elliot of Harvard, which tribut was invaluable because of its author.

The vote was taken. Senator Borah being among those who vainly voted against confirmation... .

"Hardly less historic than his contribution to the redemption of Zion was his role as founder of the American Jewish Congress. Passionately unyielding democrat that he was all his life, he found to his amazement and regret that little had been done by the beginning of the first war democratically to organize American Jews."

LLOYD GEORGE ALSO "SHYSTER, CHARLATAN," AND ZIONIST STOOGE

Rabbi Wise says of Lloyd George,

"It should never be forgotten that though the name of Balfour is most closely associated with the declaration, it was the Prime Minister, David Lloyd George who, as his memoirs attest, was most continuously eager to bring about the fulfillment of the Zionist hope. Thus, later at Paris, while boundaries were under discussion, he would repeatedly use the Biblical phrase, 'You shall have Palestine from Dan to Beersheba,' which was historically thrilling but not practically helpful in defining frontiers.

"Sir Charles Henry told me, in December, 1918, the story of Lloyd George's bidding Lady Henry, 'Julia, get together at breakfast the Jewish members of both Houses of Parli-ment who are opposed to my Zionist position that I may convince them of the rightfulness of it and the wrong of their own.' She did just that. A minyau (Jewish religious quorum of ten) was assembled at breakfast to meet the Prime Minister. After bidding Julia, 'Bring me a Bible,' which happily was to be found, he thumbed its pages, reading passage after passage from the Hebrew Prophets, prophesying the restoration of Zion to the Jewish people and of the Jewish people to Zion.

Triumphantly, he closed with these words to the Jewish members of Parliment, 'Now, gentlemen, you know what your Bible says. That closes the matter.' As far as I recall the story, no further discussion took place at breakfast, but not a few of the gentlemen continued their opposition."

The admissions of Rabbi S. S. Wise in his autobiography support my conclusion that Justice Brandeis and Woodrow Wilson were authors of the Balfour declaration and that the Zionists brought about our participation in the first World War for the creation of the State of Israel, and for its mineral wealth.

In the chapter "The Brandeis Epoch," page 185, it is stated that: "On the day after the first Congress (Basle 1897, that adopted the Protocols) he (Rabbi Wise) read in the San Francisco Chronicle a report of the session, especially the address of Herzl. He remarked to Mr. Brandeis after reading the speech aloud, 'There is a cause to which I could give my life.' That was prophecy, for he came, after a number of intervening years, to give a goodly part of his life, almost the best part, to the Zionist cause."

On page 186-7, he says,

"I had taken occasion to give to President Wilson, even before his inauguration, a rather full outline of Zionism. From the very beginning of his administration, Brandeis and I knew that in Wilson we had and would always have understanding sympathy with the Zionist program and purpose ... As I urged him one day to co-operate with the British government re the hope of the Balfour Declaration, he was touched, and soliloquized aloud, 'To think that I a son of the manse, should be able to help restore the Holy Land to its people.'"

PRESIDENT WILSON
AUTHOR OF BALFOUR DECLARATION

On page 188-9 Rabbi Wise said,

"When Mr. Balfour visited Washington in 1916 Justice Brandeis discussed the Zionist program with him on at least two occasions ... What is less well known, however, is the significant part played by the American government, and particularly by President Wilson ... Toward the end of June, 1917, when I went to see the President concerning plans to convene the fiirst session of the American Jewish Congress, we again discussed Zionism. He said at that time, 'You know of my deep interest in Zionism'... 'Whenever the time comes, and you and Justice Brandeis feel that the time is ripe for me to speak and act, I shall be ready' ... If the President had not been ready to give explicit assent to the terms of the Balfour Declaration, it would not have been made. Wilson sent the document to Justice Brandeis ... Some weeks passed, and at last, to the limitless joy of the Jewish people, the Balfour Declaration was issued in the form of a letter addressed to Lord Rothschild from Balfour, then head of the British Foreign Office."

It is estimated that we have one half of the Jews of the World and they are pouring in legally and illegally every day of the year. Practically all of those who have arrived during the Roosevelt and Truman administrations (17 years) are communists. They should be banished. In fact we should banish all socialists and communists, without regard to "race, religion or creed," for both socialists and communists are inimical to our government. Make them go some where else to establish a government that suits them.

COMMUNISTS SHOULD BE LIQUIDATED

Congress should establish a tribunal for the war trials of communists. We have precedent for it in the Nuremberg Court and trials, which the Zionists brought about. Membership in the B'nai B'rith should be prima facie evidence of guilt, and in the AntiDefamation League and the Anti-Nazi League conclusive evidence. All Jews who have arrived here since the first World War should be expelled, although a few of them may not be Zionists.

In a press interview (November 16, 1949) Morris J. Rosenwald, founder of Sears, Roebuck & Co., and president of the "American Council of Judaism," said that the Jew is a religion and not a nation, (as claimed by Theodor Herlz and Rabbi Wise), and that his organization is opposed to Zionism and the Zionist state. He said that his organization has a membership of only 15,000 out of a total Jewish population in America of 5,000,000. The estimate of 15,000 represents about the number of non-Zionist American Jews who are good citizens and they should, of course, be protected and permitted to remain. It is estimated that there are 13,000,000 Jews in America (instead of five million) and that 85% of them are Zionists.

Congress should also establish a tribunal for the trial of Zionist Wall Street Jews for they are the American Zionist Politburo and the Zionists who have directed both the Roosevelt and Truman administrations. They are traitors and should be tried and punished as such according to the common law, the penalty of which is death and confiscation of property. There will be enough of their property to more than pay the expense of the exodus of the other Zionists and such Negroes as may want to go to Liberia or as we may want to compel to go there.

I repeat that the Jews have been banished from every country in which they have resided, from England in 1210, from Spain and Portugal in 1492, and twice from France. They imply will not live peaceably with Christian people, because they are anti-Christ Their Talmud and their rabbis teach them that God has promised them that they are His "chosen people" and that the gentiles (the goi) are their inferiors and should be their slaves. We should, by all means, take possession of the minerals of the Dead Sea and surrounding country and appropriate them to the resurrection and rehabilitation of the Christian people of the world.

8.

FRANKLIN D. ROOSEVELT WAS A TRAITOR

"It stands now before the country, acknowledged by its proponents as a plan to force judicial interpretation of the Constitution, a proposal that violates every sacred tradition of American democracy...

"Its ultimate operation would be to make this Government one of the men rather than one of the law, and its practical operation would be to make the Constitution what the executive or legislative branch of the Government chooses to say it is — an interpretation to be changed with each change of administration.

"It is a measure which should be so emphatically rejected that its parallel will never again be presented to the free representatives of the free people of America."

—Report 711

Senate Judiciary Committee

Franklin D. Roosevelt was a communist and a traitor and his widow and three sons, Franklin, Jr., James and Elliot, are either socialists or communists. Every act of Roosevelt's Administration from its beginning to its end was for communizing America. His bureaucracy, which he filled with communists; his war which he brought about to make himself dictator; his regimentation, which he created to bribe and subdue the people; his internationalism and policing Europe which it is estimated now costs us 18 billion dollars annually; his extravagances and excessive taxation, and his deflation ("hold the line")—all were for the purpose of communizing America.

PACKING THE SUPREME COURT

The packing of the Supreme Court was necessary in order to communize America. It would be useless to wangle a socialist bill through Congress that did not meet the requirements of our Constitution so long as the members of the Supreme Court should remain independent and capable lawyers who believed in our system of government. It was therefore necessary that the President appoint socialist or communist lawyers, who wanted a change and who would construe the Constitution accordingly. Justice Felix Frankfurter boldly proclaimed that the Constitution is not what its "simplification of words" implied but what the Supreme Court said they meant.

The Roosevelt-Truman administrations have surreptitiously changed our republican representative system of government with limited powers to their system of socialized "democracy" with unlimited power. President Truman has forgotten, if he ever knew, that we had a Constitution, in proposing his "point 4" programme and his welfare state. There is not a word in the constitution that will authorize Congress to levy taxes and appropriate money for either of these purposes.

Roosevelt committed America to the war in behalf of Poland and China. He doublecrossed both governments. He sold the people of China and the American people to communistic bolshev-ism by his secret agreements with Stalin at Yalta.[32] He chose as his adviser the traitor Alger Hiss of the State Department, who went with him to Yalta and was also secretary of the San Francisco convention that adopted the United Nations Charter. The Yalta Agreement was deliberate treachery to our allies China and Poland, and to the American people. Truman continued Roosevelt's treacherous program through the Potsdam treaty and his agent George C. Marshall, with the result that the communists conquered Poland and the greater part of China and threaten to conquer all of Asia. What conclusion can there be other than that Roosevelt was a communist traitor and that Truman is also one?

Roosevelt was an accomplished and an artistic liar. He was an ideal Zionist ruler. He announced promptly after his election that he would "drive the money changers from the temple" and his statement was accepted as gospel by John Simpson, then president of the Farmers Union and a well informed patriot.[33] Instead of driving them from the temple, Roosevelt placed them there permanently by the Banking Act of 1935. He was an arch traitor and he selected Truman as his probable successor because he thought he was also a communist and a traitor, and Truman has been faithful to him.

BANKING ACT OF 1935

The banking act of 1935 ranks in perfidy and depravity with the betrayal of the American people at Pearl Harbor, Yalta, and Potsdam. Shortly after the Federal Reserve system was granted an indefinite extension of its charter, Roosevelt employed it to bring about the depression of 1937. He was then regimenting the farmer for the pretended purpose of

---

[32] Congressional Record, October 12, 1949, page 14625-6.

[33] The Farmers Union is now a socialist outfit with Patton as president

establishing a fair market for the products of the farm. There was no reason for this deflation except to impoverish the people and to perfect the power of the bureaucrat, and to create communism and a dictatorship.

The enactment of the Banking Act of 1935 which granted "Zionist Wall Street" perpetual power to determine and regulate our economy, was an act of planned and deliberate treachery. Truman has ratified and confirmed this act of treachery by appointing Wall Street agents to administer it.

CORRUPTION OF THE COURTS

Seven of the nine members of the Supreme Court of the United States are appointees of Franklin D. Roosevelt, and a majority of them are Fabian socialists or unadulterated socialists and one of them an unadulterated communist. They were appointed for the purpose of destroying our "antiquated" Constitution, as Roosevelt regarded it, and they have largely accomplished it. He also appointed numerous Circuit Court of Appeals and District Judges. President Truman has appointed two members of the Supreme Court, and several judges of the lower courts,— the majority of them being socialists.

These courts have construed away the Constitution; they have unblushingly reversed the decisions of all former courts. The Zionist Justice Felix Frankfurter said that the "simplification of words" did not mean what they said. He also said that the constitution is what the Supreme Court of the United States says it is and not what the constitution itself states. The courts have imposed heavy fines against property owners for violating rent control regulations and have generally upheld the rules and regulations of the bureaucrats. Rents are not interstate commerce; they are rightfully subject to control only by the states.

"NO BIBLE TEACHING HERE"

In a decision the United States Supreme Court with only one dissenting vote, held that it is unconstitutional to teach the Bible in state public schools, which is also a subject over which the States have exclusive jurisdiction. This decision was based on the petition of an avowed atheist and on the allegation that Bible teaching embarrassed her twelve year old boy. It was shown that Bible instruction was voluntary, that it was paid for privately and that the parent could select the teacher,—Protestant, Catholic or Jewish.

Until recent years we have justly revered our Supreme Court; we have regarded our National Constitution as the sheet anchor of our liberties. President Roosevelt sought early in his administration to destroy it in order to communize the American government and people. He asked for authority to remove the fudges then in office on account of their age so that he might appoint their succesors, which was denied. But death and resignations gave him this power. The Senate Judiciary Com-mittee reported upon his bold assault on our Constitution as stated in the text of this chapter.

The quotation in the text is from the unanimous report of the Senate Judiciary Committee, a majority of whose members were new deal democrats. It charges that President Roosevelt sought to "force judicial interpretation of the Constitution" and that the "proponents" of the bill admitted it. It alleges that its "ultimate operation would be to make this government one of the men rather than one of the law and to make the Constitution what the executive branch of the government chooses to say it is." And this has been its effect. "It was planned that way." The packing of the judiciary with socialists and politicians is one of the greatest crimes that Comrade Roosevelt committed against the American people,—second only to the Pearl Harbor massacre. It is humiliating to democrats to admit that we were "taken in" by this hybrid, pro-Zionist, double-crossing, lying faker, and his protege Truman.

If Congress has the constitutional power to remove the judges of the Supreme Court on the ground of age, it certainly has the power to remove them because they are socialists and communists and are antagonistic to the Constitution; Roosevelt pointed the way. Whether Congress has this constitutional authority or not the Congress should remove them and extend the removal to the Circuit Courts of Appeals and District Judges. No man, not even a Supreme Court Justice, is entitled to constitutional protection who seeks to destroy our Constitution. And no man is qualified to interpret the Constitution who seeks to change our form of government.

THE CORRUPTION OF CONGRESS

Fortunately, our congressmen and senators are elective and not appointive; they are presumed to represent our collective will. Roosevelt sought to gain control of Congress by his purges and appointments. The President has undue influence with Congress by his power to appoint judges and other officers. A majority of the members of Congress are lawyers, and many of them aspire to be judges with a life tenure of office. The only way to obtain these appointments is through faithful service to the President. Through his henchman, Harry Hopkins, Roosevelt boldly proclaimed that he would "spend, spend, and spend, tax, tax and tax, and elect, elect, and elect," and he did just that.

We have no means of knowing how much he spent or what congressmen and senators he elected. Congress granted him an expense fund of $1,000,000 to be used as he pleased, without accounting. It was revealed that W.P.A. funds were used to elect Senator Alben Barkley to the Senate. He has been the faithful henchman of both Roosevelt and Truman. He was chairman of the Senate Committee that investigated the treasonable Pearl Harbor disaster, and his committee whitewashed it.

Sam Rayburn, speaker of the House of Representatives, was also the faithful henchman of Roosevelt and Truman, and as such has ramrodded the numerous new deal measures through the House. He misrepresents his constituency. They are not New Dealers, socialists or communists. They are honest people who believe in the principles of democracy as taught by Jefferson and Jackson. He is reported to have said of the rent control bill passed in the House, transferring the agency from the national government to the states, that it was "the most reckless abdication of legislative authority I have ever seen." This so-called statesman was first elected to Congress as a states' rights democrat. What a change, and wherefore?

The proceedings of Congress as reported in the Congressional Record reveal that there are about forty communists and socialists in the House of Representatives (mostly Jews and Negroes from New York and Chicago), and at least six in the Senate. They should be expelled. We do not need socialists and communists to legislate for us. All of them took the oath of office and all of them perjured themselves, which is of itself sufficient reason for their expulsion. As between America and Israeli, they are for Israeli. The Senate and the House are the respective judges of the fitness of their numbers. It is high time for them to do some house cleaning. It is later than they think.

"Clear Everything Through Sidney." This was a message sent by Franklin D. Roosevelt, President, and candidate for a fourth term, to Robert E. Hannegan, chairman of the National Democratic Committee, at Chicago, during a

National Democratic Convention. It was the designation of Sidney Hillman as his authorized representative at this convention; it was a peremptory instruction to permit nothing to be done by the convention without "Sidney's" approval.

HILLMAN WAS A ZIONIST COMMUNIST

Sidney Hillman was a Russian Jew communist, schooled in Russian bolshevism. He was a member of the C.I.O. union and chairman of its Political Action Committee, and as such controlled the political corruption fund of that committee estimated at $6,000,000. Mr. Roosevelt's message in substance and effect directed that Mr. Hannegan and the democratic organization take orders from Sidney Hillman and his communist organization. Why?

There can be but one answer and that answer is that Mr. Roosevelt was himself a communist and desired to promote communism and sought communist support. Every act of his administration verifies that conclusion. His bosom companions, Morgenthau, Frankfurter and Rosenman were all Zionist Jew communists. They constituted the "privy council" that directed his administration and selected the managers of his numerous bureaus.

FDR RESPONSIBLE FOR PEARL HARBOR DEBACLE

He appointed communists to cabinet positions, to the Supreme Court, and to the bureaus that govern us; he recognized the outlaw Russian communist government; he prevented the deportation of the communist Bridges, and pardoned the criminal communist Earl Browder. He was a hybrid Jew and admitted it. He entertained Negroes and communists in the White House. He sought to promote social equality with the Negroes and the Jews through the creation by executive decree of the FEPC and to thereby degrade the white Gentile race. He was untruthful and insincere, which are tenets of the communist creed.

Moreover, he promised the Polish government and Churchill that we would enter the war, and the destruction of our fleet was necessary to make good these pledges. He prevented a Congressional investigation of Pearl Harbor and thereby concealed the truth from the American people. Every circumstance points directly to President Roosevelt as the man who was directly responsible for the Pearl Harbor debacle, and his communist advisers are equally guilty. No one except a communist had motive for the crime and no one except a communist would commit such a heinous crime.

There can be no reasonable question about the fact that Franklin D. Roosevelt was a traitor, in view of the revelations in "Winston Churchill's War Memoirs" published in the February 6, 1950 issue of Life Magazine. He says:

"On January 10 (1941) a gentleman (Harry Hopkins) arrived to see me at Downing Street with the highest credentials. Telegrams had been received from Washington stating that he was the closest confidant and personal agent of the President.

With gleaming eye and quiet, constrained passion he said: 'The President is determined that we shall win the war together. Make no mistake about it. He has sent me here to tell you that at all costs and by all means he will carry you through, no matter what happens to him — THERE IS NOTHING THAT HE WILL NOT DO SO FAR AS HE HAS HUMAN POWER.' "

Churchill calls it the "Grand Alliance," but it was in fact an alliance to make Roosevelt and Churchill the dictators of the world. Roosevelt, and then Truman, assisted by "Veep" Barkley, have suppressed an investigation of the truth regarding the infamous conspirators who provoked and initiated the second world War.

INSTIGATED WAR TO ESTABLISH COMMUNISM

The Associated Press, on July 24, 1945, reported that former Premier Paul Reynaud testified in the trial of Marshal Petain for treason, that on June 5, 1940,[34] he telephoned President Roosevelt and "got a promise of field guns and ammunition from the United States if France would keep on fighting," and that President Roosevelt sent "an extremely strong worded telegram to Marshal Petain saying that France would lose American friendship if she dealt with the Nazis."

President Roosevelt was unwilling for France to withdraw from the war, long before we formally entered it. This was even before the enactment of "lend lease" and at a time when we were pretending to be neutral, and one and a half years prior to Pearl Harbor. It was also before the declaration of the "Four Freedoms" and the "Atlantic Charter." Edouard Daladier testified that in 1938 President Roosevelt advised the French Government to use the money due America in preparing for war.

COMMUNISM

The communist party stands (1) for the confiscation of private property without due process of law and without compensation; (2) for the substitution of a soviet form of

---

[34] This was 11 months before the Pearl Harbor Massacre.

government based on class domination; (3) for the restriction of the rights of freedom of religion, of speech, and of the press; and (4) for the overthrow by force and violence of our government, as set forth in detail in the "official program of the American Communist Party." These were the objectives of President Roosevelt and his "privy council," and of his bureaucrats.

Would they object to the imprisonment of Tyler Kent without a public trial, as required by our Constitution ? Would they destroy our fleet in order to get us into the war and to promote a world communist super-government? Would they seek to enslave the American people through deflation and the creation of unpayable debts in order to accomplish these purposes?

President Roosevelt's communism and communist advisers explain the mysteries of Tyler Kent's imprisonment, of Pearl Harbor, of our commitment to Poland and breach of faith, of lend-lease, and of bureaucratic government. They are all consistent with the communist program and with the program of the Third International and with the protocols of the "Learned Elders of Zion" and of the Talmud.

RESTORE CONSTITUTIONAL GOVERNMENT

We can save this republic without revolution, but we can't do it by traveling the communist route. We can't do it through the Bretton Woods and United Nations schemes. We can't do it through internationalism and deflation. We can't do it through high taxes, unpayable debts, and the slavery of the people. We can't do it through either the Republican or Democratic parties as they are now constituted and financed.

We must reverse the whole Roosevelt communist program. We must get rid of bureaus and bureaucracy and their rules and regimentation. We must establish a price and wage level that will enable us to pay our debts, or else repudiate them, for repudiation is better than slavery of the people. We must disfranchise Asiatics and Africans and banish the communists, and establish an incorruptible Christian white-man's government and restore constitutional government.

THE IDEAL ZIONIST "RULER"

Roosevelt fully measured up to the requirements of a "Ruler" as prescribed in the Protocols. He always had recourse to "cunning and make believe" and he was "never frank and honest." He was an artistic and a colossal liar. He was elected President in 1932 on his solemn promise to abolish government bureaus and to reduce taxes 25%; he never made an effort to do either, but proceeded immediately after his election to increase both. He promised "again, again and again" in 1940 when he sought his third term, that he would not involve the country in war. He was an ideal Zionist "Ruler" and he had the "dark undiscovered stain" in his Jewish blood.

His wife and two of his boys, James and Elliot, profited enormously through his office as President of the United States. His wife through her advertisement of cosmetics and newspaper work, and Colonel James through his insurance fees, and General Elliot as a result of the Hartford loan of $200,000 which he solicited from an officer of an indicted firm through the President and which was settled through Secretary of Commerce Jesse Jones for $4,000 by the President's direction. The titles and perquisites of General and Colonel were not earned. They were bestowed because they were sons of the President. It is to the credit of the illustrious Presidents of the United States that no one prior to F.D.R. ever sought to commercialize the Presidency.

It was disclosed at President Roosevelt's death that he had an estate of $2,000,000 from which he received an annual income of $150,000 and that this estate was invested largely in stocks and industrial bonds and that he had only two $50 war bonds. This is consistent with the President's character; he wanted others to pay for the war and not himself.

Westbrook Pegler is authority for the statement that the Roosevelt fortune was established by their Jewish ancestor in the opium trade. Despite wars and panics and depressions and taxes, it is still a sizable fortune. The family was evidently thrifty and knew how to hoard it and preserve it; and Mr. Roosevelt was no exception.

President Roosevelt was elected to his first term upon a platform that declared for constitutional government and for economy in government. Soon thereafter he set about to undermine and destroy the constitution. He declared one emergency after another and asked for and obtained legislation unwarranted by the constitution. He sought to remove the Supreme Court as a body on the pretended ground of age to enable him to appoint successors who would sustain his emergency legislation. He appointed communists as executive officers to the cabinet and even to the Supreme Court.

His purpose from the very beginning was to communize our government; but he could not accomplish it without war. He had declared more than sixty emergencies and Congress and the people were fed up on them. He had traveled that route as far as he could go. Congress and the people did not want war and they must be betrayed into it.

REVERSE THE ROOSEVELT-TRUMAN PROGRAM

We cannot pay our enormous debts with dear money and cheap prices and wages. Deflation will bring about widespread unemployment, suffering, bankruptcy and communism. We must reverse the Roosevelt-Truman program in order to preserve our government. Roosevelt and his advisers knew what this program meant. His disciple President Truman may not know but he has, however, faithfully followed it.

9.

IS HARRY SOLOMON TRUMAN ALSO A TRAITOR?

> "In order that our scheme may produce this result ARRANGED ELECTIONS in favor of such presidents as have in their past some dark, undiscovered stain, some 'panama' or other — then they will be trustworthy agents for the accomplishment of our plans out of fear of rev elations and from the natural desire of everyone who has attained power, namely, the retention of the privi leges, advantages and honor connected with the office of of president." —Protocol 10

President Truman's character and treachery are discussed in the first part of this book, Zionist Wall Street. The following is a supplement to the argument which confirms my conclusion that he is a communist. The fact that he was selected for Vice President and Roosevelt's probable successor by the communist Franklin D. Roosevelt subject to the approval of the Zionist communist Sidney Hillman is a powerful circumstance supporting that conclusion. The three candidates for office of Vice President were Secretary Byrnes, Secretary of Commerce Wallace of the Roosevelt cabinet, and Senator Truman. Byrnes was rejected by Hill-man because he was from the South, which was considered "in the bag" and the delegates from the South supported Truman in preference to Wallace. It was "Hobson's choice," but Truman was and probably is the lesser of the three evils.

We don't know what the "dark, undiscovered stain, panama or other" was in President Truman but it was there, otherwise he could not qualify as a Zionist president. He has been a "trustworthy" Zionist agent for the "accomplishment of our plans." He has been guided by them completely and has used his great office in their behalf. It may be, and perhaps is, his blood. It is in itself sufficient reason for his selection by the Zionists Roosevelt and Hillman.

President Truman's race is unknown. He was represented as a farmer boy who could plow a straight row but that was evidently only Zionist fiction. It is entirely inconsistent with his known record. All we know about him with any degree of certainty is that he was a partner with a Jew named Jacobson in the haberdashery business which failed; and that he was a ward politician in the corrupt Pendergast machine in Kansas City. He looks like a Jew and acts like a Zionist and consorts with Zionists and advocates the program of the Zionist Jews.

The United Press on November 19, 1949 reported President Truman as saying that the book he "reads most is the Talmud." I doubt the truth of this statement but don't doubt that he said it. He was probably only bragging for Zionist consumption. If he constantly reads such trash, he must be a Zionist Jew and anti-Christ for no one has a copy of the voluminous Talmud except Jews and no one habitually reads it except Zionists. That may be and probably is the key that unlocks the mystery of Truman's pro-Zionist administration.

There can be no reasonable doubt about the fact that both Justice Felix Frankfurter and Secretary of State Dean Acheson are traitors. The traitor Alger Hiss and also Dean Acheson were appointed to their respective positions on Frankfurter's recommendation, and Acheson and Frankfurter have both supported Hiss; Frankfurter by testifying to his character, and Acheson by publicly endorsing him after his conviction.

President Truman has been guided by Frankfurter in his domestic programme and by Acheson in his foreign.

Frankfurter and Acheson are responsible for filling the Department of State with communists; and Secretary of State Acheson has assisted the bolsheviks in their war against China and seeks to bankrupt the United States. We may excuse President Truman on account of ignorance, but that excuse cannot be made for Frankfurter and Acheson.

Senator Malone said in a speech February 17, 1950:[35]

"Mr. President, the 16 ECA countries are helping the Russian Communists to consolidate their gains in eastern Europe and in China. Of course, it is history now that two of those nations have recognized Red China. Shipments going through Hong Kong now have more than doubled over those of last year, I am informed. They are being shipped everything they need to consolidate their gains in China, and also to consolidate their gains in eastern Europe and to fight World War III."

He said that shipments of supplies to the Nationalists of China were withheld at the time they were needed and that as a result they were forced to retreat from the mainland to the Island of Formosa. He said that a Russian born communist by the name of Michael J. Lee, (whose true name is Ephraim Linovi Liberman), was the man who directed these shipments, and that he was three times refused citizenship, viz: 1935, 1937, and 1939, and the grounds were, "not good character, and not attached to the principles of the Constitution of the United States."

Senator Malone said also:

---

[35] Congressional Record, 81st Congress, page 1934.

"I wish to mention at this time the 1934 trade Agreements Act, under which the Congress of the United States abdicated its constitutional authority over the national economy in favor of the State Department. I consider that action an economic "Yalta", and it will so be considered generally in a very short time. The Congress of the United States is charged, by the Constitution, with the regulation of the national economy, but through the 1934 Trade Agreements Act abrogated that authority and transferred it to the State Department.

"The 1934 Trade Agreements Acts has been extended, and is now in full force and effect. The act gives over to and industrially inexperienced (and crooked) State Department full authority over the domestic economy of this country, and puts into their hands the fate of every working man's job and every investment in this Nation. They can say, after perfunctory hearings, what industries in the United States shall survive and what will be sacrificed. That is just a part of the whole picture."

As a result of this administration the long established Waltham Watch Company factory and other institutions have been forced to quit business and the very important oil industry is seriously threatened.

When the nationalists retreated to the Island of Formosa, Acheson publicly announced that he would discontinue our support, although the island could be easily defended, being 100 miles from the mainland and surrounded by water. But without munitions and supplies the nationalists can not defend it and our withdrawal of support may mean their defeat. The General Staff (Army and Navy) were not satisfied with this decision and they visited General MacArthur to consult with him regarding the defense of Asia, with the result that he was appointed Commander of all of our forces in Asia. If he is not interferred with by the State Department, he may yet save Asia and us from a destructive war.

President Truman approves the administration of his Secretary of State; it is probably in pursuance of his Welfare State. He refused the request of the Senate to surrender loyalty files on the State Department employees. He said that he stood by his previous notification not to release these files and that Acheson is one of our greatest Secretaries of State. He protects the communists in the State Department and they continue to operate in favor of Russia and against America.

THE WELFARE STATE

President Truman stands for socialized medicine, federal aid to education which will inevitably develop into mixed racial schools and mongrelization, guarantying foreign investments to compete with American industry, and the Welfare State. If he is re-elected with a Fair Deal Congress, it means farewell to constitutional government. He has appointed socialist Judges who will sustain his socialistic program and he has already initiated his program through the R.F.C.

The welfare state necessarily implies communism with a dictatorship to assign people to their jobs and make them work. The bolsheviks have the welfare state with Stalin and his Politburo as dictator. Germany had it with Hitler as dictator and Italy with Mussolini, and Truman seeks it. The welfare state also necessarily involves the destruction of our constitutional system of government. Does not President Truman brand himself as a traitor in advocating it?

RECONSTRUCTION FINANCE CORPORATION

This corporation was created as an emergency measure to soften the blow of the Federal Reserve Board's deflation of 1930. There is no constitutional authority for it, absolutely none. But it has promoted numerous subsidiaries and its power has been enlarged by legislation and usurpation until it has developed into the over-all financial agency of the government. The press recently announced a loan of $44,000,000 by it to the Kaiser-Frazer Corporation, which added to its previous loans amounts to a total of $140,000,000 to this company alone. It is reported that $15,-000,000 of this last loan is to finance dealers who purchase Kaiser-Frazer cars. The next logical step will be to finance the purchasers!

The Kaiser-Frazer Corporation is a Zionist controlled outfit that has mushroomed into a multi-million dollar company as a result of government favors. It buys government plants from the War Assets Administration at a small fraction of their cost, and then borrows on them as security from the R.F.C. for money to operate them. What a set-up! What a beautiful slick money making scheme. It employed Winchell (whose true name is reported to be Lipschitz) to advertise its products, but despite all of this, it is said to be losing money in operating its properties. Its former investment bankers, Cyrus Eaton & Company, who are also stockholders, allege that it lost $20,000,000 during the past nine months of operation and it has reported a loss of $30,-000,000 during the past 12 months.

VICE-PRESIDENT BARKLEY ENDORSES THE ROOSEVELT-TRUMAN PROGRAM

The Associated Press reported that Vice President Barkley ridiculed the opposition to the Truman program in a speech at a democratic banquet at the Waldorf Astoria Hotel on December 2, 1949. He likened the opponents to "tree sitters and hitching post devotees" who fear the welfare state. He said they regard "every tree frog as a roaring lion and every angle worm as a spreading adder." He said that "these prophets of pessimism have not told the American people what part of the democratic program is to be replaced." May I timidly suggest that all of it should be.

And on this same date, December 2, 1949, Secretary of the Treasury Snyder is reported by the Associated Press to have admitted that we will have a deficit of $5,500,000,000 (it is now April 19, 1950 admitted to be $6,700,000,000 plus) and to have said that he knows of no way to erase it except by increasing taxes and that he is "guided by the President's position." It will probably be 20 billion or more next year. That will inevitably lead to national bankruptcy and the welfare state which is Truman's goal.

There are in fact only two other ways by which this disaster can be avoided: (1) by devaluing the dollar, which Zionist Wall Street will not permit; or (2) by appropriating the property of the Zionist traitors. The latter remedy will involve their prosecution and conviction as such. We can at the same time and by the same procedure restore the solvency of the world by appropriating the mineral wealth of the Dead Sea and surrounding countries, which by right of conquest belongs to us.

Thus, the Zionists are high pressuring us into the Welfare State. We must meet the impact in the approaching election and defeat them in the 1952 presidental election. If we fail, we may lose our freedom. We must revive the patriotism of Patrick Henry who said, "Give me liberty or give me death." If we fail we are not worthy of the great Constitution and the great government bequeathed us by our founding fathers. We must pass it on to our posterity.

ATOMIC BOMB AND H BOMB

Has President Truman known all of the time that the bolsheviks had our atomic bomb secret? He pretended to have discovered it from some sort of distant explosion that no one except he knew anything about. He revealed this information while Congress was considering an appropriation for the Atlantic Pact, for the apparent purpose of stampeding Congress to make the appropriation. It had that effect whether intended or not.

Truman and the Zionists appear to be trying to scare us with the mythical H bomb into making some sort of a deal with the politburo of Russia, which they and we know the communists will not respect. They say that the Russian politburo has the secret and may build the plant and that we must "beat them to the draw." It is no doubt true that the Russians know as much as we do, but this is nothing. They claim the H bomb is 1,000 times more powerful than the A bomb and that it will devastate cities and 100 miles of surrounding country, but that is a visionary pipe dream. There is no evidence that the bolsheviks have manufactured or can manufacture either the A or H bomb. They appear to be scare crows to stampede Congress and the people.

Our pro-Zionist dictator Truman has ordered the plant built at an estimated cost of two billion dollars. The President has no such authority; it is the exclusive province of Congress. Our dictator pretends to be alarmed and obviously wants to alarm us; and he is seeking a conference with Stalin about it, although pretending that he does not desire it.

DISPLACED PERSONS

The Senate Judiciary Committee, through its chairman Senator McCarthy, submitted a bill to admit German expellees, and to exclude communists and their spies, and to empower our immigration authorities to pass on the eligibility of D.P.'s as well as all other immigrants. Senator Jenner of Indiana in his discussion of the subject said that between six and 700,000 immigrants classed as displaced persons were admitted during and since the war, that under the displaced persons act a gigantic fraud had been committed against the American people, that the I.R.O. and the D.P. Commission were made up principally of people who were themselves displaced persons; that by "administration agreement between the Department of State and the Department of Justice they have given to the Displaced Persons Commission not only their rights but their duty to protect the security of this country"; he said "Dean Acheson is even opposed to a bill that would exclude subversives."[36] Senator Eastland said that there are between 10 and 15 million homeless destitute German expellees; that the displaced persons are well financed and maintain a lobby of $1,000,000. These statements were not disputed.

The International Refugee Organization (I.R.O.) and its administration were discussed in a lengthy colloquy between Senator Eastland of Mississippi and Senator Lehman of New York beginning March 2, 1950 and intermittently until March 10, 1950. Senator Eastland asserted and proved by undisputed evidence that the act itself excluded all German expellees from Eastern Germany; that the

I.R.O. and D.P. commissions were composed largely of displaced persons, that they had exclusive jurisdiction to pass on the eligibility of displaced persons applying for immigration to America, that there was no appeal from their decisions and that our immigration authorities were compelled to accept and did accept their certificates. These facts were established by undisputed sworn testimony before the Senate Judiciary Committee. He said that gross fraud had been committed in the administration of the act and that criminals and communists and spies have been and are being admitted. It is

---

[36] Congressional Record, 81st Congress, page 2891-7.

estimated that there are from 2 to 5 million illegal immigrants in our country (Cong. Rec, April 5, 1950, p. 4851). I venture to say that the majority of them are Zionist communists and that they have been naturalized and will vote for the Truman ticket.

THE CRUCIAL TEST OF LOYALTY OF YOUR SENATORS

Eighteen Senators led by Senator Lehman of New York proposed a substitute bill which was adopted. This bill in substance and effect endorses the corrupt administration of the law and increases the number of immigrants from 205,000 to 359,000. Such is the power of the Zionists in the Senate of the United States. It was a great Zionist and Communist victory. With a pro-Zionist senate there is no probability of impeaching President Truman.

The I.R.O. and D.P. Commissions are Zionist communist contrivances designed and administered for the purpose of admitting Zionists and traitors into our country. Some of the mem-mers of the Displaced Persons Commission were former employees of the UNRRA during the Lehman administration. Both UNRRA and the D.P. administrations have been by Zionists and for the benefit of Zionists.

What a slick political scheme for communizing our government! Zionists are flocking to our displaced persons camps from all sections of Europe where they are well cared for at our expense. It is estimated that 84% of the displaced persons are Zionist Jews. I venture to say that every member of the Displaced Persons Commission is a Zionist Jew.

We build houses for them in our larger cities; and we are unable to keep up with the demand. We respond to all sorts of drives and appeals for money for their support and they are coming to us in droves, and most of them will vote for the Welfare State in the next presidential election. What a brilliant schme! Even boss Pendergast in his palmiest days could not have improved it.

GERMAN EXPELLEES

Senator Eastland said of the German expellees:

"One of the greatest crimes in all history was the uprooting from their homes, where their people had lived for centuries, of men, women, and children, whose only offense was that through their veins flowed Germanic blood and that a thousand years ago their ancestors had been German stock. They were turned out in to the cold and snow, driven like cattle across eastern and central Europe into Germany, where many of them died on the march like flies. I say that is one of the greatest crimes in all human history, a crime to which the United States was a party. In this bill we have attempted, in a meager way, to permit some of those persons to come into the United States. They are the real sufferers. That is the real immigration problem in Europe today. I say "immigration" because, in the last analysis, that is an immigration bill. This is not a displaced persons bill. The real displaced persons have been taken care of."[37]

Germans are prohibited from coming to our country by the displaced persons act as well as by its administration. They are called expellees when in fact they are displaced persons and as a rule from Eastern Germany. They are the kind of immigrants we want and many of them want to migrate here but are not permitted to do so. President Truman and Secretary Acheson now pretend that they have reversed their

---

[37] Congressional Record, March 3, 1950, page 2776.

programme toward Germany and the Germans but the Nuremberg trials still go on and they are still dismantling German plants, thereby throwing the employees out of work and creating poverty and discontent. It is reported in the press that 138 additional plants are scheduled to be dismantled. In a letter to Secretary Acheson, Senator Eastland said:

> "It is time our State Department acted to protect the interests of the United States. It is the Russian policy to destroy these countries (Germany and Japan). The Russians know that where poverty, disease, and human misery prevail, communism is strong. We are following the English lead and we are playing the Russian game. Our own do-gooders and Anglophiles are nothing but Russian fifth columnists.
>
> "England's present policy, which it appears we are following will do grave damage to the future prosperity and security of the United States. The German people hold the balance of power between western civilization and the mongrel hordes of Communist Asia.
>
> "It is to the very highest interest of the United States that we build up Germany and Japan as prosperous strong allies and as barriers against Russian expansion. It must be remembered that they first must be conquered before the United States can be successfully attacked."[38]

This letter was presented to the Senate by Senator Jenner March 14, 1950. Commenting on it, he said:

---

[38] Congressional Record, March 3, 1950, page 2776.

"Mr. President, as I have said, I want to present nothing but the facts surrounding the policy of wanton, brutal, senseless destruction that continues to go on, at the very time when we are being told to pour out more and more billions to strengthen the economic backbone and political stability of these people who stand at the threshold of new threats of Communist infiltration and expansion."[39]

President Truman has continued to be guided by the Zionist Frankfurter and the Zionist Neyhaus, assistant to the President, and Secretary of State Dean Acheson. On the recommendation of Frankfurter he appointed Dean Acheson to the highest cabinet position, viz; Secretary of State: and John J. McCloy, a pro-Zionist Wall Street banker as German administrator. According to press reports there are 1200 communists in the State Department. It has been and is a hot bed of communism.

Commenting on the verdict of the jury in the Hiss case, Congressman Roy M. Nixon of California (who brought about the prosecution), charged that "higher officials of two administrations deliberately tried to cover up the Hiss case and that it would have come to light earlier except for these facts." He further said, "All I can tell you at this moment is that I believe that President Truman will have further reason to regret his red herring remark." This judgment will probably be reversed in view of the fact that the star character witness for Hiss was Justice Felix Frankfurter.

The legislatures of two states, Texas and Mississippi, have petitioned the President to discharge Acheson, but he remains on the job. It would not be worth while to impeach Acheson and Frankfurter, for the President would probably

---

[39] Congressional Record, March 14, 1950, page 3352.

appoint other communists to fill the vacancies. Nor is it worth while to impeach the President for Barkley would succeed him. The obvious remedy is to defeat the "fair dealers" in the approaching Congressional election.

TRAITORS

The Washington Times Herald reported in its issue of February 5, 1950 that there are still 2200 Federal officials and employees of doubtful loyalty, of which 500 hold key positions; that they are being investigated by the F.B.I. and that President Truman is still hampering the investigation by his directions to his bureaucrats to withhold documents and information. It reports that 842 of these bureaucrats "resigned and fled from investigation between 1947 and 1949 because they dared not risk heavier penalties by being exposed." It reports also that Hiss was protected for eleven years by Secretary of State Dean Acheson and Justice Felix Frankfurter and the Department of Justice.

John E. Puerifoy, Deputy Secretary of State testified that the State Department had permitted 202 of its employees to resign and that 91 of them were homosexuals. Their resignation was evidently for the purpose of escaping an investigation, and probable prosecution, and to enable them to transfer to other departments. (It was reported that there were about 4,000 of them in government bureaus March 31st, 1950.) What a revolting disgusting mess. It is safe to say that there was not a single gentile among these 91 degraded loathsome human beings. The Zionist, Morris J. Ernst of President Truman's Civil Rights Committee (FEPC), published a book in 1948 entitled "American Sexual Behavior and the Kinsey Report," defending depraved homosexual practices. We can excuse President Truman on account of ignorance but not the Secretary of State and Justice

Frankfurter who are primarily responsible for their apointment.

We have had 18 years of Zionist rule under Roosevelt and Truman. It has been 18 years of gradual transition from a republican form of government to a welfare state. Truman has now boldly proclaimed the welfare state as his goal. During this period the Zionists have bankrupted and destroyed the British Empire. They have, in fact, bankrupted us and our republican form of government is almost gone. They have taken over the two political parties, the executive department of the government and have made great inroads on the judiciary and are striving to capture the legislative branch.

The Welfare State means the destruction of our constitution with its guarantee of local government and of private property and personal liberty. It means the destruction of our state governments;— it means that we are wards of the United States and subject to the control of the bureaucrats. It means that we have surrendered our property to the state and our liberty to the commissar. It means a dictatorship of the Zionist Communists.

President Truman's advocacy of the "Welfare State" is of itself sufficient ground for his impeachment and conviction as a traitor for he seeks to destroy the constitution and the system that he swore to defend by his official oath of office.

President Truman's latest welfare scheme is revealed in his special message to Congress April 6th, 1950 recommending that Congress authorize "bigger jobless benefits to more people for longer time; that the jobless benefits should be on a uniform basis for $30 per week plus additional money for dependents and should continue for 26 weeks (6 months) and be made available for an additional 6,000,000 persons not covered by present law." Why should anybody work, particularly if he makes less than $30 per week plus compensation for dependents? What an inducement for strikes! What has become of our Constitution? Where is the money coming from and whose brainchild is this?

It is a sure route to the welfare state. It is on a parity with the Brannon plan; but the farmer refuses to swallow the bait offered by the Brannon plan. The farmer is not a communist and he prefers his liberty and independence to government service. With our protective tariff system administered by the State Department and President Truman's latest "jobless insurance" scheme we will soon have the welfare state; for the State Department will continue to destroy our industries and thereby increase the number of jobless.

WE ARE ENTITLED TO "THE TRUTH, THE WHOLE TRUTH AND NOTHING BUT THE TRUTH"

The President refuses to permit the Senate Foreign Relations Committee to inspect the reports of the F.B.I. and others as to the character of Owen Lattimore, et al. The Foreign Relations Committee is not an unfriendly committee. The majority of them are fair dealers with Senator Connally as chairman of the full committee and Senator Tydings of the sub-committee.

The President, aided by the "kept press," seeks to belittle these charges. He would have us believe that there is nothing to them except cheap politics, that they are only "red herrings" to divert us from his programme. They are in fact the most serious charges that have ever been made against any government; for treason is the crime of all crimes. Instead of co-operating with his friendly Foreign Relations Committee, he seeks to obstruct them and to suppress the truth.

A free and independent press would protest, but instead the press co-operates, and condones. The attitude of the press in this crucial test confirms the boast of the Zionist that they control it, with few exceptions. The courageous patriot Senator McCarthy has rendered our country a great service in disclosing the traitors in the State Department and particularly in revealing the fact that the communist spy Lattimore is responsible for the communist victory in China and for Truman's treachery to the nationalist government of China.

We are entitled to "the truth, the whole truth and nothing but the truth" and not Senator Tydings' version of the truth. We should not accept the certificates of character of Henry L. Stim-son, George C. Marshall, and Ike Eisenhower. They were appointees of Franklin D. Roosevelt and all of them have some responsibility for his maladministration:—Stimson was a member of his Cabinet when the Japanese attacked Pearl Harbor, Marshall was his emissary to communize China, and Eisenhower his emissary to Germany to inaugurate the Morgenthau plan. Nor should we accept the certificate of Senator Tydings that he has examined a "summary" of the evidence prepared by J. Edgar Hoover. We justly have confidence in Mr. Hoover but he is under Attorney General McGrath and no doubt prepared such summary under his direction. Let us have the truth for "the truth will make us free."

I wish to believe in the loyalty and integrity of the President of the United States but I simply cannot close my eyes to the truth. He endorses Dean Acheson because Acheson is carrying out his programme; he refuses access to the loyalty files of State Department employees, because he is himself disloyal and wants to protect the others; he continues to be guided by Frankfurter, Neyhaus, et al., because they are his kind; he seeks to bankrupt the United States and to finance foreign countries because he wants to destroy our system of government and establish a welfare state. He is obviously a communist who seeks to destroy our constitutional government and to promote communism.

ADDENDUM APRIL 26, 1950

President Truman defended Secretary of State Acheson and his administration in his speech to the Federal Bar Association in Washington on April 24th. He said that the charges against Acheson's administration were false and defamatory; that 138 communists were under deportation orders and that about 1,000 others were under investigation and may be deported. He said that there were no communists in the State Department, and he justified withholding the loyalty files because they might "reveal highly secret information vital to our national security and of great value to foreign nations."

His defense was a weak excuse for a weak cause by a weak man. What is more vital to our "national security" than to rid our government of the traitors that infest it? How can the investigation of such traitors be of "value to foreign nations." His defense is of value to us in that it reveals that he endorses the administration of Acheson and his traitor assistants.

WAR

A third war is now a serious threat. The bolsheviks have challenged us. They have shot down an unarmed plane and murdered its occupants (10 men); they have decorated the murderers and replied to our protest insultingly and with lies. We must either fight or meekly take their insult. If we accept the insult there will soon be another. War appears to be inevitable.

If we do not have war now, it will probably occur during President Truman's campaign for the presidency, for it will be necessary in order to re-elect him. It will probably not result at this time from deflation. The payment into circulation of the $2,800,000,000 G.I. insurance funds and the purchases by the

E.C.A. will sustain prosperity and our economy for the current year. We can then only avoid war by the remedies that I have proposed.

With traitors conducting the Executive Department of our government, we cannot know how well we are prepared for war. Secretary of Defense Johnson says that we are in excellent position, but General Eisenhower says that we are not. We know that we have a weak Commander-in-Chief who chooses to be advised by traitors, that our labor organizations are infiltrated with traitors, and that we have weak allies. We may lose the war on account of these traitors. Our hope of success rests upon Germany and Japan, General MacArthur and the Mohammedans.

THE ARABS

I have a recent letter (April 20, 1950) from the "Holy Land Christian Committee" which states the position of the Christian people of Palestine regarding the brutal, indefensible invasion of Palestine and the creation of the Zionist State of Israeli. It should be remembered that this invasion has been sanctioned by the Politburos of Russia and Wall Street and by President Truman and the Zionist United Nations. It is in flagrant violation of the terms of the Balfour Declaration which provides: "It being clearly understood that nothing shall be done which may prejudice the civil and religious rights of the existing non-Jewish communities in Palestine."

The following is the letter:

HOLY LAND CHRISTIAN COMMITTEE

April 20, 1950
Mr. George W. Armstrong
Woodstock Plantation Natchez, Mississippi

Dear Mr. Armstrong:

I am on a mission in this country as delegate of the Christians of the Holy Land who are descendants of the earliest followers of Christ and descendants of Crusaders. The majority of these Christians have been dispossessed and driven out of their land by invading Zionist forces. Most of them live now as destitute refugees over the hills of Bethlehem which has resisted successfully all Zionist armed attacks and has become the last Christian fortress in the Holy Land.

All the Christian hospitals, colleges and schools have been occupied by force by the Zionists who now control the new city of Jerusalem, the greatest part of which was a Christian property. The future of Christianity in the land of its birth is full of gloom.

I have been sent to this country by the Mayor (my father) and Municipal Council of Bethlehem to raise a Christian voice on behalf of the oldest Christian community in the world. I was attacked on the air by Walter Winchell, the Zionist propagandist, as the Zionists do not want the American Christians to know what is happening to their fellow Christians in the birthplace of Christ. Dorothy Thompson, Mr. Morehouse, editor of the Living Church and Bishop Gilbert of New York have defended me against these malicious attacks.

The Holy Land Christian Committee has been formed under the sponsorship of the presiding Bishop of the Episcopal Church to raise moral and material aid for the Holy Land Christians whom I represent.

I feel that you will be interested in this great cause and I will be very happy to have the pleasure of meeting you at your convenience.

Yours sincerely, (signed) Yusif el Bandak

It is reported that there are about 1,000,000 Arabs that have been driven from their homes who are now destitute and dependent on charity and that many of them have died from starvation and exposure. The Zionists have moved into their homes and taken possession of them together with their personal property. They have been robbed by the Zionists. The Zionist Henry Morgenthau has called on our government to supply these Zionists with arms to enable them to defend their ill gotten possessions. This is cold blooded savagery of the most brutal character but it is consistent with the Talmud and the alleged Zionist religion. We need a pro-American in the White House instead of a proZionist.

GEORGE W. ARMSTRONG

10.

ZIONIST VICTORY AND THE NUREMBERG TRIAL

"We are interested in the diminution, the KILLING OUT OF THE GOYIM. Our power is in the chronic shortness of food and physical weakness of the worker because by all that this implies he is made the slave of our will, and he will not find in his own authorities either strength or energy to set against our will. Hunger creates the right of capital to rule the worker more surely than it was given to the aristocracy by the legal authority of kings. By want and the envy and hatred which it engenders we shall move the mobs, and with our hands we shall wipe out all those who hinder us on our way.

"When the hour strikes for our SOVEREIGN LORD OF ALL THE WORLD to be crowned, it is these same hands which will sweep away everything that might be a hindrance thereto."from Protocol 3.

Stalin is now the dictator of the world. He has the job that President Roosevelt aspired to get. Roosevelt was only another Kerensky preparing the way for him. How true the prophecy announced at the communist dinner attended by Professor Wirt! Under Jewish manipulation Stalin developed from "Comrade" Stalin to "Marshal" Stalin to "Generalissimo" Stalin; and from a blouse and with trousers stuffed in his boots to a well groomed gentlemen in appearance. The rulers of all nations pay him homage and get inspiration from him. It is a far cry from his early criminal record to the dressed-up "Generalissimo" who dictates to the world. He is reported to have been arrested nine times, jailed eight times, deported seven times, escaped six times, and changed his name four times.

What a change in appearance, but it is the same old Stalin in the blouse and with trousers stuffed in his boots, and with a criminal mind and heart. The one thing that he has always been honest and sincere about is the extension of bolshevism. He has maintained huge standing armies for the purpose and fought wars for it; he maintains a huge and expensive political organization, the Third International, for its propagation throughout the world. He has never compromised or faltered, and he has pursued his objective relentlessly, ceaselessly and ruthlessly—in season and out of season.

We do not know anything about the terms of the secret agreement that he made with General de Gaulle, representing the French Government, and Dr. Soong, representing the Chinese, except what they tell us. But we do know what Generalissimo Stalin wanted and we know that he obtained it, otherwise he would not have made the treaties. He continues to enlarge the bolshevist empire, by wars or treaties as may best suit his purpose —United Nations or no United Nations. The only thing that he will respect is the atomic bomb.

President Truman is now in the "swift stream" without the ability or the will to stem it. The result would be the same if Mr. Roosevelt were living. His plan to rule the world supported by Mr. Churchill had gone on the rocks prior to the time of his death. He created a Frankenstein monster that thwarted his ambition and appropriated his job.

CHURCHILL PROPHECIES WORLD BOLESHEVISM

Mr. Churchill's case is pitiful. The Zionists used him until he was no longer needed, and then ditched him. In one of his campaign speeches Mr. Churchill prophesied that all Europe and Asia would go bolshevistic in case of his defeat. He has the reputation of being frank and conservative, and he knows Atlee and Bevan and Europe and Asia better than we do. The Associated Press reported that on the first assembly of the new members of the House of Commons the labor members rose en masse and sang "The Red Flag."

We can not estimate the effect of the 1945 British election. Mr. Churchill appears to be correct in his forecast. If so, it means the disintegration of the British Empire and its absorption by the Soviet Union. It means the destruction of free government throughout Europe and Asia, and worst of all the enslavement and debasement of the people. What a tragedy!

CHURCHILL'S PROPHECY VERIFIED

We already have forebodings of it. Stalin would not permit our soldiers to enter Berlin for several weeks after the collapse of Germany and until after the Russians had dismantled many important German factories and moved the machinery to Russia. They proposed to repair all the war damages to Russia and France with German labor at $3.00 per month, which means starvation, slavery and death; and to try all German fascists as war criminals.

A secret conference at Potsdam extending from July 17 to July 25, 1945, was held between Joseph Stalin, President Truman and Prime Minister Atlee, for the purpose of imposing penalties upon the German people and dividing the spoils of war. The conferees issued a 6,000 word report which they claim fully represented their conclusions. They proposed to control Germany's economy and educational and judicial systems; to destroy German industrial plants and promote German agriculture; to impose all of the reparations that the people can pay and "subsist without external assistance."

They proposed to "arrest and intern all Nazi leaders, influential Nazi supporters and high officials of Nazi organizations and institutions, and any other persons dangerous to the occupation or its objectives." In fact every man who is objectional to the communists. When the Zionists get through with their arresting and killing and interning there will not likely be enough people and industries left to pay very heavy reparations.

PROPOSED CABINET OF WORLD EMPEROR

They set up a "Council of Foreign Ministers" composed of one representative each from the "United Kingdom, Soviet Republics, China, France, and the United States," with headquarters in London, who will sit continuously either in person or through their "high ranking deputies and secretariat." This Council is invested with authority to administer on Germany, to define the boundaries of countries, and with other broad powers. It was probably intended as a cabinet for their "King Despot," as he is called in the protocols.

The only apparent limitation upon the power of this Council is the fact that the Polish Government as created by the Soviets is recognized. The only thing left for the Council to do is to determine how much German territory the Poles shall have as compensation for the territory taken by Russia. This, however, is an unimportant detail since the Soviets will dominate the Council.

The terms of the peace conference made no disposition of the other conquered countries, viz: Italy, Austria, Jugoslavia, Czechoslovakia, Greece, Finland, etc. According to the press reports the bolsheviks have set up governments in most of these countries. The peace settlement left the bolsheviks in undisturbed control of them. There was a pious expression about elections but the elections were under bolshevik control and we knew the result beforehand.

BOLSHEVIK BRUTALITY

We do not know what is transpiring in these countries, for the bolsheviks refuse to tell us or permit us to investigate. The Time magazine succeeded in getting two of its reporters in Austria and published their reports in the issue of August 13, 1945, p. 36-38. The following are their reports of conditions in Austria: "LOOTING CAMPAIGN. — Wrote Correspondent

Durrance: Since the Russians entered Vienna they have carried out a looting campaign which has left it stripped to the bone. Red deployment troop trains leave the marshaling yards loaded with soldiers' loot—armchairs, sofas, bicycles, statues. Gangs of soldiers have gone through entire apartments from top to bottom, forcing their way into each apartment, taking what struck their fancy. In the early days of their occupation, Red soldiers made it a habit to stop civilians in the open streets at the point of a gun, demanding their watches, bracelets, jewels, money. Three months after their entry, this still continues.

"Rape stories are rampant and it is difficult to verify most of them. I do know one Viennese girl who is in the hospital now after two Red Army soldiers had killed her father and raped her. I have heard from several sources that during the first weeks here the Russians would approach an apartment house and, judging from its size, demand from the landlord that a certain number of women be delivered to them for their pleasure. Whether true or not, it is certainly true that 99 out of 100 Viennese girls live in mortal dread of the Russians.

"Correspondent Walton reported that a middle-aged Vienna woman said to him wearily: 'I suppose it will be impossible for even America to send us all the food we need to survive. But the least the Allies can do is to distribute poison to those who want it. Now we don't even have any way to commit suicide. You will see when the gas is turned on again how many of us will kill ourselves before we starve to death.'"

Time reported the condition in Russian occupied Germany as follows:

"At least 10,000,000 hungry Germans were being uprooted from their old homes in East Prussia, Pomerania, Silesia, Sudentenland, by the new Polish, Czech and Russian owners.

"The wanderers choked the roads in Russian occupied Germany. Ragged, barefoot, with children in their arms, and the shabby remains of homes stacked on perambulators, carts and wheelbarrows, they trudged westward. But they were barred from the British and U. S. zones. No UNRRA was on hand to help, though their problem immensely outscaled that of Displaced Persons elsewhere in Europe ...

"Many a wanderer was beyond appeal or succor. Typical was a scene in Berlin's once fashionable Dahlem, now part of the U. S. zone. A grey old man stood on a curb. Beside him a tattered cadaverous woman leaned apathetically against a shell-scarred tree. On the pavement before them lay a long bundle wrapped in a frayed black dress and held together by a string drawn around the ankles and neck of the corpse inside. The three were refugees from the East. They were thumbing a ride out of town to a spot where the dead could be buried and the living could move on."

VINDICTIVE PEACE SETTLEMENT

It was a cruel, vindictive, savage and inhuman peace settlement, dictated by the bolshevists, and will mean either the extermination of the German people or another war. The Russian press boast of their great victory, and so it was. It did not require President Truman with his retinue of high officials to concede it. Secretary Byrnes' assistant, Benjamin Cohen, could have done so just as well and in much less time. But President Truman summoned Rosenman from Washington to Potsdam for advice, and thereafter signed the document.

It was reported in the Swedish press and republished here August 7, 1945, that

"The publication of the Potsdam communique has been followed by an enormous wave of (German) suicides, principally business men and industrialists: 1200 in Berlin; 600 in Leipzig; 300 in Cologne, 458 in Hamburg, and a larger figure in Frankfurt on the Main."

And no doubt thousands unreported.

What despair must have seized the hearts and minds of the German people! What hope can there be for them? All of this human misery for the purpose of creating a world super-state to be ruled by the Zionists. This war was waged for the establishment of a world super-government, and the San Francisco charter provides it. That was the purpose of Roosevelt and Churchill and of their Zionist advisers in initiating it.

The agents of the Rothschild money trust have directed the war and they have profited enormously by it. They are interested in all of the principal war plants and war contracts and will likely acquire the government plants when they are sold—the most of them at junk prices. The war will prove to be the most profitable war that the Rothschilds have enjoyed.

PRISONERS

It was estimated by the press in November 1946, almost two years after the conclusion of the war, that Russia has 3,500,000 German prisoners, France 1,000,000, and the British 500,000. These are slaves performing slave labor upon starvation rations.

It is improbable that this number are still alive, for it is the plan of the communists to either destroy the German people or convert them to bolshevism; this is the Morgenthau plan. It is in flagrant violation of the Geneva convention and an offense against decency, humanity and civilization. It was estimated, January 1, 1950, that the Bolsheviks have more than 1,000,000 Japanese prisoners.

President Truman appointed ex-President Hoover as his special envoy to investigate conditions in Germany. He reported on February 27, 1947, that

> "the Germans in food, warmth and shelter have been sunk to the lowest level known in a hundred years ... that there is widespread starvation appearing in the children, and appalling increase in deaths among the aged; and general loss of weight, vitality and ability to work."

Mr. Hoover recommended $951,000,000 of "supplementary exports" to Germany.

This is the result of the Morgenthau-Eisenhower plan. It is a striking example of the difference between Zionist-Talmudic hate and cruelty, and Christian charity and mercy.

REPORT OF TRIAL

Charles W. Alexander, official director of photography for the "Nuremberg Trials," published and copyrighted a pictorial history of the trial. The foreword was written by Justice Jackson in which he says that the book "constitutes a faithful and vivid record of the Nuremburg trial." In his foreword Justice Jackson also says that "it is the first trial of its kind ever undertaken and is certain to be of considerable interest in history." He says: "The accusers were four victorious nations, viz: America, Russia, Great Britain, and France, which had it in their power to execute the defendants without trial but which considered it more in keeping with the principles for which they fought to give the defendants the benefit of hearing and establish before the world their guilt. The crimes charged were uncommon offenses; first, crimes against the peace of the world by commencing a war of aggression. Second, conducting it in ruthless violation of the rules of war which gave rise to innumerable war crimes; third, crimes against humanity— the slaughter of millions."

Each of the four nations appointed a Judge and alternate and a prosecuting attorney and an assistant. President Roosevelt appointed Francis Biddle, former United States attorney, to represent America as a Judge and Robert H. Jackson, United States Supreme Court Judge as attorney. Twentyfour Nazi leaders and seven Nazi organizations were indicted, viz: Reich Cabinet, Leadership Corp of the Nazi party, S. S., S. D., Gestapo, S. A. and the General staff and high command of the German armed forces. The indictment which exceeded 23,000 words in length was signed by Robert H. Jackson, et al.[40]

There was no evidence shown in this record supporting the first two charges, viz: that the German government initiated the war and conducted it in "ruthless violation of the rules of war." The evidence supporting the third consisted wholly of alleged crimes against the Jews.[41] It was in fact a Zionist trial prosecuted by pro-Zionist attorneys before a pro-Zionist Court against the defendants, for the offense of being opposed to Zionism and communism.

It is true, as stated by Justice Jackson in his foreword that the victorious allies had the power to kill the German cabinet and officers of the German Army but that is not civilized warfare. That is bolshevik, Zionist warfare.

The Judges made the law, prescribed the penalty, and enforced it. If it is to serve as a precedent for the future, it means that the officers of the defeated in war must be punished. Ex post facto law is prohibited by British Magna Charta as well as by our Bill of Rights. It is contrary to justice and to our Christian civilization. The mass trial was contrary to every principle of law and justice and Christian civilization. There is no precedent except the Russian purge trials.

There is also no precedent for the treatment of the unfortunate victims who were convicted, except the Bolshevik code. The foreign correspondent, Constantine Brown, reported that "of those convicted only two have retained a degree of sanity." Admirals Karl Koenitz and Elrich Raider, Rudolph Hess and Walter Funk are said to be shouting in their cells that they be put to death to end their sufferings.

---

[40] "Justice at Nuremberg," page 5.
[41] "Justice at Nuremberg," page 175-185.

Their cells have small blackened windows, their food is just little more than bread and water diet ... they are allowed to receive no visitors and only a lew of them one letter each month. Their guards make regularly hourly inspections during the night, flashing electric torches in their faces thus preventing a continuous nights rest."

MALMEDY TRIAL

There is also no precedent for the Zionist Malmedy trial except the Zionist communist code.

I agree with the British author, C. F. Green, who states in the January 1, 1949, issue of his periodical "The Independent Nationalist" that "the slaughterings of Nuremberg were foul enough but the sadism of Malmedy seems to be that of slow death by mental and physical torture." That is bolshevik justice and punishment based on the Talmud; it is in pursuance of the cruel vindictive Morgenthau plan. It is the penalty sanctioned by the Zionists.

Judge Gordon Simpson of the Texas Supreme Court and E. Leroy Van Roden of the Delaware County Orphans Court reviewed 139 death sentences in connection with the "Malmedy Massacre:" and recommended that 29 be commuted. Judge Van Roden said that the prisoners "were placed in solitary confinement for several weeks or months and allowed no visitors or conversation and that there was evidence of brutality in that a dentist employed by the government had to work overtime taking care of prisoners whose teeth were knocked out and jaws broken."

America has been ruled by Zionist international bankers during the entire Roosevelt and Truman administrations. Justice Jackson and Attorney General Biddle were appointed to the Nuremberg Court because the Zionists desired it. It was at Zionist instance that Dean Acheson was appointed Secretary of State. It was at Zionist instance that we double-crossed Poland and China, supported the Zionist invasion of Palestine, recognized the state of Israeli, and loaned it $130,000,000. It was the Zionist Jews who degraded and bankrupted the British and French Empires and who now threaten to degrade and bankrupt the American republic.

Mr. Arnold Leese reported in "Gothic Ripples," January 30, 1950: "The Jew M. Perlzweig, an official of the World Jewish Congress, is reported in the 'Jewish Chronicle' (16th Dec. 1949) to have recently stated in an address at Glasgow: 'It was the World Jewish Congress which had secured the holding of the Nuremberg trials at which it had provided expert advice and much valuable evidence; it was the World Jewish Congress that had such lines of communication throughout the war, extending even into the German Foreign Office, that they received information long before either the British Secret Service or the American Intelligence did ...

"Prisoner's counsel, Mr. R. T. Paget, put these 'war criminal' trials in their proper prespective. He pointed out that these 'trials' were the first of the kind for 500 years, when Joan of Arc was found guilty and burned at the stake. We sought to brand her as a witch, and made her a saint, he said. History is apt to repeat itself."

This Zionist trial is a precedent for a mass trial of Zionist American traitors. We should give them a dose of their own medicine.

11.

WAR CRIMINALS

HANG THE CONSPIRATORS AND BANISH THE TRAITORS

PEARL HARBOR.—Senator Barkley bravely promised us a thorough investigation of the Pearl Harbor disaster whether the truth reflected upon "the living or the dead." But under his direction, assisted by Senator Lucas, the investigation was not a search for the truth but an artistic cover-up under a voluminous inquiry into the conduct of subordinates and not of the principals. No inquiry was made as to the motive for the crime, or the planning that led up to it. Every crime is the result of motive and it can not be understood and appraised without knowledge of the motive.

Tyler Kent was back in the United States and willing to disclose the truth but was not called to testify. Ex-Prime Minister Winston Churchill was also here. He could have told us about his secret meetings and agreements with President Roosevelt, the "Atlantic Charter," the "Four Freedoms," and the trial and imprisonment of Tyler Kent; but by a vote of 6 to 2 he was not called as a witness. ExAmbassador Bullitt was also here and could have told about the negotiations with the French and Polish governments that resulted in repudiation of the Munich agreement, the overthrow of the Chamberlain government, and the war.

ROOSEVELT BROUGHT ABOUT PEARL HARBOR DISASTER

The investigation, however, did reveal that the Washington high command had actual notice of the Pearl Harbor attack two days prior thereto and in ample time to prevent the disaster. It revealed also that Admiral Kimmel and General Short were not guilty of negligence despite the fact that they had been officially and unjustly accused by President Roosevelt's board of inquiry headed by Justice Roberts.

You can not escape the conclusion that President Roosevelt had actual knowledge of the "winds" messages and of the planned attack and that Admiral Kimmel and General Short were not notified because the President wanted the attack made and the fleet destroyed as a means of arousing the Congress and the people to war. You must conclude also that in order to escape responsibility he sought to put the blame on Admiral Kimmel and General Short.

The committee headed by the shrewd Alben Barkley gave us the third whitewash, but the truth, like Banquo's ghost, will not down. The American people want the truth and they are entitled to have it whether it reflects on "the living or the dead." They want an impartial, judicial investigation, and not a biased political one.

Senators Ferguson and Brewster, republican members of the Pearl Harbor senate investigating committee, sought to develop the truth about the Pearl Harbor disaster. They desired the correspondence, memoranda, reports, etc., of Roosevelt, Morgenthau, Stimson, Ickes and Harry Hopkins, and found that they had all disappeared. It is probable that the incriminating parts of them have been destroyed. Senator Ferguson said:

"Some 900 volumes—not pages or papers, but volumes — of memoranda, photostats, correspondence, reports and transcripts of conferences can hardly be classed as fragmentary data ordinarily used to refresh a weak memory. Nor is it possible to conceive how an official so busy with public affairs as was Mr. Morgenthau could find time to accumulate 900 volumes of purely personal data. Even Colonel House, who had plenty of time unburdened by the cares of public office, and who kept a methodical diary for a great many years in the stirring times of Wood-row Wilson, barely squeezed out two volumes of data and reminiscences. The Morgenthau material, so far as we know, is exceeded only by the boxcars of public papers said to have been removed by Franklin D. Roosevelt to the self-created shrine at Hyde Park."[42]

It was Morgenthau's claim that these 900 volumes were his personal diary and that he was entitled to them. Think of it a moment: 900 volumes containing an estimated 60,000,000 words of personal notes, and that this huge quantity was exceeded by the "box-car of public papers ... removed by Franklin D. Roosevelt to his 'shrine' at Hyde Park."

It is an obvious lying excuse for the theft of public property. A man who will steal and lie about it is capable of the Pearl Harbor disaster. And why should he have done so if he was not afraid of the truth? And who would commit these thefts except a communist? Senator Alben Barkley, chairman of a former Pearl Harbor investigating committee, and Senator red-Pepper defended Morgenthau, et al.[43]

---

[42] Congressional Record, February 11, 1947, page 1017.

[43] Congressional Record, February 11, 1947, pages 1017-27.

NUREMBERG TRIAL

Herman Goering, et al., were tried at Nuremberg because they were anti-Semitic and not because of anything they did to bring about the war. There was no law or precedent for this trial. It is not only the right but the duty of the soldier to serve his country,—right or wrong; and of the statesman to serve it according to his own conscience,— right or wrong. They were only soldiers who obeyed the orders of their Commander-in-Chief, Adolf Hitler.

Hitler did not seek war; he sought the return of the pre-war possessions of Germany by agreement. He accomplished it by the Munich settlement (called the "Munich appeasement"). Roosevelt, Churchill and the Zionists repudiated this agreement and brought about the overthrow of the Chamberlain government. But for their interference there would have been no war.

This evidence was available to the Nuremberg attorneys and court. It is in the official records of the United States, Great Britain, France, and Poland, but the attorneys did not introduce any of these records. Winston Churchill and Tyler Kent could have given important evidence on this subject. They chose to try anti-Semitics instead of the real criminals. It is another cover-up of the truth and a whitewash of the criminals.

The plight of the Polish people is one of the saddest tragedies of this cruel war. They were double-crossed by Churchill and Roosevelt. They sent their armies to fight with the Allies. It is estimated that 300,000 of them were in Italy at the conclusion of the war, fearing to return and be killed or made slaves by the Russians. The brave people of Poland know who started the war, for despite Russian protection the Jews are being driven from Poland.

The criminals who should have been tried in the Nuremberg trial were the conspirators who brought about the war. It was not Goering, et al., for they were merely soldiers obeying the orders of their government. They may have been anti-Semites, for which they were tried and convicted, but that is not against international law. The Zionists are trying the other German anti-Semites, who comprise most of the adult population.

The real criminals were the gentlemen who influenced Poland to repudiate the Munich settlement and promised the assistance of their respective governments. They were FRANKLIN D. ROOSEVELT and WINSTON CHURCHILL and THEIR ADVISERS.

Roosevelt is dead, and Churchill is beyond our reach, but Morgenthau and Frankfurter and the other Zionists are still on hand and are still engaged in their nefarious enterprise. TRY THEM. They are the conspirators who influenced Roosevelt to repudiate the Munich settlement and who brought about the Pearl Harbor disaster. Try them and punish them as traitors to our government.

The Nuremberg trial and the conviction of the German officers was a tragical farce. There is no precedent for it in the history of the world, unless the Soviet purge trials may be considered as such—yet the press has not condemned it and none of our statesmen have done so. They were tried and convicted as anti-Semites in a tribunal created by Semites and before Semitic or pro-Semitic judges.

One of the alleged crimes was cruelty to Jews in concentration camps. Obviously Goering and the other army generals had nothing to do with these camps and there was no evidence supporting this charge. They were simply prominent and active anti-Semites. War is cruel and destructive at best. We must give Hitler credit for waging it according to the rules of civilized warfare. It was not Hitler who initiated the campaign of bombing women and children, but it was the British and ourselves. It was not Hitler who used poison gas, but we at Hiroshima. It was not Hitler who attacked ships in neutral ports, but the British at Oran. No effort was made during the war to assassinate Roosevelt or Churchill, but two attacks were made upon the life of Hitler. It is not saying much for Hitler to say that he was a better man than Roosevelt, Churchill or Stalin; nor is it saying much for the Germans to observe that they are better than the Zionists.

MORGENTHAU-ZIONIST HATE PROGRAM

According to press reports we have changed our Zionist policy of HATE. It was a policy inaugurated by Roosevelt and Morgen-thau at the Quebec conference and followed by Truman at the Potsdam conference, and put into effect by Eisenhower while governor-general of Germany. In pursuance of this program he stationed Negro troops in the city of Berlin who were guilty of rape and every other kind of rascality. It was a Zionist-Communist programme.

Strange to say, Stalin is entitled to credit for the change in our policy of hate. He first announced that the Soviets would undertake to restore Germany and we followed suit in an effort to prevent Germany from going communist.

Stalin is smart enough to see that if he could win Germany he could conquer Europe. Our Zionist communists are also that smart, but Morgenthau, et al., wanted Stalin to win and so they had us adopt and pursue a hate, extermination program. Oh, what a miserable criminal mess our New Dealers have brought upon us and the world! The German people and the German Nation stand in the way of the extension of bolshevism and the creation of the Zionist Empire and the Zionists therefore desire their extermination.

We are not, however, in very good position to ask the Germans to help us save the world from bolshevism. In pursuance of the Morgenthau plan to degrade and destroy the German people we have policed Germany with pro-Zionist officers and Negro soldiers. It was reported that 80% of the Negroes had venereal diseases. The magazine "Life" in its issue of Feb. 10, 1947, published a full page of small pictures of unfortunate, miserable German white women with venereal diseases. The magazine apparently was biased in favor of the Negro soldiers for it stated that the Negroes "were more victims than culprits."

Every soldier, white or black, who has ravished a helpless starving woman should be court-martialed and shot. The officers in charge should also be court-martialed and if found to be accessories or grossly negligent they should be appropriately punished. The precedent for such trial and severe punishment was established in the Nuremberg trials of Goering, et al. They should at least be dishonorably discharged from the army for they are a disgrace to it and to humanity.

Germany is the key to bolshevism in Europe, and Japan in Asm. If the bolsheviks obtain the co-operation of the Germans, as they are striving to do, it is goodbye to freedom in Europe and to the British Empire.

REPORT OF HERTER
INVESTIGATING COMMITTEE

In a speech in the House of Representatives on Nov. 24, 1947, Congressman Vursell of Illinois, a member of the

Herter Investigating Committee, reported on conditions in Germany and Austria as follows:

"Some have said in support of the Marshall plan, if it is not approved, we may lose the peace. It is my candid opinion, if we lose the peace, the responsibility for losing the peace must be placed on the door step of the Yalta conference, and the failure of all British and American troops to go on in and take Berlin. And, the Potsdam agreement has contributed to the debacle as well as the Morgenthau plan."

The Morgenthau plan was the second great mistake.

"Because of it we have lost 2 years' time in the rebuilding of Germany as an industrial state, and have furnished 50 per cent of the food for 45,000,000 people out of the pockets of our taxpayers. The Morgenthau plan in all will cost our Government a loss of over a billion dollars.

"Finally, after realizing the recovery of western Europe depended largely on the coal of the Ruhr, the manufacture of steel and the re-industrialization of Germany, the Morgenthau plan was thrown out of the window ...

"It has cost western Europe and the United States billions of dollars through the mistake of the Morgenthau plan. We are now upon the first rung of the ladder moving toward the rehabilitation of all western Europe."

He reported further:

"The German people, however, have not lost their will to work and they are making a supreme effort. Those in heavy industrial and mining sections are receiving a higher ration of food because of the necessity of greater industrial production in Germany. The farmers in Germany are working intensively.

All of the people in Germany and Austria as well, are putting forth in my judgment their best efforts ...

"We found that the German people and the Austrians, by religious convictions and habits, are opposed to communism.

"In the last mayoralty election in Berlin; that part of Berlin which is controlled by Russia voted overwhelmingly against the Communist candidates for mayor and city offices. If a free election was held in all Germany and Austria today, it is my personal opinion that less than 5 per cent of the people would vote Communist."[44]

This report is fully confirmed by Congressman Dirksen of Illmois, who said:—

"But to this imperial dream of the Politburo and the Communists there is an obstacle. It is Germany. Once Germany falls, France and Italy will be easy. Lenin, whose body lies in state in Red Square in Moscow, once said that 'whoever controls Germany controls Europe.' He is the same Lenin whose gospel is still the faith of communism and whose textbooks, so recently revised by Stalin, are still faithfully adhered to by the Communists. He is the same Lenin who was the author of chaos and hate.

"The coal and steel of the German Ruhr when coupled with Soviet resources would be an invincible combination. Of course, slave labor would do the work. Already 15,000,000 or more slave laborers work UNDER GUARD in the Soviet Union. Few of them ever came back."[45]

---

[44] Congressional Record, November 24, 1947, p. 10814.

[45] Congressional Record Nov. 18, 1947, p. 10758.

Congressman Vursell recommended that we should reject the Marshall Plan and continue to aid in the rehabilitation of Germany and Austria; that we demand that Russia move out of Germany completely "so that the nation can be reunited as an economic whole as was so agreed at the Potsdam conference;" that we prohibit the further dismantling of factories in Germany, stating,

"One move can, and certainly should be made without further delay. The President and the Department of State should insist on prohibiting the further dismantling of any factories in Germany. Six hundred and eighty-two factories and plants have recently been marked for dismantling under reparations agreements. Since the agreements have been broken and since the United States, England and France have agreed to the rebuilding of Germany. It is madness and unnecessary to tear down these manufacturing plants and at the same time ship steel, machine tools and other supplies, a part of which later on will likely be used in building new plants.

"Mr. Speaker, Members of the Congress who have visited Europe are alarmed as are the German people with the destruction of these plants now so much needed in the revival of the economy of Germany. Under past agreements, by our State Department and Administration leaders, we have been tearing down Germany, holding down the production of coal and steel, rather than building it up, which at the same time is costing countless millions of dollars."[46]

More than three years of dismantling German plants and removal of them to Russia and her satillites have passed since this report was made. It has been within the last 90 days that this vandalism was said to be checked. Most of the plants

---

[46] Congressional Record November 24, 1947, p. 10913-18.

have, no doubt been moved and our government has done nothing about it.

It is the irony of fate that we must now call on Germany and Japan to aid us in saving the world from the consequences of our folly in entering the war, and from communism. Germany is the bulwark that protects southern Europe and northern Africa from the deadly march of bolshevism, and Japan is the bulwark that protects Asia. If the Soviet succeeds in communiz-ing Germany, then the balance of Europe will be communized; if they communize Japan, then Asia is gone. It is reported in the press that there are numerous anti-Semitic riots in England and that "heil Hitler!" is often heard.

It was reported in the press that there were several hundred mulatto children in Berlin. The Negro soldiers were stationed there by order of General Ike Eisenhower. He was originally in actual command of the occupation forces in Berlin. They were obviously stationed there for the purpose of degrading the German people in pursuance of the Morgenthau-Eisenhower Plan.

General Patton was in charge of the occupation forces in Bavaria. Eisenhower demoted him because of his humane treatment of the defenseless Germans. General Patton's Operations Executive, Colonel R. S. Allen, said in his book, "Lucky Forward," that Patton would have won the war much sooner and with much less bloodshed except for Eisenhower's interference.

HANG THE TRAITORS
AND BANISH THE COMMUNISTS

We have passed the stage for appeasing, pussyfooting and halfway measures. We are on the verge of war. Nothing can save our young men and our government except radical remedies that will exterminate the disease and its cause. Our critical situation requires a major operation. We must have the intelligence and courage to adopt it, otherwise our government will be lost. We must hang the traitors and confiscate their property, and banish the communists. They are not entitled to constitutional protection or the presumption of innocence. There should be a mass Nuremberg trial of our traitors and communists. Membership in any of the communist and Zionist organizations should be conclusive evidence that the member is a communist.

In 1216 the British banished the Jews from Great Britain and for 400 years thereafter no Jew was permitted to enter the kingdom. These were years of peace and prosperity. The act of banishment provided that any Jew found in the realm after a given date should be punished by death; and the Jews migrated. We should enact a similar law as to the Zionists. The Rothschilds and their agents and agencies, the traitors who engineered the Pearl Harbor disaster, and the traitors in our government should be hanged and their property confiscated, if found guilty.

The confiscation of enemy property will pay our national debt and thereby relieve the over burdened taxpayer. These traitors are responsible for its creation and it is only just that they pay it. Such confiscation would give us our railroads, steel industry, metropolitan press, New York banks and trust companies, cinema industry, radio, etc. Our government should then exercise its constitutional duty to issue money and regulate its value.

If the British had adopted this plan they would not need our help, for the Rothschilds owned practically everything in the British empire that was worth owning. Instead, the socialist government gave our money to the Rothschilds in payment for their Bank of England and other properties, and they are crying for more. Britain's Chancellor of the

Exchequer, Sir Stafford Cripps, in his "Economic Survey for 1948" stated that the British Empire is bankrupt.

They are slated to receive five billion out of the seventeen billion that President Truman proposes for European recovery, the greater part of which will likely go to the Rothschilds and through them to their proposed World Empire. It was the Rothschilds through their agency Kuhn, Loeb & Co., that financed the Russian revolution and created the Soviet Empire. They now seek to expand it into a World Empire. Make them pay with their lives and their property for their crimes against Christian civilization.

We have higher authority for the punishment of traitors than Nuremberg law. The common law, which we adopted as a part of our judicial system, provides that traitors shall be punished by hanging or beheading and confiscation of property, and for the banishment of undesirable citizens. We must indict and try and punish the traitors who brought about the last war, and banish all communists, Jew and Gentile. This will include practically all Jews who have been admitted into our country since the first World War. The communists seek to destroy our government and to murder us, and appropriate our property. They are traitors and criminals and they should be shown no more mercy than they have shown the Germans.

APPROPRIATE THE MINERALS OF THE DEAD SEA

I repeat for emphasis that the Dead Sea and its fabulous mineral wealth belongs to us and our allies by right of conquest. We wrested it from the Sultan of Turkey in the first World War for we won the war and thereby prolonged the life of the British Empire. It did not belong to the British, who gave it to the Zionists, and who only had a mandate to govern the country. It does not belong to the Zionists whose title rests on a gift from the British.

It belongs to the Allies, who won the first world war. It is the title by which we acquired America. We have the same title to all of the oil fields of former Turkish countries valued at six hundred billion dollars. In equity we have the principal interest because we won the war. But we should recognize the equities of the oil companies that have developed the property and of our Allies.

Moreover, Lord Balfour did not promise Lord Rothschild the minerals of the Dead Sea. He only promised Palestine as a Jewish home, subject to the vested interest of the Arabs. The minerals of the Dead Sea cannot be used as a home and the promise cannot be construed to include them. Lord Balfour could not make the gift without the consent of the allies. It was only a personal deal between these two British lords, as on its face it appears to be.

If the Dead Sea and the nearby oil fields have one tenth of the value they are reported to have, it will be sufficient to reimburse us for the expense of the two wars and the costs and extravagance of the Roosevelt and Truman administrations. It will rescue us and our posterity from debt slavery. In fact, our freedom and the freedom of the peoples of the world depend on whether we get the wealth of the Dead Sea with adjacent oil fields or the Zionists and Communists get it.

The Zionists and the Communists now have it. It is true the state of Israeli proclaimed its neutrality in the event of a war between Russia and its satellites and the United States and allies, but we should not be deceived by such declaration. It will be respected like the Litvinov promises to Roosevelt to gain our recognition of Russia. It will be just as neutral as the Rothschilds and the Russian Politburo want it to be. It will be neutral in words and belligerent in acts, which is the communist Zionist political creed.

Our safety and the safety of the Christian peoples of the world depend on our appropriating the mineral wealth of the Dead Sea and the adjacent oil fields. If the communists perfect their title to them, as they seek to do, they will perfect their control of all Asia, Africa and Europe. They are strategically located; much more than our tide lands,—and it is much more important to us and the world that we own and control them than that the federal government appropriate our tide lands. And moreover, we have a perfect title to them, and the bordering states have a perfect title to our tide lands.

GEORGE W. ARMSTRONG

12.

MARSHALL & LEVITSKY PLAN

There is no constitutional authority for the so-called Marshall Plan. Our national government has no constitutional right to lend or give money to foreign countries or to levy taxes for these purposes. There is not one word in the constitution that will support the International Bank, the Export-Import Bank, the R.F.C. and its numerous subsidiaries and the United Nations and its various agencies. That should be sufficient argument against these schemes.

Congressman Tackett of Arkansas said of the Marshall Plan, "It was conceived in iniquity and born in sin at the hands of some Wall Street bankers and war profiteers ... Right now a move is on to give more billions to the British and to have us assume the debt of Britian to India, Egypt, and other foreign countries."

The Marshall Plan was conceived by the Zionist State Department and its author, Leon Levitsky, while Marshall was Secretary of State, and was sold to the American people as the "Marshall Plan" to promote the recovery of Europe. It has been employed to promote socialism and communism in Europe and America; indeed, that was the purpose of its Zionist promoters.

BRITISH LOAN

The British squandered the $3,750,000,000 we gave them, and they have been abusing "Uncle Shylock" and asking for more. The effect has been to enable the British labor government to buy the Bank of England and other properties from the Rothschilds but the loan has not benefitted the British people. The British laborer loitered because there was no incentive to labor, and he thereby reduced production. The Atlee government threatened to conscript labor, which is dictatorship and Russian communism.

Mr. Churchill said of the proposed Atlee "Crisis Bill":

"I warn you solemnly that if you submit to totalitarian compulsion and regimentation of our national life and labor there lies before you an almost measureless prospect of misery and tribulation of which national bankruptcy will be the first result, hunger the second, and the dispersal or death of a large proportion of our population, the third.

"The choice which lies before the British nation is between a system of competitive selection and a system of compulsion.

"Neither of these systems offers an easy passage, but I am sure it is only by personal effort, free enterprise and ingenuity, with all its risks and failures, with all its unequal prizes and rewards, that anything like 47,000,000 people can keep themselves alive in this small island, dependent as it is, for half its food on selling high quality goods and rendering necessary services to the rest of the world."

He declared, "There can be no dispute about the Socialist failure or its gravity," and accused the government of having permitted the $3,750,000,000 American loan to be "unwisely and improvidently spent." (Churchill is primarily responsible for this calamity to his country).

The British loan agreement contained a joker. It provided that British money (the pound sterling) should be converted into dollars, thus deflating the British Empire. The cause and the effect was similar to our deflation of 1920 when the Federal Reserve management contracted currency and credit; and it was brought about by the same gang in the same clandestine way. The Rothschilds promptly took advantage of this clause in the contract and converted their sterling into dollars.

It is reported that the greater part of the money left after buying the Rothschilds' Bank of England and other properties has been used in this conversion. Thus, our much heralded loan to relieve the distress of the British people has been, in fact, a gift to the Rothschilds and has been used to deflate British values and to communize the people. The simple relief measure for the British was to confiscate the Rothschild wealth, but instead the government gave the Rothschilds our $3,750,000,000 and made Lord Rothschild head of the labor party.

We are not on the gold standard for gold is out of circulation. The Federal Reserve management has created a fictitious and imaginary gold standard by simply counting a certain quantity of our buried gold as a gold reserve for federal reserve notes. While our dollars have less value than formerly, they are still so scarce and high as compared with the monies of other countries that no country can buy our products unless we give it the money. They can and do trade with Russia and other countries having cheaper monies.

JOKERS

What assurance can we have that loan agreements under the Marshall Plan will not also contain jokers and that our money will be used to promote communism rather than to check it? The $2,750,000,000 we gave UNRRA was administered by the Zionists, Lehman and La Guardia, and went that route. President Truman is surrounded by the same people.

Any plan that James Warburg and other Rothschild agents advocate is subject to suspicion: General Marshall is not above it. He was a Roosevelt pet. He was only pried loose from Ben Cohen and other socialists and communists by Congressional action. He had some responsibility for the Pearl Harbor disaster for he had knowledge of the "Winds Messages" and did not notify General Short and Admiral Kimmel but instead went horseback riding. And he sought to communize China.

The British laborer is a living example of socialism. We are all inherently lazy; none of us will work unless compelled to do so by force or by the necessity of making a living. There must be an incentive to work. Socialism can only succeed through a dictatorship, and inevitably leads to a dictatorship. The French laborer also reduced work and the French Government nas sougnt further loans and will no doubt continue to do so until the source of supply is exhausted. The only countries involved in the war that appear to be willing to work to support themselves are Germany, Japan, Holland, Belgium and Finland.

The Marshall Plan promotes socialism at the giving as well as the receiving end of the line. It is estimated that it will cost us 30 billion dollars during the next four years, but this is only a guess—it may cost ten times that amount. It necessarily means confiscatory taxation. The rate is now so high as to stifle enterprise. Under the present rate of taxation the government will eventually acquire all private property and we will be a socialistic, bureaucratic state, and headed for a dictatorship.

President Truman said in one of his speeches that we would have a surplus of four billion dollars at the endof the fiscal year (June 30, 1950), which he proposed to apply on the public debt, but instead it is estimated that the deficit will be $6,700,000,000. He is striving by propaganda and otherwise to reduce the price level which will necessarily reduce the government income. But at the present rate of taxation and price and wage level it will require approximately 100 years to pay our national debt, during which time we will likely lose our present form of government. Thus President Roosevelt and his Zionist friends will have accomplished their objective in involving us in the war.

It was claimed that these loans and gifts would promote foreign trade, but they have not done so. There is no profit in selling goods, and then giving the purchaser the money to pay for them. It is estimated that only 10% of our products are sold abroad. We had better do without this foreign commerce than tax ourselves to support it.

We are faced with the alternative of cancelling the national debt or losing our constitutional form of government. Our remedy is clear. We must cancel the national debt by issuing legal tender currency in payment of our government bonds and thereby promoting inflation and prosperity, or make the Zionists pay it. Deflation and want will communize and enslave us, and Soviet Russia and the communists are looking hopefully for that to happen. By inflation we will save about 5 billion dollars annual bond interest, will promote foreign commerce and save our government;—by deflation we will lose it and enslave ourselves and our posterity.

GEORGE W. ARMSTRONG

13.

UNITED NATIONS

This is a supplement to the chapter "World Empire" discussed on pages 66 to 94 of Zionist Wall Street.

We are probably paying the entire expense of the United Nations, which has been estimated at $100,000,000 anually. It will be far more than that sum when the United Nations exercises all of the powers granted to it. The UNESCO (United Nations Educational Scientific Cultural Organization) is not yet functioning except on paper, our representative being Mrs. Eleanor Roosevelt. It is impossible to estimate the cost of this service, for it will depend on the extent of the UNESCO set up. It is estimated that President Truman's social service program will cost thirty to forty billion dollars annually and $1,250,000,000,000 in fifty years.[47]

The UNESCO is intended to exercise jurisdiction over schools, labor, health and everything else ("other"). The United Nations is intended to establish an international socialistic superstate to be supported by the earnings of labor and industry and the wealth of the world. It was written by the communist Alger Hiss and associate communists of the State Department. Its Secretary General is Trygvie Lie, a Norwegian communist. A District Court of Appeals in California recently held that the United Nations Charter is a treaty with foreign

---

[47] See Congressional Record, 1949, 4785-6.

governments and as such supersedes our National Constitution!

The pretense of the United Nations is the promotion of peace; and the pretense of the "Atlantic Pact" is for defensive war. They are both mere pretenses, they are both for the same purpose and that purpose is a Zionist World Empire. "Union Now" with the British Empire, and the "Atlantic Pact" are only stepping stones in that direction. "Union Now" was promoted by Thomas Lamont, deceased, of J. P. Morgan & Co., and the Fabian socialist Nicholas M. Butler, deceased, its first president, and Justice Roberts, and Clarence Streit who was its second president. The "Atlantic Pact" is a war measure and the socialistic United Nations is an alleged peace measure. Obviously we do not need both the Atlantic Pact and the United Nations and obviously they are inconsistent, the one for peace and the other for war; and obviously also we are top heavy on governments, and over taxed for their support.

ATLANTIC PACT

Secretary of State Acheson estimated the cost of the "Atlantic Pact" for 1949 at $1,130,000,000 and for 1950 at $1,450,-000,000. This was the biased estimate of a socialist who sought to get the scheme adopted. It is only the "ante" and there will be much more to follow. It necessarily means additional taxes or inflation, for Congress appropriated about seven billion more than the estimated income ($42,000,000,000) for 1949. This estimate was based on 1948 values, tax rate and income. These values were deflated under government pressure and will likely be reduced 25% or more. If so, our income and the government's income will be reduced accordingly. It must be remembered that this is the program of Zionist Wall Street, the program of the Rothschilds, of Morgan & Co., Kuhn, Loeb & Co., and the other commumsts. Its purpose is to bankrupt and destroy our government and to establish their empire. Its ultimate purpose is to enslave the "goyim" (gentile cattle).

I recognize that it is our duty to save the Christian peoples of the world from Bolshevism, Zionism and slavery if we can. We are at least partially responsible for their condition for we have permitted Zionist Wall Street and Baruch and Frankfurter and Roosevelt and Truman to bankrupt and impoverish them. We cannot save them by bankrupting our government and ourselves or by socializing their governments and our own. We cannot do so through the United Nations, Atlantic Pacts, W.F.U. and their other schemes. It is probable that Zionist Wall Street and the Zionist Politburo of Russia are cooperating together, for they both seek to accomplish the same end. We must undo as far as we can everything that has been done under their direction.

GENOCIDE CONVENTION

The slick Zionists seek to undermine and destroy our government by treaties, which will be paramount to our Constitution and thereby transfer jurisdiction over us from our courts to international courts. One of the most offensive of these treaties is the declaration of the General Assembly in its resolution 96, December 11, 1946, proposing a "Genocide Convention." In Article II they define genocide, a newly coined word, to mean serious "bodily or mental harm" to members of a "national, ethical or religious group." If this booklet about the Zionists should be distasteful to any member of such a group, and probably it will be, the author could be prosecuted (under the "Genocide Convention") in some international court in Russia or Switzerland or other foreign country. It is the obvious purpose of this so-called Convention to suppress discussion of the Zionists and their schemes. It has been endorsed by the House of Representatives and is pending in the Senate.

There is also pending in Congress the International Bill of Rights sponsored by Mrs Eleanor Roosevelt. There is also pending the International Trade Organization (ITO) and International Labor Organization (ILO). The obvious purpose of all of these alleged treaties and conventions is to supersede our Constitution and deprive our courts of jurisdiction. Mr. Merwin K. Hart said of them:

"Overshadowing all of these alphabetical agencies and the foster parent of them all is the United Nations. This organization, the brainchild of Franklin D. Roosevelt, was drafted in a preliminary way at the Dumbarton Oaks Conference at which the Executive Secretary was one Alger Hiss."

Then it was referred to the San Francisco Conference in the late spring of 1945. The Secretary General of the San Francisco Conference was Alger Hiss. He was also the right hand man of Mr. Roosevelt at the Yalta Conference.

WORLD FEDERALIST UNION, INC.

Evidently the Zionists are not fully satisfied with their United Nations. They have organized the World Federalist Union, (WFU) a new scheme sponsored by James P. Warburg of Kuhn, Loeb & Co., the Rothschild agency that financed Lenin and Trotsky. L. L. Strauss, a member of the Atomic Commission, is also a member of this firm. The sponsorship by Warburg of itself should condemn this enterprise for he and his firm are Zionist Jews who seek to subordinate our government to their United Nations.

But it means also that the World Federalist Union is supported by unlimited funds. The wealth of Kuhn, Loeb & Co., has been estimated at 11 billion dollars. The purpose is alleged to be to prevent war, and to preserve peace, and that is also the alleged purpose of the United Nations. Both require communist Russia participation. Then why the World Federalist Union? What can they do through it that they cannot accomplish through United Nations?

There are two good reasons for it. One is that the United Nations has failed and it is now generally recognized as a failure. It has not preserved the peace but has promoted war in Palestine. The other is that they desire a new American Constitution that will supplant our present Constitution. They have made great progress in obtaining their objectives. They have already received the endorsement of 23 states, but the State of Georgia has withdrawn, leaving a net of 22. With 14 additional states a new Constitution can be written making us a province of a Jewish Empire and transferring civil rights and all other controversial questions to the tribunal of the United Nations and establishing the Welfare State. There can be no appeal from decisions of this "Genocide convention" except revolution.

The World Federalist Union (W.F.U.) is a Zionist communist scheme as was the League of Nations and "Union Now" with the British, and as are the United Nations and the Atlantic Pact. The Zionist Professor Arnold Toynesbee truly stated their plan at the 4th annual conference of the "Institution for the Scientific Study of International Relations" at Copenhagen. He said:

"We are working at present DISCREETLY BUT WITH ALL OUR MIGHT, to wrest this mysterious political force called 'Sovereignty' out of the clutches of the local national states of our world. And all the time we are denying with our lips what we are doing with our hands!"

This is the Judaic system and the plan of the Protocols. They must get rid of state sovereignty before they can establish international authority.

Their Welfare State means social equality as well as political equality. It means the mongrelization of the races. There will be no Anglo-Saxons, Jews, Negroes, and Chinese but we will develop a mongrelized race as a result of the mixture of these races. It is their plan to have absolute social and economic equality. There will be no trade barriers such as a tariff. The same standard of wages will prevail in Africa, Asia, Europe, and America. The United Nations, the World Federalist Union, or the State of Israeli will be the employer. There may be no strikes or wars. We may have peace, without liberty, but we will have little else except slavery, for there will not be much production. We will be slaves of the Super-State.

This subject is fully discussed by Joseph P. Kamp in his booklet "We Must Abolish the United States," published by the Constitutional Educational League, Inc., 342 Madison Avenue, New York. He says that the budget for this enterprise [WFU] last year (1949) was $550,000,000 and that it is financed by very rich people, viz: the Warburgs, Goldsmiths, and other Zionists. One woman contributed the sum of $1,000,000. He says that while there are some gullible gentiles who are members of these world government schemes, e.g. Henry Wallace in America and Sir Stafford Cripps in England, that most of the members are Zionists and that they propose to have a "World. Constituent Assembly" meeting in Geneva in 1950 and that this assembly will be asked to approve the following platform:

> (1) A monopoly of armed forces to be used as a world police force. Participating states to be disarmed to the level of their internal policing commitments.
>
> (2) A monoply of the processes involved in atomic development and other scientific discoveries capable of mass destruction.
>
> (3) The establishment of a World Bank for the

purpose of creating a common currency throughout the world, and of holding funds for the Central Authority in order that it may initiate and finance on a large scale economic planning such as that operated by the TVA.

COMMUNIST ENDORSEMENT

A "communist" world peace conference was held in New York for three days during March 1949 under the auspices of the "Cultural and Scientific Conference of World Peace." It was attended by 23 accredited delegates including Gerhardt Eisler and other American communists and communists from other countries. The State Department refused to admit a few of the British and French communists because they did not have proper credentials. It branded the convention as a "sounding board for communist propaganda," but it could not have been held without the approval of President Truman and Secretary of State Acheson. It had an estimated 2,000 delegates and the convention was picketed by an estimated 5,000 patriots. It adopted the following resolutions:

(1) To do everything possible to strengthen the United Nations as the best hope for peace.
(2) To transform the conference into a "cultural and scientific committee of arts, sciences and professions," [UNESCO], for the promotion of the socialist programme.

ISRAELI

The Zionists of Wall Street have now created their puppet government of Israeli and have taken posession of the minerals of the Dead Sea. The futility of the United Nations was demonstrated by the removal of the capital of the State of

Israeli from Tel Aviv to Jerusalem. According to the Associated Press report of December 15, 1949, Premier Ben Gurion truthfully said: "Israeli is against the whole world,"— (except Soviet Russia).

The Zionists can safely defy the United Nations. Who is to enforce its decrees? Suppose America undertakes the job. What will the Soviets do? If the United Nations cannot enforce its decrees against a small rebellious state such as Israeli, of what use is it as a peace agency? Is it worth the $100,000,000 that we contribute annually to its support?

It is not likely that Mr. Ben Gurion would have been so defiant if he had not known that he would have Russia's support. The State of Israeli is only a Zionist set-up to take over the mineral wealth of the Dead Sea and of Asia. The establishment of Israeli was celebrated on its first anniversary by Senator Lucas and other pro-Zionists in Congress. (Congressional Record, April 24 and 25, 1950).

We must repudiate the Communistic United Nations, and restore Constitutional Government.

THIRD ZIONIST WAR

GEORGE W. ARMSTRONG

TO: THE CONGRESS OF THE UNITED STATES

The People of the UNITED STATES

vs.

HARRY S. TRUMAN, ET AL.

PETITION

Now comes Geo. W. Armstrong, and respectfully represents the following:

1. That President Harry S. Truman, Secretary of State Dean Acheson, and Justice of the Supreme Court Felix Frankf urter are traitors and should be impeached and prosecuted;
2. That the members of the firms of J. P. Morgan & Co., Kuhn, Loeb & Co., and Lehman Bros. Co., and the members of the B'nai B'rith, Anti-Defamation League, Anti-Nazi League and American Jewish Committee are traitors and should be prose- cuted as such;
3. That the Zionists are aliens and are citizens of the State of Israeli and that they are communists and should be banished;
4. That the purpose of said traitors and Zionists is to destroy our system of government and create a Zionist super state; that in pursuance of said purpose they fraudulently established the United Nations and created the Atlantic Pact, and caused our government to intervene in the Korean war.

WHEREFORE, I pray you to impeach and prosecute the traitors and to cancel our membership in the United Nations and the Atlantic Pact.

I respectfully submit the following brief and argument in support of these allegations.

GEO. W. ARMSTRONG

March 1, 1951

BRIEF AND ARGUMENT

GEORGE W. ARMSTRONG

1.

THIRD ZIONIST WAR

Our present war with Russia ·and China is obviously our Third Zionist War. All threé of them were for the same purpose, viz: to· establish a Zionist World Empire. AU of themwere initiated by a·shocking disaster to arouse us to war: the first one by the sinking of the passenger ship Lusitania; the second by the destruction of our Pacific fleet at Pearl Harbor; and the third by the Korean attack. The first resulted in the League of Nations, the second in the United Nations, and the third is obviotisly in.; tended to convert it into a Zionist World Empire for the *pretended* purpose of preserving peace.

THE ZIONISTS OF NEW YORK AND MOSCOW INSTIGATED THE WAR

The North Koreans as well as the South Koreans are victims of the machinations of the Zionist communists. It is unfortunate that the Koreans must suffer. They have been betrayed into this fratricidal war by the Zionist communists of New York and Moscow. We should strike boldly to destroythe head of the snake and not its tail. *Bomb Moscow* with the atomic bomb and not the Chinese or the Koreans, and hang the New York and Washington Zionist traitors. There will never be peace on earth until Zionism is destroyed. Its mission is to destroy Christianity and to destroy and enslave Christians.

WHY THIS WAR?

The Zionists pretended that the Korean war was to establish free elections and a democratic government in Korea They represented that the North Koreans are communists and the South Koreans are democrats. That is all we know about them. The North Koreans are savages and the South Koreans may be also. The North Koreans murder their prisoners and the South Koreans murder non-combatants, according to press reports. They fight to the death rather than surrender. *It is at best a brutal savage war with savages, for the alleged purpose of compelling them to establish a democratic government. It is in fact a Zionist war for the purpose of establishing a Zionist Empire.*

The armies of communist China joined the North Koreans and at this time (March 1, 1951) they are reported to be losing and retreating. Our casualties have been heavy and we appear to be in for a long destructive war. 1t may be a life and death struggle between Christians and communists, and between freedom and slavery.

While the President called our intervention "police action," his message to Congress and his press interviews and his conduct reveal it as *war*. It was necessary to color it as "police action" to give it the semblance of legality, for the President under our Constitution has no power to declare war; that is the exclusive province of Congress. It is in fact war, and a war initiated by the President and his advisers, Dean Acheson, Felix Frankfurter, David Niles, and other Zionist traitors.

We are a gullible, charitable, unsuspecting Christian people, and are easily deceived. We excuse Roosevelt because he was in poor health, and Truman because of his early training as a Pendergast ward heeler and because of his ignorance. But they both had sense enough to select their associates, and they both selected Hiss, Niles, Acheson, et al.

CHINESE NATIONALISTS

The Associated Press of Nov. 30, 1950 reported General Claire Chennault, retired, formerly of the Flying Tigers, as saying that the Chinese Nationalists are good soldiers and will fight with and for us; and that only 1% of the 450 million Chinese are communists. That is less than the percentage of traitors in our own country. He said also that Chiang Kai-shek is a patriot of great integrity.

Chiang Kai-shek offered to send 33,000 trained soldiers to Korea, which is more than ail of the other 52 nations offered or contributed. Truman and Acheson not only rejected the offer but stationed a part of our Navy in the strait between China's mainland and Formosa on condition that the nationalists stay out of the war. In spite of it, the nationalists appear to be waging a successful guerilla war.

Truman and Acheson evidently plan to deliver Formosa and the Chinese nationalists to the communists through the United Nations or a four -or seven-power treaty. The British government is a socialist, pro-Zionist government dominated by the Rothschild money trust, as is our own. It recognized communist China for the alleged purpose of protecting its interests in Hong Kong and Malaya. It would, no doubt, vote to deliver Formosa and the nationalists to the Bolsheviks. France is at best an uncertain and unreliable member of the United Nations and the Atlantic Pact.

It is reported that the French have changed their government sixteen times since 1944. The government of France is now engaged in a losing war with the communists of Indonesia and want and need our help. The French and British governments are so indifferent to their own security as to oppose the re-armament of Germany, which is necessary for their protection. Both the French and British will agree to surrender Formosa to the communists if by doing so they can promote their commercial interests. They are not interested in protecting Formosa for the protection of the Chinese Nationalists or for our protection; nor are President Truman and Dean Acheson and Secretary of Defense George C. Marshall and the Zionists interested in doing so. They want to change our system of government and to establish a "welfare state."

Be it remembered that the Nationalist Government is in Formosa because of the treachery of our State Department. We promised to furnish them munitions and supplies for waging their war against the communists on the mainland. They were compelled to go to Formosa because our State Department failed to carry out its agreement at a critical period of the war. It was cold-blooded treachery for the purpose of communizing China, for which no one has yet been punished.

It is the duty of the 82nd Congress to establish an impartial tribunal of competent men to ascertain the truth, the whole truth, and nothing but the truth about the criminals who initiated the Second World War and also the Korean War. They should be empowered to investigate the Zionists and their organizations, viz: the B'nai B'rith, Anti-Defamation League and Anti-Nazi League, et al. If they are found to be Communistic, their members should be banished.

2.

THE PRESIDENT'S MESSAGE OF JULY, 19, 1950

President Truman sent a message to Congress '.on July 19, 1950, requesting authority to mobilize the resources of the United States in support of the United Nations. In his message he said 52 of the 59 nations had pledged their support. He de- scribed our support of the South Koreans as *"police action"* to enforce the orders of the United Nations. On the request of President Truman the United Nations appointed General Doug- las MacArthur commander of the United Nations Army. It is estimated that we supplied 150,000 combat troops; ·South Korea 100,000, all other countries 24,300; and that to date we have had about 50,000 casualties. This is more than twice the number of troops furnished by the other 52 nations of the United Nations that signed the resolution on Korea.• It is estimated that we have furnished 95% of the supplies for the army. Less than a dozen nations have supplied anything.

The President, in his message to Congress of July 19th, said: "Already aircraft of two nations: Australia and Great Britain, and naval vessels of five nations: Australia, Canada, Great Britain, the Netherlands and New Zealand, *1uz;ve been available,* for operations in the Korean area."

He also said:

"This outright breach of the peace in violation of the United Nations Charter created a real and present danger to the security of every nation; • • • it was a clear challenge to the basic principles of the United Nations."

He also said:

"The speed, the scale and the co-ordination of the attack left no doubt that it had been plotted long in advance."

He said that the United States was "going to the aid of the nation (Korea) established and supported by the United Nations and unjustifiably attacked by an aggressor force."

*Congressional Record Jan. 12, 1951, page IOO.

He said further:

"For our part we shall continue to support the United Nations action to restore peace in the Korean area... We are determined to support the United Nations in its effort to restore peace and security... We have also taken action to bolster the military defenses of individual free nations, such as Greece, Turkey and Iran."

The President also said in this message:

"I will transmit to Congress specific requests for appropriations in the amount of approximately ten billion dollars."

He asked Congress to enact legislation authorizing the government "to establish priorities and allocate such materials as necessary to promote the national security and the increase of taxes, as our basic weapon in offsetting the inflationary pressure exerted by enlarged government expenditures, and to control credit." He said further that "if a sharp rise in prices should make .it necessary, I shall not hesitate to recommend the more drastic measures of price control and rationing."[48]

These are the powers of a dictator which the President proposes to invoke to enforce the "police action" of the United Nations. If granted they will not end soon. Certainly not until the "police action" is ended. He obviously aspires to be our dictator.

The President's message was received with aeclaim by Congress and the press. They approved the defiance of Russia and the *apparent* repudiation of the Asiatic program of the Secretary of State and the appointment of General MacArthur as Commander-in-Chief.

The President's message plainly implied that the Korean invasion has been and is being prosecuted and directed by the Kremlin. If so, it means a long and costly war. It may mean the death of millions of men and the probable destruction of our government.

"POLICE ACTION"

Less than 25,000 combat troops of other nations have been used and only a limited number promised, except by the Nationalists of China, which offer was rejected. Only a limited number of .small naval vessels and a limited quantity of supplies have furnished or promised. This alleged "police action" has demonstrated the impotence of the United Nations as a peace agency and the hypocrisy of the Marshall Plan. We have given the people and governments of Europe and Asia more than fifty billion·dollars to restore their economy. They are all interested in protecting themselves but

---

[48] Congressional Record, Slst Congress, page 10781-5.

they have put the heavy burden of the alleged "Police action" on us.

The contribution of the 52 nations is mainly limited to an expression of good will. The government of France says they are engaged in Indonesia, and the government of Israeli that she is busy at home with the Arabs. The governments of the world evidently do not accept our intervention as "police action" to enforce the orders of the United Nations. They regard it as our war with the communists and they prefer to remain neutral. They may suspect that it is another Zionist war for a super government (which in fact it is). We have practically nothing to show for the billions we have spent through the Marshall Plan, the UNRRA, and in support of the United Nations, except a few pious expressions of good will and the promises of limited assistance at some indefinite future date.

If it was in fact mere "police action" to enforce the orders of the United Nations, then we are obviously the world's policemen. The President and not Congress, has assumed for us the obligation of enforcing the peace of the world. The President had no authority to do so; it was exclusively a subject for congressional action and Congress was then in session. It has already involved us in about 50,000 casualties to our young men and an estimated 18 billion dollars. It has involved us in war with Russia and China, a temporary suspension of constitutional government, and a threatened dictatorship which may become permanent.

IT IS IN FACT A THIRD WAR TO PROMOTE A ZIONIST EMPIRE

There are many circumstances that support this conclusion:

1. The President's message to Congress which was written by his Zionist advisers, is a strong circumstance. He bas requested more power than Roosevelt enjoyed in the last war. He seeks to complete the bankruptcy of America through deflation, debt and taxation. Korea is connected with Russia and China by land and by two railroads, - one to Mukden and the other to Vladivostok, and is separated from us by about 6,000 miles of ocean and was probably selected for our defeat.
2. Our government has known for more than a year that this attack would be made. Rear Admiral Roscoe Hickenloetter, until recently chief of our central intelligence agency, testified before the House Armed Services Committee that Russia and North Korea made a secret agreement in May 1949 under which fifty Russian military officers were sent to the North Korean capitol. This number was later increased to one hundred. The duties of these military officers was to plan strategy for the coming invasion and it was agreed that Russia would provide North Korea with ammunition, artillery, aircraft, tanks, trucks and other war equipment.

This was reported by the Intelligence Agency to the proper officials fifteen months before the attack. Truman and Acheson were warned until two days before the invasion, that the attack would come any day. They were not surprised but they were totally unprepared.[49] Admiral Hickenloetter was made the "scape goat," and has been discharged.

Congress appropriated $112,000,000 for the defense of Korea but only $200,000 was used for South Korea,

---

[49] Congressional Record, 81st Congress, page 9373.

the balance being used "directly and indirectly" for North Korea.[50]

The State Department's representative, Owen Latimore, described by Senator McCarthy as "the architect of our Far Eastern policy," said on January 15, 1950 that "the problem in Korea is to allow Korea to fall but not appear that we pushed her.[51]

Our State Department had known for more than a year that the communists have been training and arming the North Koreans for war, but *it* disarmed the South Koreans and withdrew our troops and support.

3. One of the most potent circumstances is the fact that Dean Acheson is still Secretary of State with the power of handicapping General MacArthur. If the President actually repudiated Acheson's administration of our Asiatic program, as he apparently did, Acheson would have indignantly resigned or the President would have demanded his resignation.

4. The appointment of the pro-Zionist George C. Marshall as Secretary of Defense and his appointment of the Zionist Jewess Anna Rosenberg and Jew Max Leva as his assistants reveal Truman's sympathies and character. They have the power to defeat General MacArthur.

5. War is necessary to preserve the socialist United Nations and to mobilize our manpower and resources and to establish a dictatorship and to silence critics, all of which the Zionists desire. The endorsements of Henry Morgenthau, the head of the American Zionists, and of the Zionist Bernard Baruch, chief high priest of the Zionist Sanhedrin, are significant.

6. The Zionists planned this Zionist war through the traitors Roosevelt, Marshall and Hiss at Yalta, and

---

[50] Congressional Record, 81st Congress, July 24, 1950, page 11001.

[51] Congressional Record, 81st Congress, page 9862-3.

through Truman and Hiss at Potsdam. It was disguised by the traitors Roosevelt and Hiss and Stettinius in the creation of the socialist United Nations at San Francisco.

WAS OUR DEFEAT PLANNED BY TRAITORS?

The foregoing circumstances indicate that our defeat in Korea was planned. The Zionist "saint," F. D. Roosevelt, was authority for the axiom that "things don't just happen, they are planned that way." Have the Zionists planned our defeat? They armed North Korea and disarmed South Korea. They knew that an attack would be made and selected the weakest point for it. Evidently the Zionists of America are cooperating with the Zionists of Russia.

They will profit whether we win or lose. If we lose, we will have lost our government and our liberty and they will have gained their communistic United Nations and World Empire, and will acquire undisputed title to the enormous mineral wealth of Palestine, Iran, and other countries.

If it was in fact *"planned* that way" the scheme originated immediately following World War II. We then had billions of dollars of war equipment and material. The Zionists caused the greater part of it to be destroyed. The Yalta and Potsdam agreements and the United Nations were all in pursuance of it.

UNDECLARED WAR

The communists of Russia and China are waging an undeclared war on us and not on the United Nations or Britain or France, and we can't rely on them to win it for us. The Reds have defiantly and insultingly declared war on the United States through their special envoy Wu. He said that we must get out of Korea or be driven out. Our *alleged* allies, the

British and the French, through their representative the British Prime Minister Attlee, sought to influence us to surrender Korea and Formosa and Asia to the communists. The British have already recognized the communist Chinese government of Mao and are supporting him with munitions and supplies, some *of* which came from us through the Marshall Plan, and are now being used against us.

Senator Eastland said of this appeasement:

"It would check off the vast resources of Asia to communism, and would tremendously weaken the United States throughout the world. In fact, if we lose Asia with its vast manpower and resources, the foundation is laid for Communist control of the world. The truth is that if the Communists are permitted to absorb and digest Asia, their conquest of Europe will be simple. The control of Asia will place them 75 percent of the distance on the road to world control for communism. I note that the British and French desire, among other things, to take Communist China into the United Nations, and want us to sacrifice Formosa.

"Mr. President, to take Communist China into the United Nations would be like placing a rattlesnake in a playpen with little children, and would raise the crime of blackmail to one of the cardinal virtues of mankind. Communist China, in conjunction with the Soviet Union, is bent upon world conquest. We must recognize this fact and act before she becomes any stronger."[52]

Both the British and French have coalition socialist-communist governments. The British Secretary of Defense Emanuel Shinwell and Minister of Labor and Supplies Aneurin Bevin are avowed communists. France's Secretary of

---

[52] Congressional Record, December 5, 1950, page 16264.

Defense is the communist Louis Kahn; the French have taken no part in the Korean campaign; they are themselves waging a losing phony war with the communists in Indonesia. Neither of them is a loyal or sympathetic ally. We do not need them for our defense and we cannot rely on them for help.

The French government is an off and on proposition. At the moment it is a socialist communist coalition government; it has changed sixteen times in the past six years. The British government is controlled .by the Rothschilds, who finance ·the labor party, and it is also a socialist communist coalition government.

We are able to protect ourselves and incidentally Christianity and the greater part of the world without the help of the British and French or the United Nations; nor do we need the "hydrogen bomb," which is only a figment of the imagination and may be a Zionist scheme to divert our resources and weaken us. What is the use of having a bomb if we do not use it? And how many years will be required to develop this visionary destructive bomb? It is by no means certain that Russia has the A bomb.[53] We have only President Truman's and Senator McMahon's word for it, and they are both pro-Zionist and are not reliable witnesses. It may be only a bugaboo to scare us into accepting their plans.

COMMUNISM OR FREEDOM

Senator Eastland said that we must support the nationalist army of Chiang Kai-shek, which was betrayed by the traitors Roosevelt, Acheson and Truman; and we must arm the Japanese. Chiang recently stated that he had 750,000 trained troops in Formosa and that he could raise about 2,000,000

---

[53] Congressional Record, December 8, 1950, page 16565-6.

more on the mainland of China. The traitors hogtied him by not furnishing him with munitions and supplies which they had promised, otherwise he would have won the war with the communists. They also defeated MacArthur temporarily by enabling Mao to divert his troops from Formosa and China to Manchuria and Korea.

Senator Eastland also said in this speech of December 5, 1950:

"Our whole military strategy in the Orient bas to be revised, and the time to do it is now, without waiting for 62 different nations to submit 62 different interpretations of a new Munich by which to guide us. The American people must understand tbat with America's future banging in the balance, with American boys pouring out their lives, with the American people financing with their earnings and savings the struggle to stop the spread of communism in Europe the time bas come for the American Government to stand on its own feet with a realization tbat it is our destiny with which we gamble...

"We must immediately clamp an iron blockade upon the China coast and seal her ports to all commerce with anyone. American air power must attack and destroy Chinese industrial potential and China's transportation system. In fact, she has no highways, but depends upon a thin spread of rail lines to supply ber industries and feed and clothe her people. This transportation system can be destroyed by American air power from bases which we now possess. These two things, Mr. President, will do more damage than a great armed invasion of the China land mass. In addition, we must aid Chiang Kai-shek and assist him in returning to the main-land and destroying the communists. We must aid and help the million anti-communist guerrillas now in China and thus create havoc and confusion there."[54]

Senator Eastland points out the only way that we can win the war with Russia and China. We cannot win it by diverting our resources to Europe. The Europeans can protect themselves with Germany's aid and a capable commander and capable governments without our help, but they cannot win it without Germany and we should not extend help unless Germany is included.

Senator Eastland's view is supported by General Claire Chennault, retired, former commander in China of the "Flying Tigers." He is reported by the Associated Press of November 29, 1950, to have said that he is well acquainted with Chiang Kai-shek and that he is a courageous, incorruptible, patriot who earnestly seeks to protect his country from communism, which is more than we can say of our government. It is also supported by former President Hoover.

It is obvions that if Chiang attacks Mao from Formosa that his army will soon be moved from Manchuria and that MacArthur can then occupy both Korea and Manchuria. It is the sure route to victory. It is our war and we are in it up to our necks and we must win it.

---

[54] Congressional Record, December 5, 1950, page 16265.

GEORGE W. ARMSTRONG

3.

UNITED NATIONS A SHAM AND A FRAUD

The United Nations is a sham and a fraud, designed and promoted by traitors and scalawags for the purpose of destroying our government and merging it into a Zionist World Empire and dictatorship. The annual cost of the United Nations is estimated at $100,000,000.00. The United States is assessed 40% of it, Britain 11%, Russia only 7%, and the remaining 44% is divided among all of the other nations. We are underwriting the outfit and probably paying the greater part of its cost.

We have financed the Korean War and supplied about 150,000 troops, the other countries of the U.N. an estimated 24,300. We have suffered about 50,000 casualties and they are increasing daily. There are no reported losses for any other country except about 200 to Great Britain. Our casualty and financial cost for this alleged "police action" are more than the casualty list and cost of our first three wars, viz: the American Revolution, the British War of 1812, and the War with Spain; the total casualties of these three wars are estimated at 28,000.

The United Nations was conceived by the traitor Roosevelt and his Zionist assistants and written by the traitors Pasvolsky, Hiss, and other Zionists of the State Department. It is "a snare and a delusion," and a very costly one. There is nothing to be gained by our continued membership in it, and everything to be lost. We can protect the Americas without the help of our alleged allies and they can protect themselves without our help. We must return to our Constitution and our time-tested foreign policy of isolationism and the Monroe doctrine.

The Zionists seek to undermine and destroy our Constitution under Article VI of the Constitution which provides that "all treaties made under the authority of the United States shall be the supreme law of the land." The United Nations Charter (Chapter IX, Article 55) provides that "the United Nations shall promote... universal respect for and observance of human rights and fundamental freedoms for all without distinction as to race, language or religion." Article 55 has been expressly adopted by the United Nations General Assembly. The District Court of Appeals in California held that the adoption of this declaration of "human rights" by the United Nations Assembly superseded our Bill of Rights and transferred jurisdiction over these subjects to the United Nations! Fugii vs. State, 217 Pacific 2nd, page 481.

The Zionists have submitted to the states and to Congress the "Genocide Convention;" and to Congress also treaties on the subjects of labor, known as I.L.O., and the tariff, known as I.T.O., which if adopted will, under the decision mentioned, transfer jurisdiction on these subjects from Congress to the United Nations, and from our courts to the United Nations Courts.

GENOCIDE CONVENTION

The "Genocide Convention" (or treaty) is particularly obnoxious for it makes anti-Zionism a felony, punishable in foreign courts. Under the terms of this convention I would, if charged with anti-Semitism, be subject to prosecution in a foreign country and in a foreign court, despite the fact that I have carefully sought to distinguish the Zionist communist Jew from the Christian Jew, who believes in our Lord and Savior, Jesus Christ, and our system of government. The Genocide Convention will become the supreme law of the land if adopted by 36 states. It was adopted by 22 states before its real purpose was known, and seven of them have since withdrawn. The campaign was promoted and financed by the Zionist James Warburg, of Kuhn, Loeb & Co.

The Zionists sought to suppress criticism of the Jews during the last war by the War Securities Act. The bill actually passed the House of Representatives. They will seek to do so again for that is one of the purposes of the present war. They have had similar laws adopted in several of our cities and states. If they are innocent, why do they object to criticism? No other race or class of people seeks such exemption.

President Truman appointed the socialist Eleanor Roosevelt as one of our delegates to the United Nations and she is at the head of its "Human Rights" branch. Her division declared the following "human rights," viz :

"The right of social security;" "the right to just and favorable conditions of work;" "the right to protection against unemployment;" "the right to rest and leisure;" "the right to food, clothing, housing, and medical care and necessary social services;" "the right to security in the event of unemployment, sickness, disability, widowhood and old age;"and "the right to education."

These rights are, of course, to be enforced through the United Nations. No penalty for disobedience, or method of providing the money are stated, but they will be provided later.

There are three known communists on Mrs. Roosevelt's committee and the balance of them are socialists. Their program is a socialist-communist program and for the purpose of promoting socialism and communism. That is in fact the purpose of the United Nations and not the prevention of war, as pretended. Trygve Lie, its manager, is a Norwegian socialist, and his subordinates are either socialists or communists.

THE CELEBRATION

The President stated the purpose of the United Nations in his speech at Flushing Meadow, November 4, 1950. He said that "our soldiers died in order that the United Nations might live," and that as a result the United Nations is "stronger than ever before." He said also:

"The people of the world look to the United Nations as a source of direct help in their daily lives, to them it is a case of food or a box of school books or a doctor who vaccinates their children. It is an expert who shows them how to raise more rice or wheat. It is the flag which marks a safe haven to the refugee, an extra meal to a nursing mother."

Where does the President find authority for transferring us and our government to such a "glorious" super-government? Where will it get the money to carry out his seductive promises? What is left for our national, state and city governments to do, and why not abolish them? How can the President reconcile his advocacy of such a government with our Constitution and his oath of office? His entire speech adds up to socialism and communism. If the President understood the meaning of his speech, which is doubtful, he is either a socialist or a communist and is unfit to be President of these United States.

The Flushing Meadow meeting was a celebration of the fifth anniversary of the United Nations and the occasion of the "Freedom Bell Crusade" sponsored by President Truman, General Ike Eisenhower and the Zionist Senator Herbert H. Lehman of New York. In preparation for this great hullabaloo our Department of Agriculture sent materials to county agents throughout the country to be made into United Nations flags and distributed through the school children. The "victory" bell was sent to Berlin and a great celebration was reported to have been held there on "United Nations Day," viz : October 24, 1950.

What did we celebrate? And what did the Germans celebrate? We are the freest people of the world and are guaranteed freedom of life, liberty and property by our Constitution, and we are satisfied with it. The Germans had no occasion for a celebration, and Truman, Lehman and Eisenhower would not have sponsored a real German celebration. It was in fact an insult to the Germans.

The excitement appears to have been a celebration of surrendering our system of government to the Zionist United Nations, but it was premature. They have not yet established the "Genocide Convention," their I.L.O. and I.T.O. treaties. When and if they are ratified our pro-Zionist Supreme Court will probably hold that they supplant our National Constitution and then the Zionists will have an occasion to celebrate.

Congressman Wood of Idaho said of the United Nations flag: "The United Nations flag is not American. It has no heredity back of it except that of crime, treason, lies, hate, suspicion and double-dealing. It has nothing in it which is American, except our money, and it holds little promise of ever being anything but a wilted, blood-stained rag against the glorious history and tradition of our flag of America - our beloved Stars and Stripes."[55]

"AMBASSADOR" DULLES

President Truman appointed the republican Zionist stooge, John Foster Dulles, as our Ambassador plenipotentiary, and sent him on a mission to General Douglas MacArthur. His firm (Sullivan & Cromwell) are reported to be attorneys for J. P. Morgan & Co., agents for the Zionists firm of N. M. Rothschild & Son. At a conference of the Federal Council of Churches (a communist front) in Delaware, Ohio, Dulles submitted the following resolution, which was adopted "as a requisite principle of peace," to-wit :

"World government, strong immediate limitations on national sovereignty, international control of all armies and navies, world wide freedom of immigration, elimination of tariffs and quota restrictions, and an international bank."[56]

That was the purpose of the Roosevelt-Stettinius-Hiss United Nations and of the Truman-Acheson-Frankfurter Russian Chinese War. That is the program of J. P. Morgan & Co., Kuhn, Loeb & Co., and of the Rothschild money trust. It is the program of the Zionists and communists. While the Russian representatives often appear to be recalcitrant and antagonistic to the United Nations, they are not so in fact. They are only shadow-boxing for public consumption and to deceive the gullible Christians. There can be no harmony between Christ and anti-Christ, or between Christian and anti-Christian.

---

[55] Congressional Record, Feb. 6, 1951, page 1073.
[56] Time Magazine, March 16, 1942.

"World government" as advocated by President Truman's Ambassador-at-Large Mr. Dulles, and as established by the United Nations, involves the *absorption of our government and its subordination to the United Nations*. There is no need for two governments "controlling our Army and Navy." Their interests will conflict and in that case the super-government will of course control. Mr. Dulles' "world government" will abolish our immigration laws and protective tariff, and that is practically what the Truman "fair deal" administration has accomplished. Mr. Dulles' world government scheme correctly represents President Truman or he would not have been appointed Ambassador-at-Large to deal with other governments.

GEORGE W. ARMSTRONG

4.

THE FIRST TRAP

The victory celebration with its victory bells and United Nations flags was premature. The Chinese hurled an estimated 1,350,000 troops from Manchuria against the United Nations Army and drove them back regardless of their own losses. The Chinese troops were said to have been doped to make them reckless. They surrounded a part of the United Nations Army and cut them off from their base of supplies. General MacArthur was prohibited from attacking the Chinese base of supplies on the alleged ground that such attack might provoke them to war!

The Zionist press of the world, of course, blamed General MacArthur. They were particularly gleeful over the fact that he was said to have expressed the hope that he would be able to send our soldiers home by Christmas (of 1950). The Zionists never intended for General MacArthur to win the war and it will be a miracle for him to do so, handicapped as he has been by Truman, Acheson, Frankfurter and Niles. The loudest critics were the Zionist British Defense Minister Emanuel Shinwell, and the French, whose government has not contributed a soldier or a dime, and the Zionist mouthpiece Drew Pearson.

The Associated Press reported December 2, 1950 that General MacArthur said that "he had received no suggestion from any authoritative source" that his North Korean drive should have been halted some distance short of the

Manchurian border. He was asked whether "military operations" were handicapped by orders not to attack Chinese bases. He replied that "the order was an enormous handicap and without precedent in military history." He said that the communist "sanctuary of neutrality behind their lines protected them from air attack and gave them the advantage of moving troops at night in difficult terrain."

He declined to discuss the use of the atomic bomb and expressed the belief that the situation was not hopeless. It was revealed that the order to refrain from attacking the Chinese bases was given by Truman and Acheson and not by the United Nations. It was also revealed that the Chinese assembled an estimated 1,350,000 seasoned troops on the Manchurian border at night during a period of several weeks prior to the attack.

This was unknown to General MacArthur, who had been prohibited from sending planes across the Manchurian border, but it was probably known to Truman and Acheson. In an open letter to President Truman, published by the Associated Press December 2, 1950, Senator Joe McCarthy said: "If this treasonable farce of insisting that only American boys can die while refusing the help of the soldiers of allies continues, then the time is long overdue for the Congress in the name of America to stand up and be counted and immediately impeach you." *Amen! Amen! Amen!*

Senator McCarthy added that it is "beyond conception that your State Department, which either bungled or *planned us into this war* now bars the use of any of Chiang Kai-shek's troops in Korea." No, it is not beyond conception if they *planned* us into the war, for that is precisely what to expect. He said that Chiang had "358,000 well-trained and well-equipped soldiers" that he was ready and willing to contribute. This treacherous Korean attack is consistent with the Zionist and communist system of warfare; and the treachery of Truman and Acheson with that of Roosevelt, Stimson and Marshall. This "treasonable farce" is exactly similar to the Pearl Harbor and Lusitania treasonable farces. A traitor is a loathsome creature that will commit any crime to accomplish his treacherous purposes. He is as a general rule a Zionist and an anti-Christian.

The trap was set by President Truman and Dean Acheson. They stationed warships in the strait between Formosa and China upon the agreement with Chiang Kai-shek that he would not attack the Chinese army on the mainland. Obviously the purpose was to protect the army of Mao, and to enable him to transfer it to Manchuria, which he did. They prohibited General MacArthur from sending planes over Manchuria and required him to stop at the Manchurian border for ten days, to enable Mao secretly to send an estimated 1,350,000 fully equipped soldiers into Korea.

It is difficult for the Christian mind to comprehend the depravity of treachery but it is a part of the religion of the Zionist. It is their method of warfare. They are taught it by their Talmud and Protocols and Rabbis. It explains Truman's peevish, childish letters to the music critic Hume and to Congressman Hebert; they were the outbursts of a guilty conscience and a disordered mind.

GEORGE W. ARMSTRONG

5.

DOUGLAS MACARTHUR, SOLDIER AND PATRIOT

The Zionists made the mistake of permitting President Truman to recommend General Douglas MacArthur as commander in chief of the United Nations forces. They did not think that he could win, disarmed as he was, and with them directing the campaign and in control of his supplies. They underestimated him.

He was, of course, the logical man for the job. He was not only on the ground but he was the recognized military genius of the age. They sought to revive the decadent and useless United Nations and they thought they could rally its members and the American people to its support more effectively through him than the pro-Zionists Mark Clark or Ike Eisenhower. Moreover, they wanted to discredit him by defeat.

He said in his short address at Seoul to the people of Korea : "It is through the spirit that we must save the flesh ... In humble and devout manifestation of gratitude to Almighty God for bringing this decisive victory to us I ask that all present rise and join me in reciting the Lord's Prayer," which they did. We cannot imagine such humility in Mark Clark or Ike Eisenhower or Truman.

What a contrast between this great Christian American patriot and our vain little pro-Zionist President who seeks to be our dictator, cavorting around in his private yacht, "The Williamsburg," and his private plane, "The Enterprise," maintained at public expense. What a contrast between MacArthur and our real rulers the traitors Felix Frankfurter and Dean Acheson.[57]

Acheson evidently planned that we should lose the Korean War; and such was the scheme of the Zionists. They disarmed the South Koreans and armed the North Koreans. They selected General MacArthur as commander for the purpose of rallying the American people to the war, and if lost, of eliminating MacArthur as a probable presidential candidate on the republican ticket. If the demand in 1952 is for a military president, they want Eisenhower.

But MacArthur, the great soldier and patriot, refused to be crushed. What a pity he is not now our President. He will win the war if given a free hand. The only possible way to defeat him is by the treachery of Truman and Acheson and their Zionist assistants.

The President, at the instance of Acheson, endeavored to suppress an address of General MacArthur to his fellow Veterans of Foreign Wars at their annual convention in Chicago. In this speech General MacArthur said:

"Our line of defense is a natural one and can be maintained with a minimum of military effort and expense. It envisions no attack against anyone nor does it provide the bastions

---

[57] Our dictator Truman said that he would not appoint John L. Lewis "dog catcher," to which Mr. Lewis replied that if he did he would have more brains in the dog department than in the State, and that one of his first acts would be to discharge the "pusillanimous pups in the State Department." If we must have a labor dictator Mr. Lewis is preferable to Mr. Truman.

essential for offensive operations, but properly maintained would be an invincible defense against aggression. If we hold this line we may have peace,-lose it and war is inevitable."

He said also:

"To pursue any other course would be to turn over the fruits of our Pacific victory to a potential enemy. It would shift any future battle area 5,000 miles eastward to the coasts of the American continents, our own home coasts; it would completely expose our friends in the Philippines, our friends in Australia and New Zealand, our friends in Indonesia, our friends in Japan, and other areas, to the lustful thrusts of those who stand for slavery as against liberty, for atheism as against God."[58]

It is reported that this is also the view of former Secretary of Defense Johnson and General Omar Bradley and the "high command." General MacArthur bowed to the command of his commander-in-chief and did not authorize the delivery of the address. Senator Wherry said of Truman's attempted gag:

"In the press and over the radio we hear reports of President Truman's order putting a gag on General Douglas MacArthur's message on Formosa to the meeting of the Veterans of Foreign Wars in Chicago yesterday. Such action is outrageous and will be resented by every American.

"Apparently there are fundamental differences over Far East American policy between Secretary of State Dean Acheson and General MacArthur, but General MacArthur, as a good soldier, is obeying and carrying out the orders of the

---

[58] Congressional Record, Aug. 28, 1950, page 13769.

Commander in Chief as dished up to him by the bungling Acheson."[59]

Senator Knowland said of it:

"Our moral leadership was undermined by the secret deals of Yalta, regarding which neither the Congress of the United States nor the American people had information until later years. The suppression of the Wedemeyer report on China for two years, and the report of General Wedemeyer on Korea, which has now been held in secrecy for three years, has allowed the State Department to lose for us in the Far East all that our fighting men had won in World War II at great sacrifice... Now once again the administration is gagging a patriotic soldier, who sees the danger facing our Nation in the Far East, and want to warn our people before it is too late."[60]

If this war was in fact only a "police action" to enforce the orders of the United Nations, as Truman proclaimed, then General MacArthur would be the commander and not President Truman, and his effort to gag MacArthur was sheer impertinence. General MacArthur is entitled to credit for accepting the job and obeying orders. But the Korean War is not now regarded as police action by the members of Congress, as revealed by their speeches, nor by the President, as revealed by his messages.

Truman said of the Marines that they were the "Navy's police force" and that they maintained a "propaganda machine that is almost equal to Stalin's." The Marines resented it and the President saw that it might cost votes for the democratic "fair deal" candidates for Congress. On the following day he wrote to General Clifton B. Cates, the Marine Corps

---

[59] Congressional Record, Aug.28, 1950, page 13678.
[60] Congressional Record, Aug. 28, 1950, page 13770.

Commander: "I sincerely regret my unfortunate choice of language," etc., and later appeared before the Marine convention and made an abject apology, which was featured pictorially in the daily press.

THE TRUMAN-MACARTHUR WAKE ISLAND CONFERENCE

There was much speculation as to President Truman's purpose in calling for the Wake Island conference with General MacArthur pending the war. The pro-communist columnist Drew Pearson wrote that it was Truman's purpose to tell Douglas MacArthur "who was boss." The commentator Fulton Lewis said that Truman's purpose was to prevail on General MacArthur not to resign his command. The President may have revealed his purpose in his San Francisco speech following the conference. If so, it *was to dramatize his dictatorship and to promote the United Nations.*

He said in substance:

"I, Harry Solomon Truman, hereby pledge the people of the world that the American people will preserve the peace of the world through the United Nations and that we will defend any and all countries against aggression."

He had no authority to make any such commitment, for that is a subject over which Congress has exclusive jurisdiction, and Congress had not spoken.

The 82nd Congress may not be willing to assume such a grave responsibility without submitting the issue to the people. It is true that a prior Congress subscribed to the United Nations, but it was without authority to subordinate our government to the United Nations. The Zionists and communists and socialists wish to do so, but the white

Christians are the majority and can and should repudiate the membership. Congress did not then know that the United Nations charter was written by the traitor Alger Hiss and other traitors in the State Department. They did not understand that its effect would be to make our government a minority state in a world Zionist super government and abolish our own government.

It now appears that this dramatic Wake Island conference was to use General MacArthur and his victories to promote the United Nations and the democratic party. The meeting was planned by the bunch of traitors who seek to destroy our government. On October 8, 1950 they announced their program to increase our army to three million men, according to the Associated Press and United Press of that date. It was reported that this program has the support of Chairman Vinson of the House Armed Services Committee. It means a military government and confiscatory taxation; it means bureaucracy, bankruptcy, and a dictatorship.

General MacArthur declined to comment on the conference with President Truman further than to assure the Asians that America would protect them against Russia, which was his mission.

General MacArthur performed a miracle in rescuing more than 100,000 of his men in sub-zero weather who were surrounded in mountain passes by an overwhelming number of well clothed and well equipped Chinese red bandits. The hands and feet of many of our men were frozen and had to be amputated. The United Nations was requested to denounce this treacherous Chinese attack. Some of its members objected and the decision was postponed. It is within our power to punish the depraved traitors who designed the trap, but no punishment is adequate; the most that we can do is to try them for treason and if convicted execute them in disgrace and confiscate their property.

6.

POLITICS

In his St. Louis campaign speech, Nov. 4, 1950, President Truman said, "Isolationism and greater strength and prosperity are the major campaign issues." The Associated Press reported that there were several hundred vacant seats and that "hundreds of police, detectives and secret service men guarded the auditorium." Obviously they constituted a large part of his audience. He paid tribute to the many "honorable men and women in the Republican Party who have backed bi-partisan foreign policy."

Truman condemned the republicans who attacked the bi-partisan policy and who attacked his administration "and sought to destroy the United Nations and labor unions through the infamous Taft-Hartley law." He promised its repeal. He boasted that the Democratic Party had "broadened and increased social security and raised the minimum wage from 40c to 75c an hour." He asserted that a "vote for isolationism would be a vote for national suicide." This speech was made over a nationwide radio three days before the 1950 election and was paid for by the National Democratic Committee. It was the platform and program of that committee.

ISOLATIONISTS

We must return to our ancient moorings, viz: Constitutional Government and isolationism. Dean Acheson sought to reflect on Senator Taft by saying he is an "isolationist." If he is, in fact, it is to his credit. It is to be hoped that some of our alleged states-men will have the courage to stand for constitutional government and our ancient isolation foreign policy. We were a happy and prosperous people with a solvent government until they were abandoned by Roosevelt, followed by Truman. We are now at war and are an over-taxed people with a bankrupt government seeking to find something else to tax.

Isolationism was not the issue in the 1950 campaign; it was discussed only incidentally. The issues were Dean Acheson, Felix Frankfurter and the other traitors in our government, the C.I.O., of L., the Taft-Hartley Act, the Truman administration, and Truman and his Zionist-labor government. They were all repudiated, even in the strongholds of organized labor.

The democrats of the South are as strongly opposed to Truman and his "fair deal" and "welfare state" and his pro-Zionist Wall Street labor administration, as are the people of the West, who turned against him. In Oklahoma, where the democrats elected the governor, they repudiated the United Nations and the World Federalist "Genocide Convention" by a vote of more than four to one, despite the fact that the Genocide Convention had previously been approved by the legislature. The American people are obviously satisfied with their Constitution and system of government but not the present administration of it. That is the correct interpretation of the election.

There was no political party or candidate that would stand for our system of government in preference to the United Nations, or for isolationism as against internationalism; these important issues were not, therefore, directly involved in the election. Senator Taft accepted the challenge as to the repeal of the Taft-Hartley Act, and won by a majority of more than 430,000 votes. William Green, president of the A.F. of L., and Philip Murray, president of the C.I.O., campaigned to defeat him. The Zionist communist, Jack Croll of the C.I.O., undertook to raise a campaign fund of $12,000,000 by an assessment on the C.I.O. membership. He reported a campaign contribution of $460,000. The balance, if collected, was obviously misappropriated. The election results must be interpreted as an approval of the Taft-Hartley Act and a repudiation of their leaders by the membership of organized labor, which is to the credit of the membership.

ELECTION RESULTS

The election of Senator Taft in Ohio and the defeat of the President's spokesmen, Lucas in Illinois, Myers in Pennsylvania, and Tydings in Maryland, was a repudiation of his administration, but it did not faze him or change his plans.

The Associated Press reported on November 15, 1950, that Truman wrote Chairman Doughton of the Ways and Means Committee to prepare an excess profits tax bill at the short session of Congress that would provide for $4,500,000,000. He recommended that profits be subject to this tax after July 1, 1950. He also recommended that government agencies begin "blueprinting at over a new multi-billion dollar foreign aid program for presentation to Congress in January." Thus it appears that the President adopted Lenin's plan of communizing America, viz: to cause us to *"spend* ourselves into bankruptcy." It is a slow but sure route.

The American people have impeached Truman, Acheson, and Frankfurter as shown by the results of the November election. Self-respect and decency should compel them to resign. It was a vote of want of confidence in the Truman administration. In England or France it would have meant an election to bring about a change of government in order that the government represent the will of the people. Our system does not require it. It demonstrates a weakness in our Constitution. Congress should elect the president every two years instead of the politicians electing him every four years. Under our present system the president dominates Congress through his power to give jobs to them and their friends. The suggested change would make the president responsive to the will of Congress. They would dictate to the president instead of he to them, for they would have the power of removal without impeachment.

THE TRUMAN PROGRAM

President Truman in his message to the adjourned session of the 81st (lame duck) Congress, which convened on November 27, 1950, urged Congress to grant statehood to Hawaii and Alaska, and to appropriate $17,800,000,000 for the Korean War, continue rent control and levy an excess profits tax. He scheduled statehood for Alaska and Hawaii as the first order of business. Congress rejected it on the ground that it was packing the senate for the adoption of the Truman program. It would also be important to Truman and Acheson in case of impeachment by the 82nd Congress.

Senator Wherry, the republican minority floor leader, said that the first order of business should have been the "removal of Dean Acheson," to which should be added Truman and Frankfurter. Congress should promptly create an impartial non-partisan board or committee to investigate the Pearl Harbor disaster (which has been twice white-washed), the Korean War, and Zionist responsibility for them. It should then take the necessary steps to relieve us of traitors and to restore constitutional government.

The House of Representatives adopted an excess profits tax bill providing for a tax of 77 per cent, retroactive from July 1, 1950, on profits above "normal" as defined by the bill, which is estimated to raise about $3,000,000,000 additional revenue. The taxpayers, as represented by the United States Chamber of Commerce and the National Manufacturers Association and about 100 voluntary witnesses, appeared before the House Ways and Means Committee in opposition. It is an unjust and discriminatory method of taxation that will discourage private enterprise and be harmf ul to our country. The representatives of the tax-payers proposed an increase in the rate as an alternative, which has been adopted, but not as an alternative; both plans were enacted.

A better plan is to issue $4,000,000,000 of currency and thereby relieve the overburdened taxpayer of the added tax load.

This would increase prices and wages, called inflation, but inflation is better than deflation and bankruptcy. It is better than debt, slavery and communism. Our money is inflated as compared with the monies of other countries. They cannot trade with us unless we give or lend them the money. The dollar ought to be deflated.

A still better plan is to withdraw from the Roosevelt-Hiss-Zionist United Nations and from the Atlantic Pact. Let the Europeans create their own "United States of Europe" or pacts, without us. They can defend themselves against Soviet Russia with Germany's help, but can't without it, - not even with our help. We should protect Formosa and arm the Chinese nationalists so that they can defend themselves.

Major General Claire Chennault, retired Air Force Commander in China during World War II, says that the nationalists of China can win with our support and that all that is necessary is to equip them. We should equip Chiang's men and let them finish the war. Congress should then demand the retirement of General Marshall as Secretary of Defense and the appointment of General MacArthur as his successor.

The President, in his economic message to Congress of January 12, 1951, called for huge new "pay as you go taxes, strict price and wage and rent controls." He said everybody will have to make "big sacrifices for years to come, all the way down to using towels and sheets longer." He estimated that we will "require $140,000,000,000 in this and the next fiscal year," and asked Congress to "drastically increase taxes and to curb speculation." He told Congress that "1,000,000 more men and women may be added to the armed forces within the next few months," and he claimed the power to add them without consulting Congress.

Stalin could not have devised a better and more certain program for communizing America and for the destruction of our government. We have reached the saturation point on income taxes, called "diminishing returns," where increasing the rate will reduce production and create less revenues. The democratic "fair deal" House leader McCormick proposed through the press of the same date (January 12, 1951) a national sales tax. This is an indirect, disguised and comparatively painless tax upon the consumer. We have reached the limit or nearly so, of providing revenue by income taxation, and must adopt a sales tax if the President creates another emergency or sends a large army to Europe.

There are in fact two better methods of providing the required revenue, viz:

1. To confiscate the wealth of the rich Zionist traitors who euchered us into this war. Justice, as well as our necessity, requires the adoption of this plan. It will involve a trial of traitors and an adjudication. We are entitled to know the truth about this war and also World War II. Wben we know the truth the remedy will suggest itself, "and the truth will make us free."
2. To pay in currency "as we go" and not by taxes and bonds which will produce inflation, unless prices and wages are frozen. But inflation is better than deflation and bankruptcy and price and wage controls and communism. Inflation simply means high wages and prices, and cheap money. It benefits the debtor, the producer and the farmer, and it injures the bond holder, the creditor and salaried people. But it does not produce poverty and bread lines and soup kitchens and socialism. It is admittedly bad, but is better than deflation.

The President's plan will result in communism and a dictatorship, if indeed that is not the purpose of it. He has practically established himself as a dictator by usurpation. In a press statement on the same date (January 12, 1951) he asserted that he had power to send troops to Europe in support of the Atlantic Pact and that while he would consult Congress, he would do as he pleased regardless of Congress, and if Congress refused to appropriate the money to pay for the troops he would "go to the mat" with them; that he "had licked them once and could do so again."

The press commentators have interpreted this to mean that Truman would seek re-election. But it is also subject to the interpretation that he would *abolish Congress,* which I think is what he meant, for it is what he wants and what his Zionist advisers want, and is only another step -a very long one- in his program to make himself our dictator. He can only obtain that goal by usurpation and theft, for he cannot obtain it by the ballot.

7.

SABOTAGE

The Associated Press reported on August 14, 1950 that four republican members of the Senate Foreign Relations Committee, viz: Wiley of Wisconsin, Hickenlooper of Iowa, Smith of New Jersey, and Lodge of Massachusetts, charged that "the Truman administration policy invited Russia to grab whatever it could in China, Korea, and Formosa." Attacking presidential agreements at Yalta and Potsdam, they said "the Roosevelt and Truman Far Eastern policy consistently temporized with and capitulated to the ruthless program of the communists." They said further that they "disintegrated onr armed forces in 1945" and caused the senseless destruction of billions of dollars worth of military equipment which the United States and its friends so desperately need today.

OR WAS IT "PLANNED THAT WAY"?

They ascribe this conduct to "incompetence and bungling," which is a charitable view to take. Was it in fact "incompetence and bungling" that caused Roosevelt to select Alger Hiss as his adviser at Yalta, and as Secretary of the San Francisco convention that created the United Nations Charter? Was it "incompetence and bungling" that caused Roosevelt to select Stettinius of J. P. Morgan & Co., as Secretary of State; Henry Stimson, attorney for Kuhn, Loeb & Co., as Secretary of War; the Zionist Henry Morgenthau as Secretary of the Treasury; the Zionist Felix Frankfurter as

United States Supreme Court Judge; and the Zionists Neyhaus alias Niles, and Baruch as "assistant presidents"?

Was it in fact "incompetence and bungling" that caused Roosevelt to doublecross Chiang Kai-shek and to cede Manchuria to the communists at Yalta ? Was it "incompetence and bungling" that caused him to select the communist Sidney Hillman as the dictator of the Chicago democratic convention and Truman as Vice President and his probable successor?

Was it "incompetence and bungling" that caused Truman to ratify Roosevelt's program at Potsdam, and to divide Germany into four zones giving the bolsheviks the eastern fertile agricultural section and agreeing to the confiscation of the property of the inhabîtants of the eastern zone and the expulsion of 12,000,000 of them from their homes? Was it "incompetence and bungling" that caused Truman to continue Roosevelt's Zionist advisers and program; to select Dean Acheson as Secretary of State and the pro-communist George C. Marshall as Secretary of Defense and the Zionist Jewess Anna Rosenberg Assistant Secretary?

We may excuse Truman on the ground of "incompetence and bungling" and ignorance, but it is a lame excuse for *a President of the United States* and not a valid one. We are all legally responsible for the consequences of our conduct. It is a severe tax on our charity and credulity to find an excuse for President Truman but no excuse is valid for the conduct of Roosevelt and Acheson.

The Zionists designed and partially executed a most adroit and cunning plan to communize the world, including America, and it is now in process of accomplishment. A very large part of Europe and Asia have already fallen, and our government is seriously threatened. If we lose the war with Russia and China, we are sunk; if we win, we still have the Zionists and the Socialists to deal with. If we lose, we lose our liberty and our system of government and our Christian religion. We will not be safe until we hang the traitors and banish the communists, 95 per cent of whom are Jew Zionists. We must imprison them in concentration camps until we can transport them.

Congress should repudiate the Yalta, Teheran, Quebec and Potsdam agreements; the bolsheviks have already done so. Their intent and purpose was to communize the world. President Truman in his radio report to the Nation on September 1, 1950 now admits that this is true. He said,

"The Soviet Union has repeatedly violated its pledges of international cooperation. It has destroyed the independence of its neighbors. It has sought to disrupt those countries it could not dominate. It has built up tremendous armed forces far beyond the needs of its defense."

He said in substance that the Soviet politburo are liars, that their purpose is to communize and dominate the world, and that they are the instigators of the Korean War.

All of that is true but the President is rather late in recognizing it. If it is true, then what in the name of common sense is the use of having a conference with them about a Japanese treaty and the disposition of Formosa?

GERMANY

It was Truman and not Roosevelt who made the Potsdam treaty that gave Berlin and East Germany to Stalin, which resulted in the forced migration of 12,000,000 Germans and the confiscation of their homes and property. Senator Langer, who recently returned from a visit to Germany, says of their condition:

"Those familles were driven from their homes, away from their churches, away from their schools. Where are they today? We have heard a great deal of the displaced persons; but the situation of these millions of people is just as bad as the worst we have ever heard about displaced per sons. I saw them. They live in single rooms, three or four familles in a room. They live in camps and shacks. Children are without proper food, and are getting no education. How can they when the heads of familles are without work and fathers and mothers see no hope of re-establishing a home?"

He also said that the fate of Europe is dependent on the Germans.

"Let me repeat the warning that if Western Germany should fall a victim to Russia, the hundreds of millions of dollars which we have spent in France, Italy, and England will have been spent in vain, for those nations, too, will fall before Communist aggression."

He said of the Nuremberg trials:

"Moreover, the rules under which the defendants were tried were not the rules and laws prevailing in Germany, but were the rules written specifically for the purpose of the trials. Though the laws were drafted by Americans they did not follow American standards of procedure at all...

"There bas been much discussion, both pro and con, with respect to the war-crimes trials which we held in Nuremberg. I am not now speaking of the first Nuremberg trials, in which the Russians openly participated, to try Goering and the other Nazi leaders. I am speaking of the subsequent war-crirnes trials, which were conducted by American judges, under American law written especially for the purpose. The prosecutors were Americans...

"The other trials were conducted by American judges and American prosecutors according to American laws specifically enacted for that purpose. The difference between them was as great as the difference between day and night. For the second Nuremberg trials we sent from all over the United States judges to try between 2,000,000 and 3,000,000 Germans who were arrested and tried at what were called the denazification trials...

"If the payrolls of the Nuremberg prosecution staff were subpoenaed by the Judiciary Committee, headed by the distinguished Senator from Nevada, it will be seen that PRACTICALLY THE ENTIRE PROSECUTION STAFF WAS COMPOSED OF LEFTISTS AND MEN WHO SINCE THEN HAVE BEEN EXPOSED AS COMMUNISTS, AND MEMBERS OF COMMUNIST-FRONT ORGANIZATIONS. They were, and still are, leftists. The tactics they pursued at Nuremberg were partisan. They were not the sort of tactics we expect to see followed in an American courtroom. They acted under the Moscow principle that the state can do anything to its enemies, and they decided who were those enemies."[61]

The Christian Germans cannot be enthusiastic over the appointment of the pro-Zionist Ike Eisenhower as commander. He restrained General Patton from taking Berlin; he was the first administrator of the Morgenthau Plan and was responsible for stationing Negro soldiers in Berlin.

LEHMAN

Senate Resolution 187, providing for a review of the policy of dismantling German industrial plants, was before the

---

[61] Congressional Record, Decerober 18, 1950, page 16872-4.

Senate on the consent calendar on August 8, 1950. Under the rules of the Senate no resolution or bill can be considered on the consent calendar if there is objection by any senator. The New York Zionist international banker, Senator Lehman, objected. The following is a colloquy between Senator Wheery, minority leader, and Senator Lehman, regarding this resolution:

MR. WHERRY: I was assured by various members of the Senate Foreign Relations Committee that Senate Resolution 187 would be given early consideration. I had hoped it would be agreed to during the call of the calendar. Of course, I realize that any Senator has a right to object...

The first resolution for this purpose had the signatures of approximately 50 senators upon it. All that it calls for is a review of the dismantling program in Germany... We have had this matter before us for two years. For two years we have tried to have this resolution agreed to and now it is here before us on the consent calendar, and it will be impossible to bring it up again before the adjournment of Congress...

MR. LEHMAN: I object.

MR. WHERRY: What is the objection to the resolution, may I inquire?

MR. LEHMAN: I object to both the declarations and conclusions of the resolution and I do not think its adoption is necessary.

MR. WHERRY: Of course, the Senator from New York knows that it will be impossible to bring up the resolution for debate at any other time in the present session.

MR. LEHMAN: I continue my objection to the present consideration of the resolution.[62]

The dismantling and destruction of German factories continues in both the British and French zones. The French profess to fear the revival of German military power, and the British her economic powers, but both need German help to check the March of Bolshevism. Indeed, it is necessary; for if Germany lines up with the comrnunists, Europe is doomed and America is seriously threatened. Senator Lehman knows that this is true. His objection to the consideration of the resolution was to help the communists. It brands him as a communist sympathizer and traitor.

DUAL CITIZENSHIP

Senator Lehman provides an apt illustration of dual citizenship. The Zionists claim to be dual citizens wherever they reside. It is reported that the governments of Greece, Austria, Sweden, and Denmark have acquiesced, and that Britain, France and America will not revoke citizenships on the ground that the Zionists are citizens of the State of Israeli. Never has such privilege been granted to any other nationality or race of people. It is contrary to sound public policy.

No man can serve two masters for he will "forsake the one and cleave to the other." No man can be a Zionist and a Christian, for the Zionists are anti-Christ and anti-Christian. No man can be a communist and a loyal citizen of the United States,- and all Zionists are communists or socialists. The international banker Zionist Senator Lehman, the reputed father-in-law of Henry Morgenthau, should be expelled from the United States Senate and from America.

---

[62] Congressional Record, August 8, 1950.

Lehman is loyal to the State of Israeli and the Zionists, and he is disloyal to America. If the communists win, Zionists and Zionism will win, and we will lose our Christian religion and our Constitutional system of government. His objection to the consideration of the senate resolution served to neutralize Germany in the present war and to help the communists to win it.

Lehman and the other international Zionist bankers are the head and front and the master minds of the American traitors. They secured the appointment of Jno. J. McCloy of the Chase National Bank, and the Zionist Benjamin Buttenweiser of Kuhn, Loeb & Co., as West German administrators in pursuance of the Morgenthau-Eisenhower program. The West Germans are white Christians and would be our friends, despite our brutal treatment of them. What a contrast between the humane administration of Japan by General Douglas MacArthur, and the Morgenthau-Eisenhower administration of Germany!

GEORGE C. MARSHALL
SECRETARY OF DEFENSE

I have doubted the loyalty of General Marshall since the Pearl Harbor disaster and his attempt to communize China. He revealed his true character in the appointment of his two assistants, viz: the Zionists Anna M. Rosenberg and Max Leva. General Marshall was a Roosevelt pet and is now a Truman pet. He appears to be a sanctimonious hypocrite.

8.

VETO OF INTERNAL SECURITY ACT[63]

This bill provided a practical and correct test of loyalty of our government employees. It was not only actively opposed by all of the Zionist members of Congress, but by all of the Zionist political organization, viz: American Jewish Committee, American Jewish Congress, Anti-Defamation League of B'nai B'rith, Anti-Nazi League, Jewish Labor Committee, Jewish War Veterans, and Union of Hebrew Organizations. All of these organizations are political Zionist communist organizations. President Truman vetoed the bill for them and at their request, which is in itself sufficient ground for his impeachment.

Promptly after the President's veto message was read in the House of Representatives, Congressman John E. Rankin of Mississippi said, "This document should be answered on the floor. I have never heard so many mis-statements (lies) in the saxne number of words. I am sure the President did not write it and I doubt if he even read it. It sounds like communist propaganda." (And was).

"The rumor is that Felix Frankfurter wrote it. They say that he and a man named Russell from the Justice Department spent a large part of yesterday and this morning in the White

---

[63] H. R. 9490, Congressional Record, September 22, 1950, page 15672-76.

House preparing this message."[64] Fulton Lewis, Jr., suggested over the radio that the rumor was that the message was written by the President's assistant, the Zionist David Niles (Neyhaus).

Whether the message was written by the Zionist Frankfurter or Niles or some other Zionist, it was a Zionist communist message and a disgrace to the office of president. It is a disgrace to the office of president that the occupant must have Zionist approval of an act designed to restrain them. The President said in his message that the act would *help the communists and not restrain them*. The communists and "fellow travellers" in the House and Senate and the patriots in Congress did not take that view of it. The veto was rejected by a House vote of 286 to 48.[65]

Every communist and communist sympathizer, led by the Zionist Emanuel Celler and the pro-Zionist Franklin D. Roosevelt, Jr., and the communist Marcantonio, voted to sustain the veto. The same was true in the senate, where the vote to sustain was supported by the vote of every communist and pro-Zionist, led by the Zionist Lehman. It was rejected by a vote of 59 to 10.[66]

The President's veto of this bill is another ground for his impeachment. By a vote of about 6 to 1 our representatives in Congress, irrespective of party, have sought to protect our security. Their principal purpose was to intern traitors pending war, as revealed by the act and the discussion of it.

The President, in his lengthy discussion of the bill, did not mention the all important subject of incarcerating

---

[64] Congressional Record, 81st Congress, page 15672.
[65] Congressional Record, 81st Congress, page 15676.
[66] Congressional Record, Sept. 23, 1950, page 15872.

communists. That was the chief objection of the Zionists to the bill. He discussed elaborately (in 5500 words) "thought control business" and the "freedom of expression of opinion." He said, "We need not fear the expression of ideas but we do need to fear their suppression." He said also: "To permit freedom of expression is primarily for the benefit of the majority because it protects criticism and criticism leads to progress." Granted, but what a mockery, coming from Truman, Frankfurter or Niles.[67]

Truman said as to the section of the bill that limited the immigration of aliens: "The bill would deprive our government and our intelligence agencies of the valuable services of aliens in security operations." As charitable as we may want to be toward his Zionist message, we cannot concede that their services are so very valuable. We did pretty well without them before the Roosevelt and Truman administrations and we can manage somehow to worry along without them.

Nor can we accept his assurance that there are no communists in the Executive Department as long as he retains Acheson and Niles. The Executive and State Departments are "lousy" with them. It should be remembered in this connection that Truman still "sits on the lid" and refuses to permit congressional committees to examine their records. By his message the President convicts himself of being pro-Zionist and pro-communist. He obviously prefers them and their welfare to that of the American people, and obviously the Zionists have more influence in our government than our elected representatives in Congress.

---

[67] I hope that the Zionists will take that view of this brief and argument.

PERVERSION OF INTERNAL SECURITY ACT

This measure was designed by Congress to prevent the influx of .Zionist Communists and was opposed bitterly by the President and the Zionists of Congress. Since its enactment the President has not only refused to enforce the law but has perverted it; not a single communist has been confined; and his judges continue to release the convicted communists on technicalities. The immigration officials have applied the law with great severity to the homeless and friendless Germans. Senator Langer said in his speech regarding his visit to Germany:

"However, that is not all. Mind you, Mr. President, more than 200,000 of those persons had applied to come to the United States, under the quotas; but following the passage of that act, their visas were canceled. Why was that done? At one time at Ellis Island, 1,200 persons were stopped. Some of them were the brides of American soldiers. Some of them had sold their furniture. Many of them had given up their jobs to come here."[68]

The immigration officials acted under the authority and by direction of Attorney General McGrath, whose duty it is to enforce the law. A joint committee of twelve Congressmen headed by Senator McCarran from the Senate and Congressman Woods from the House, both democrats, protested this perversion of the act to Attorney General McGrath. He did not deny responsibility but said it was the law and that he was not responsible for writing the law.

This can not be true. The act was scrutinized and debated for a long period of time by the members of Congress, many

---

[68] Congressional Record, Dec. 18, 1950, page 16875.

of whom are able lawyers. It was supported by all of the Christian patriotic members of Congress and opposed by all of the Zionists and pro-Zionists. It was vetoed by the President, presumably on McGrath's advice. He would not have vetoed it if it applied only to the Germans. If it is true then evidently some scoundrel changed the Act after its adoption, and the President was the last person to handle it.

Senator Langer states that the Germans deeply resent their exclusion from America, and justly so. This is confirmed by the recent elections in Bavaria and the other German states in which rearmament was an issue, and the people by an overwhelming majority voted against it; they repudiated Adenaur who advocated it. The allies have proposed that they will lift controls and grant them independence if they will co-operate, but still they refuse. The situation is not helped by the appointment of Eisenhower, their arch enemy, as European commander.

GEORGE W. ARMSTRONG

9.

THE SECOND TRAP

President Truman and his mentor, Dean Acheson, seek to provide a *second trap* for our defeat. They seek to surrender Formosa and China to Russia, and to fight Russia and China *in* Europe where we have no dependable allies.

With the help of the Chinese Nationalists we can defeat them in Asia; but without the help of Germany which we have no right to expect and can not get, we can not do so in Europe. No war is necessary in Asia other than to retain our position in Korea and to arm the Japanese and Nationalist Chinese; but the Zionists urge that we must promptly send an estimated 100,000 troops to Europe in order to protect Europe.

In addition thereto we are told that we must draft our 18 year old boys and tax ourselves to the extent of confiscation; and mobilize our resources and submit to Zionist bureaucratic government and practice self denial. It is to be observed that President Truman, with his yacht and plane and *tax exemptions* and his high salaried Zionist bureaucrats, -does not participate in the privations of war. And he proposes to wage a losing land war in Europe and to send our troops there regardless of Congress and of Germany.

GENERAL IKE EISENHOWER

I do not know whether Mr. Eisenhower is a Swedish Jew as he was reputed to be by his schoolmates at West Point. All that I know about him is "what I read in the papers." And they give him a great deal of publicity. He is a socialist and is president of Columbia University, which has a number of socialist professors and is supported in part by the communist government of Poland. He was a receptive candidate for president on the democratic ticket in 1948 and supported by the A.D.A. and Franklin D. Roosevelt, Jr. and other Zionists. He is now a receptive candidate for president on the republican ticket and is supported by "me too" Dewey and the Zionists. Drew Pearson proposed that he be drafted as a bi-partisan candidate. He reported that President Truman said that "if Ike wants the job I'll nominate him myself."

He was appointed commander of the European Army by Truman and Acheson and the socialist governments of Britain and France. He was Franklin D. Roosevelt's choice for commander of our European Army in the last war. He gave the order that required General Patton to halt his army in order to permit the bolsheviks to capture Berlin, which later made it necessary for us to employ the air lift to feed the people. He stationed Negro soldiers in Berlin who rounded up 4,000 German girls in a tunnel and ravished them. He did not punish these infernal black friends for their terrible crimes.

President Truman sent him on a tour to Germany and our other proposed Atlantic allies. He is reported to have shed crocodile tears over the grave of General George Patton, of whom he was intensely envious, and to have told the German people that he once hated them but now needs their help and that he is willing to "let by-gones be by-gones."

EISENHOWER'S REPORT TO CONGRESS

The Associated Press of Feb. 1, 1951 stated that General Eisenhower "in glittering military uniform" reported the results of his European trip to a joint session of Congress.

He stated that the French would furnish 25 divisions by 1952 or 1953; and that Great Britain and Norway would fight, but did not specify the troops; that he tbougbt he could assemble an army of 6 or 700,000 soldiers; that he was opposed to "dragooning the Germans;" that we *must* send troops to Europe or "wither away and suffer economic atrophy and then finally collapse."

Commenting on Eisenhower's oration, Senator Johnson, democrat of Colorado, said :

"The general character in the General's report was very general. I could find no disagreement with the generalities."

It is to be observed that the General recognizes that he can only get German support by "dragooning" them, which he does not want to do. Congressman Gross of Iowa expressed his estimate of the Eisenhower report as follows:

"According to Eisenhower, if England, if France, if Italy, if all the rest can rise to the patriotic grandeur, we might not need some help.

"Does he mean the kind of help we are not getting in Korea? In other words and according to the Eisenhower formula, if we will provide the ham we will be sure to have ham and eggs, if we will also provide the eggs."[69]

The European countries can not be defended without German help, and the Germans are not likely to enlist under Eisenhower. His selection as commander is, of course, acceptable to the communist British Secretary of Defense Shinwell and to the communist Louis Kahn, France's Secretary of Defense, and to our Secretary of State Dean Acheson, and Felix Frankfurter, for it insures the communism of Europe and probably of the world; and it insures our defeat.

AMERICAN TROOPS TO EUROPE

President Truman appears to have asked Congress for authority to send four divisions, 72,000 men, to Germany, despite his defiant statement that he would send them regardless of Congress. It is reported that we now have two divisions in Germany. The Zionists claim that such a small force is insufficient and that in case of attack may be destroyed. Obviously this is true, and it is also true that six divisions may also be destroyed if the attacking force is large enough.

What do these 36,000 men do in Germany ? What business have we or they in Germany? How much have they cost us and are they now costing us? Who is keeping them there and by what authority and for what purpose? Why not bring them home, together with John J. McCloy and the Zionist Benjamin Buttenweiser, and permit the Germans to govern themselves?

---

[69] Congressional Record, Feb. 5, 1951, page 1023.

The 72,000 troops are not enough to defend Europe against the many millions of Russia and China. President Truman has warned us that the Europeans will soon need a million men for their defense and that we must increase our army to 3,500,000 men and further increase our taxes,-but that still will not be enough.

We are headed for another destructive war. What is the purpose of it, and who are the aggressors? Stalin accuses "Wall Street" which he aptly and truthfully calls our "ruling class." Wall Street accuses Stalin and his Politburo, saying that they are constitutional liars, will not abide by their compacts and plan to conquer the world. They each tell the truth about the other. They are both governed by Zionists and their objectives are the same. They both seek to establish a Zionist Empire and to enslave the Christians. The war is primarily directed against the United States because we are now the principal bulwark of Christianity and freedom. Destroy us, fortify the United Nations, and they have their Empire.

These four divisions (72,000 men) are but an entering wedge, -the beginning of an endless demand for troops for the defense of Europe. The Europeans will eventually get the most of our troops, our munitions and our wealth. It is a lying treacherous scheme to destroy and enslave us. It is a *second trap* by the same traitors who set the first one, and for the same purpose.

England, France, Italy and East Germany are partially communist. The greater part of Europe is now governed by either socialists or communists. It is their privilege. The Europeans have the right to have the sort of government they want without let or hindrance from us. Communism will defeat itself if the people do not want it. Wars will not destroy it; they will only aggravate it. America will not "wither away and die" if we refuse to send an army to Europe, as General Eisenhower asserts. We have lived and thrived with all kinds of European governments and will continue to do so provided we ourselves maintain a good government.

STALIN'S THREAT

It is reported that Stalin threatens that if we re-arm Western Germany that Russia will invade her. We can not regard this as an idle threat, for it is the logical move for Russia to make. Nor will the Germans and our alleged allies so regard it. The probability is that if President Truman sends troops to Europe, as he threatens to do, he will initiate war on the European front while we are as unprepared for it there as we were in Korea.

BOMB RUSSIA

If it is true, as the President asserts, that the communists are determined to conquer and rule the world, and that they will not abide by their agreements, -then there can be no negotiated peace with them, and war is inevitable, and the sooner we have it and get it behind us the better. We can now win it with the A bomb. As destructive as it is, we should employ it, for it is not any more so than a long war. We should bomb Russia without delay.

Major General Orville A. Anderson, commandant of the Air War College, is reported by the Associated Press on September 1, 1950 to have said:

"To assume that the Russians won't use their A bombs if we sit by and watch them build them is a dangerous assumption... Give me the order to do it and I can break Russia's five A bomb sites in a week. And when I went up to Christ I think I could explain to Him that I had saved civilisation."

Why has not the order been given? Why is it necessary to draft one million men and increase taxes and empower the President to control prices and our economy if the war can be terminated in a week's time? The obvious answer is that Truman does not want to destroy the bogey-man. It would destroy his prospective "welfare state."

No one has challenged the truth of General Anderson's declaration, but the Administration answered it by discharging him. By bombing and destroying Russia's five bomb factories they would destroy the bogey-man by which they scare us into appropriations and into war, and the eventual "welfare state" and a communist dictatorship with Zionist dictators. It has been suggested that we use the bomb on the Chinese soldiers who have crossed the Yalu River. But these ignorant soldiers do not know what it is all about. If we must use the bomb in war, the Kremlin in Moscow is the proper target.

THE WELFARE STATE

The purpose of all these shenanigans is the establishment of a Truman dictatorship and a Zionist welfare state. That is what the Zionists have in Russia, with Stalin as dictator. That is what Congress has delegate in the War Production Act of 1950, proposed by Baruch and advocated by Morgenthau. That is what Truman advocates.

God alone can save us from a dictatorship and communism. He will do so if we will only do our part and trust Him and serve Him. We do not deserve His help for we elected Roosevelt and Truman, and the representatives in Congress who have granted Truman the powers of a dictator.

GEORGE W. ARMSTRONG

10.

DICTATORSHIP

In a radio speech December 15, 1950, the President announced an emergency and the appointment of Charles E. Wilson as Director of Mobilization to mobilize our resources and man-power. Soon thereafter he departed in his private yacht, the Williamsburg, for a pleasure cruise. He said in his pronouncement that certain articles were in scarce supply (steel and copper) and should be rationed immediately and that he would specify others later. This is the Baruch Zionist scheme for the purpose of creating a dictatorship, and not for increasing production, as they pretend.

This plan of "increasing production" originated during the Wilson administration and Baruch was our first "War Production czar." It has never yet "increased production" but it has always hampered it and created bureaucratie government with Zionist bureaucrats, and that is the present purpose.

PRICE AND WAGE CONTROL

The President actively opposed the resolution to empower a congressional committee to determine when and to what extent wage, price and rationing controls should be imposed on our economy. He sought to obtain a free hand to regulate it, when and as long as he pleased, and Congress granted it to him by a bi-partisan vote. This means that Frankfurter, Rosenman, Neyhaus (Niles), Acheson, and other Zionists and pro-Zionists will be our dictators. This means also that the communist Zionists will be in control of our government and our economy during the period of the war and probably long afterwards.

Price and wage control and bureaucracy are wholly unnecessary. If this war is in fact only "police action" to enforce the order of the United Nations, we can accomplish it with 200,000 or 300,000 soldiers and without straining our economy; and we can prepare for a still greater war without doing so. In fact, price and wage controls will hamper us.

Truman said apologetically as to price and wage control that "in these fields where price control is imposed, the government will also *undertake to stabilize wages, as the law requires.*" He said also, "in the immediate future a series of control orders will be issued by the Economie Stabilization Agency." DiSalle is the stabilizer, Symington is the Coordinator, Valentine was then at the head of the N.R.B. or the N.P.A., and Ching of the E.S.A. All of these bureaus have been created by the President and salaries fixed and duties prescribed, in violation of our Constitution. The principal purpose appears to be to hold down prices and wages, which is also the purpose in part of the Director of Mobilization.

Truman showed his contempt for Congress by usurping these powers while Congress was in session. The members of Congress are our elected representatives. They alone can create offices, prescribe their duties and fix their salaries. They have the power to remove the president, withdraw from the United Nations and the Atlantic Pact. They have the exclusive power to create emergencies and the office of Director of Mobilization and to prescribe his salary and duties; the President can only recommend.

In his speech of December 15, 1950 he said: "I *am establishing an office of Defense Mobilization. I am appointing* Charles Wilson to be director of this office." Observe the *"I am establishing an office,"* not that "I establish it *subject to the approval of Congress."* He announced that Wilson had accepted, and gave him power to ration certain materials, which he said were scarce; and said that he would ask Congress for additional power.

We don't know much about Wilson other than that he is president of the General Electric Company, that this company is a huge monopoly and that it is controlled by the Zionists of Wall Street. He will be more useful to the Zionists as our dictator than as president of this company. The press reported that Wilson appointed Sydney Weinberg of the international Zionist banking firm of Goldman, Sachs & Co., as his assistant and that Weinberg would select his staff. It does not require the gift of prophecy to predict that they will all be Zionists, and that Weinberg will be our actual dictator. Wilson and Clay, who is at the head of the Continental Can Company, another Zionist outfit, are only ornamental Christian (?) stooges. The firm of Goldman, Sachs & Co. is a Rothschild agency. The Rothschild money power has bankrupted and destroyed the British Empire and they plan to bankrupt and destroy our government.

We do not need a dictator to make us work or to increase production. If given the incentive we will do the work. Congress should dismiss the director of mobilization, and economic and price stabilizers and permit the just law of supply and demand to operate. We will produce more if permitted to do so under our free enterprise system than under bureaucratic control. One is freedom, which we love; the other is slavery, which we abhor.

We work for profit as an incentive, and not from compulsion and fear of punishment. God made us that way.

What if we do make money! The government gets a large part of it in taxes. What if we have a little inflation! It makes it the easier to pay our taxes and debts.

It is infinitely more important to get rid of the traitors in our government than to increase production, or create a bureau for that purpose. We can't win the war with traitors running it; or through the United Nations or the Atlantic Pact.

I nominate General Douglas McArthur for commander-in-chief of our armed forces with power to use the atom bomb when and where needed. If appointed, we will win the war speedily; I predict that it will not continue ninety days longer, and will save multiplied thousands of our young men and our government.

MOBILIZATION PLAN

The Magazine *Time* reported in its issue of Jan. 29, 1951, that:

"The same day that Mobilizer Wilson sounded the call for industrial control President Truman announced that if 'voluntary measures failed' he would use bis present powers and ask Congress for additional ones... to tell employers the numbers and kinds of workers they may have, 2) see that individuals serve in the jobs for which they are best fitted, 3) require the hiring of women and members of minority groups, 4) *import workers* from friendly countries if necessary."

This is the scheme of Frankfurter and other Zionists to establish their dictatorship and to enslave us. It will be put into effect unless Congress intervenes.

The plan appears to be to send our able bodied men and boys, 18 years old and up, to Europe, and put the women to work in the factories and to import aliens (minority groups) to take their places. Thus we will lose our government and our liberty.

This action is the result of an "emergency" which the President illegally declared, and to enforce "police action" by the United Nations which he illegally undertook to do. It is the scheme of a power mad President and his power mad Zionist advisers to overthrow our government. It is for the pretended purpose of increasing production for a war that Russia has not declared and is not in position to wage.

USURPATION OF POWER

These acts of usurpation are in themselves sufficient grounds for the impeachment of President Truman. He flaunts our Constitution and ignores our Congress. He delivers our Government to the Zionists of Wall Street and the Zionist United Nations.

> *"Upon what meat doth this our Caesar feed,*
> *That he is grown so great? Age, thou art sham'd!*
> *Rome, thou hast lost the breed of noble bloods!*
> *When went there by an age, since the great flood,*
> *But it was fam'd with more than with one man?"*[70]

We do not need a dictator to mobilize us and our activities, but we do need a patriot to purge our government of traitors and to win the Russo-Chinese war. I nominate fighting Senator Joe McCarthy for that job. The emergency now exists and the President has declared it. Congress should confirm it and adopt the remedy. Give Senator McCarthy all of the authority that Truman has given or proposes to give Wilson,

---

[70] From Shakespeare's *"Julius Caesar."*

with the authority to withdraw from the United Nations and the Atlantic Pact, to use the A bomb, and to purge our government of traitors and to prosecute them.

IMPEACHMENT AND PROSECUTION

Truman intervened in the Korean War for the purpose of creating a dictatorship. There is strong demand for the impeachment of the President and Acheson, and they should be impeached and prosecuted. Truman's administration was impeached by the electorate in the November election. Congress should confirm it.

The prosecution of Truman's administration should include his appointees and assistants, Frankfurter, Acheson, et al. There is ample ground for Truman's impeachment and prosecution in the fact that he was selected by the traitors Roosevelt and Hillman to betray the United States, and he has done so. Every important act of his administration has been one of treachery and deceit; his selection of the communist traitor Niles, Frankfurter, Acheson, et al, as his advisers; his adherence to the socialist treacherous United Nations; his euchering us into the war with Russia and China; and his usurpation of power.

I grant that these are radical measures but our liberty is at stake. However, they are not any more radical than those proposed by the President and those by which he and his predecessor have brought us to this unhappy state. We must undo, as far as possible, everything they have done during the past twenty years of their rule, and put Truman where he cannot continue to injure us.

INDICTMENT

Harry Solomon Truman should be impeached and prosecuted as a traitor, upon the following grounds:

1. He seeks to subordinate our government to the United Nations, a world super government;
2. He has selected communist traitors as his advisors, viz: Dean Acheson, Felix Frankfurter, David Niles, et al., and his administration is governed by their advice;
3. He seeks to destroy our government by war and excessive taxation;
4. He seeks to establish himself as a dictator and has usurped the powers of one;
5. He involved us in the disastrous Korean war with Russia and China without authority of Congress;
6. He bas ratified the treachery of Dean Acheson who seeks to bring about our defeat in this war;
7. He has not the moral character or intellectual ability or the integrity to fill the highest office of government: he is either a Zionist or a Zionist stooge;
8. He is a socialist or communist and seeks to destroy constitutional government and to establish a welfare state;
9. He failed or refused to enforce the Internal Security Act; and
10. He made the Potsdam agreement with the communists, giving them control of Berlin and East Germany for the purpose of destroying Germany and promoting communism.

Impeachment is a slow and an inadequate remedy. President Truman and his accomplices, including Acheson, Frankfurter; Lehman, Niles, Marshall, Morgenthau, et al., should be prosecuted and punished for treason and as conspirators to commit treason, and the President should be suspended from office pending trial. We are fighting for our lives and our liberty and Christianity, and we cannot win with delays and technicalities and with traitors controlling our government. We can have a mass trial of them as conspirators, where the acts of one is evidence against the others. It may be preferable to have two tribunals and two mass trials, one of the traitors and the other of the communist Zionists.

Congress should then elect a president to serve out Truman's unexpired term. This is indeed a beter system than our present electoral system. It is defensible as an emergency measure at this time, and more so than price and wage control, for there will be a real emergency and not a "cooked up" one. We need a *patriot* as President, who believes in our system of government.

President Truman's first message to the 81st Congress is sufficient ground for his impeachment, for his "Point Four" program is in plain violation of our Constitution and his oath of office. He swore to uphold and defend the Constitution, which he has not done. His Point Four program was not only unconstitutional but involved a change of our government to a *Welfare State*.

There can be no reasonable doubt about the treachery of Dean Acheson. He has surrounded himself with traitors, and his foreign administration has been in the interest of Bolshevik Russia and Zionist Wall Street and Zionist Israeli. His administration of our tariff has been and is to destroy American industries. He condoned the treachery of Alger Hiss; and his law partner is the communist Donald Hiss.

President Truman clings to Acheson knowing him to be a traitor, and despite universal protest. He is reported to have defiantly said in one of his press conferences that Acheson would remain Secretary of State as long as he (Truman) remained President. Let them both go together, for they are "birds of a feather."

What more could an enemy have done to us than Acheson and Truman have accomplished surreptitiously? They disarmed us so that Russia might communize the world. They seek to give Russia all of Asia for that purpose. They seek to destroy our economy and to communize us by free trade and deflation and their Point Four program. *Impeach them and prosecute them as traitors.*

GEORGE W. ARMSTRONG

11.

ZIONISTS

Zionists simply cannot live peaceably with Christians, primarily because they are anti-Christ and anti-Christian. Our moral and political principles and our laws are based on our Christian religion, to which the Zionists are opposed. The moral and political principles of the Zionists are based on their Talmud, which is anti-Christ and anti-Christian. The Protocols represent their political code. They explain the history of the world since they were promulgated, for the Zionist Jews have directed it.

The remedy is obvious. It is the age old remedy that has been adopted by every Christian country, and some of them twice,- England, France and Spain: It is the expulsion of the Zionists. It has always been followed by long periods of peace and happiness in the country that applied it.

Jewish historians admit that it is their religion and rabbis that have prevented their assimilation with other races. They denounce segregation on the part of Christians, but they themselves practice it; segregation is a part of their religion. The Christian is a rare exception who attends a Jewish synagogue or has ever been present at a B'nai B'rith meeting; and no Christian is or ever has been a member of the anti-Defamation League or anti-Nazi League. They are strictly closed to Christians for they are anti-Christian and anti our system of government.

ZIONIST DEPRESSIONS

I have personal knowledge of all of our depressions since 1907 and including it, and can, therefore, write with authority regarding them. In 1907 I was president of the Stock Yards National Bank of Fort Worth and owned three private banks, viz: Geo.W. Armstrong & Co., at Sour Lake, Saratoga and Batson. Suddenly and without warning the officers of all of the banks of the country woke up to the fact that they could not get the money with which to conduct their business.

Under the system that then prevailed, the banks were required to deposit their reserves in banks in reserve cities, and the banks of New York City were the central reserve banks. The New York banks refused to pay their customer banks which in turn caused all other banks to refuse to pay their customers. The New York banks were then the ultimate reservoirs of both currency and credit. Congress created the Pujo Committee to investigate the cause, and the Aldrich Commission to find a remedy. George F. Baker, president of the First National Bank of New York, James B. Forgan, president of the First National Bank of Chicago, and George M. Reynolds, president of the Continental Commercial of Chicago, were witnesses before the Pujo Committee. All of them testified with singular unanimity that there was a "money trust" and that it should be curbed. The Aldrich Commission conducted an extensive investigation and recommended a system which is substantially our present Federal Reserve system.

The frame work of the bill was written by Paul Warburg of Kuhn, Loeb & Co., (who was the actual author of the bill), Davidson of J. P. Morgan & Company, and F. A. Vanderlip, president of National City Bank, at a rendezvous on Jekyll Island. The bill, in its original form, provided for a central banking system, but there was opposition to it by Wm. J.

Bryan and Senator Robert L. Owen of Oklahoma and others, with the result that it was amended, and the original act provided for a decentralized, locally controlled system. It was, in fact, a good banking measure, but these amendments were all soon changed.

The system is now a slick money and credit hoarding and manipulating device and it now controls the economy of the country. It brought about the depressions of 1920, which bankrupted me, and of 1930 and 1937. The Zionist New York banks still dominate it and still control our volume of money and our economy. Tom McCabe, president of a Morgan institution, is now chairman of the Federal Reserve Board and is the active head of it. They have recently applied the screws on installment buying and warned the banks to restrict credit, which they will not disregard. We will have a depression when the management of the Federal Reserve System decrees it, which will be when the Zionist bankers want it.

IMPORTANCE OF VOLUME OF MONEY IN CIRCULATION

Our prosperity is dependent on the volume of money in circulation. Increase the volume and we will have high prices and wages, called "inflation." There is no need for an O.P.A. to regulate them. The Zionists manipulate our Federal Reserve System and inflate to "let the suckers in," and deflate to "squeeze them out," and thus the Zionists have acquired through their control of the exchanges, the greater part of the wealth of the world.

I became a student of the money system and its Zionist authors following my bankruptcy in 1923. I wrote "The Crime of '20," "The Calamity of '30," "The Iniquitous Dawes Scheme," and "A State Currency System, -To Hell With Wall

Street," which were followed by my discussions of the Zionists and their wars...

I made an independent race for governor of Texas in 1932 upon "A State Currency System-To Hell with Wall Street," as my platform, and was defeated. I entered the race for the democratic nomination but withdrew upon the nomination of Franklin Roosevelt for president upon a so-called "sound money" (gold standard) democratic platform.

BANISH THE ZIONISTS

Jewish usury and deception and greed became so offensive to the Christians of other countries that they brought about Jewish pogroms where Jews were killed without trial and without exception. The mere fact that they were of Jewish blood was a warrant of death or expulsion. We, however, have a few good Jews and there were a few good ones at the time they crucified our Saviour. It takes rare courage to be a *Christian* Jew, for they are always ostracized by the Zionist Jews. Christian Jews should not be punished simply because they have Jewish blood.

It is quite easy to segregate them for they have separated themselves into groups of "reformed" Jews and "synagogue" Jews. They have further separated themselves in their societies, the B'nai B'rith, the Anti-Defamation League, the Anti-Nazi League, etc. Every synagogue Jew and every member of the B'nai B'rith should be presumed to be a Zionist communist until proven otherwise; and *contra,* every reformed Jew is presumptively a good American citizen. All members of the A.D.L. and A.N.L. should be expelled.

The Zionists have pointed out the judicial remedy in their Nuremberg mass trial. Congress has taken a long step in the right direction in the enactment over President Truman's veto of the Internal Securities Act of 1950, but which is not likely to be enforced as long as Truman is president. It commands the Administration to imprison the traitors in concentration camps. Our sense of justice and our judicial system require that they be tried before impartial judges and punished according to their guilt. The active traitors should be executed and their ill-gotten wealth confiscated, and the others banished.

This will be a vast improvement over the Zionist Nuremberg farce where the judges were all Zionists or pro-Zionists and made fascism (anti-Semitism) and the service of government, crimes, and prescribed penalties for them. Ignominious death and confiscation of property is the ancient common law penalty for traitors. It is a just penalty for the rich Zionist Wall Street Jews because they have acquired our wealth fraudulently and illegally through their Zionist made wars and depressions.

The effect will be not only to rid our nation of traitors, but to restore its solvency. We should restore the solvency of other Christian countries by appropriating the wealth of the minerals of the Dead Sea and surrounding countries, and dividing it among them, which would *ipso facto* destroy the State of Israeli. This wealth belongs to us by right of conquest, and if it is as rich as it is reputed to be, it will revive every Christian country. If it is taken from the Zionists they will quickly abandon the State of Israeli and migrate elsewhere, and will also abandon their United Nations.

INDICTMENT

I indict the Zionists of Wall Street and their stooges upon the following charges:

1. That they initiated the First World War by sinking the passenger ship Lusitania during the war between Germany and England and France, blaming the act on the Germans. We entered the war for the pretended purpose of establishing the freedom of the seas, as declared by President Wilson; and it resulted in the League of Nations;[71]
2. That they initiated the Second World War through the treacherous destruction of our Pacific fleet with about 3,006 of our Navy at Pearl Harbor during a second war between the allies and Germany and Japan;[72]
3. That the purpose of both the League of Nations and the United Nations was to destroy our nationality and system of government, and to subordinate them to a world government;[73]
4. That the United Nations charter was created under the auspices of Secretary of State Edward Stettinius, of the firm of J. P. Morgan & Co., at a convention in San Francisco, of which the traitor Alger Hiss was chairman. The charter is reported to have been written by Jacob Pasvolsky and Alger Hiss, both of the State Department. The purpose was to establish a Zionist World Empire;
5. That the Zionists were responsible for the concessions made by Roosevelt at Quebec, Teheran and Yalta, and Truman at Potsdam; and for the Morgenthau plan;

---

[71] The Zionists' responsibility is admitted in the British Secret Report No. 1919, called the "Col. E. M. House Letter" which is discussed in my pamphlets *"High Treason"* and *"The Zionists."*

[72] There has never been an impartial investigation of the traitors responsible for this catastrophe. It has been white-washed and hushed up twice. It resulted in the United Nations.

[73] The League of Nations Charter was created by Woodrow Wilson, Lloyd George of England and Clemenceau of France. Wilson's adviser was Bernard Baruch; Lloyd George had as his adviser Philip Sassoon, and Clemenceau's adviser was Georges Mandel (Jeroboam Rothschild). Sassoon and Mandel were descendants of Amschel Rothschild.

6. That they promoted the infamous Nuremberg trials which resulted in the imprisonment and death of thousands of innocent men;
7. That they seek to destroy our system of government and to communize us and our children;
8. That they suppress the truth about their treacherous plans to destroy our government, by intimidation and corruption. The following is a sample of their method.

THE ANTI-NAZI LEAGUE

One of the letters issued by the Anti-Nazi League to its members under date of October 20, 1960, fell into the hands of a friend of mine who passed it on to me. It is here reproduced:

Non-Sectarian

ANTI-NAZI LEAGUE
TO CHAMPION HUMAN RIGHTS, Inc.
165 WEST 46th STREET • NEW YORK 19, N.Y

Cable Address: NOSAN Telephone: PLaza 7-8430

FOUNDED IN 1933
BY SAMUEL UNTERMYER

Officers and Board of Directors

PROF. JAMES H. SHELDON
Administration Chairman

HERMAN HOFFMAN
Chairman, Board of Directors

REV. HENRY A. ATKINSON
Chairman, National Advisory Board

RABBI LEON FRAM
JOHN FREDERICK LEWIS, JR.
Vice-Presidents

ISIDORE LIPSCHUTZ
Vice-President & Treasurer

JULIUS L. GOLDSTEIN
General Counsel

JOSEPH R. APTE
ALGERNON D. BLACK
ADOLPH BRAUN
ABRAHAM CAHAN
AUGUST CLAESSENS
MRS. BERTHA V. COATS

October 20, 1950

Subject: Did the Jews Start the Korean War?

Dear Member:

This is an emergency letter.

Since the start of the Korean war, there has been an unprecedented outburst of anti-Semitic and racistic agitation all over the country.

This propaganda -- which is very heavily financed -- ranges all the way from openly provocative headlines in the CHICAGO TRIBUNE to lurid pamphlets called <u>The Jews Have Got the Atom Bomb</u>.

296

Non-Sectarian

ANTI-NAZI LEAGUE
TO CHAMPION HUMAN RIGHTS, Inc.
165 WEST 46th STREET • NEW YORK 19, N.Y

Cable Address: NOSAN Telephone: PLaza 7-8430

FOUNDED IN 1933
BY SAMUEL UNTERMYER

Officers and Board of Directors

PROF. JAMES H. SHELDON
Administrative Chairman

HERMAN HOFFMAN
Chairman, Board of Directors

REV. HENRY A. ATKINSON
Chairman, National Advisory Board

RABBI LEON FRAM
JOHN FREDERICK LEWIS, JR.
Vice-Presidents

ISIDORE LIPSCHUTZ
Vice-President & Treasurer

JULIUS L. GOLDSTEIN
General Counsel

JOSEPH R. APPEL
ALGERNON D. BLACK
ADOLPH BRAUN
ABRAHAM CAHAN
AUGUST CLAESSENS
MRS. BERTHA V. COATS

October 20, 1950

Subject: Did the Jews Start the Korean War?

Dear Member:

This is an emergency letter.

Since the start of the Korean war, there has been an unprecedented outburst of anti-Semitic and racistic agitation all over the country.

This propaganda -- which is very heavily financed -- ranges all the way from openly provocative headlines in the CHICAGO TRIBUNE to lurid pamphlets called <u>The Jews Have Got the Atom Bomb</u>.

For example: THE BROOM -- West Coast weekly once indicted for war-time sedition -- has just appeared with this full page headline: Prospective Draftee Confused on Jew Problem, Asks For Advice.

This dangerous agitation is already so far advanced as to have become a subject of official concern by the Congressional Committee Investigating Propaganda and Lobbying Activities in Washington.

Gerald L.K. Smith, ring-leader of these trouble-makers, is holding meetings all over the country, stirring up the public to blame the Korean war on "Jewish influences". Taking advantage of press hysteria aroused by the "atom spy" exposures, Smith is pushing a particularly scurrilous pamphlet called Is Communism Jewish?

The same line is reflected by anti-Semitic and former Bundist trouble-makers all over the country.

Behind much of this propaganda is money supplied by the Texas multi-millionaire, George W. Armstrong. This is the man who last year tried

MARK B. DUNLE
MORRIS D. FORASECH
MORRIS N. FRIED
P. GINGOLD
MRS. ANNA GREENBERG
MRS. IRENE HARARI
MRS. LILLIAN HARRIS
ARTHUR J. HARVEY
ABRAHAM H. HOLLANDER
REV. STEPHEN M. JAMES
E. M. LOEW
REV. DONALD G. LOTHROP
ARTHUR L. MALKINSON
IRVING MANZS
EZEKIEL RABINOWITZ
DAVID ROBINSON
GERHARD G. SCHROEDER
PROF. WILLIAM P. SEARS, JR.
MRS TONI SENDER
MRS LISA SERGIO
MAX SILVERSTEIN
HERMANN STERN
DEAN WILLIAM E. TAYLOR
MILTON A. TEPLIN
ANDREW VALUSEK
JOSEPH WHITE
MAX ZARITSKY

to finance a "hate college" with a $50,000,000 endowment -- a huge plot successfully exposed and stopped by the Anti-Nazi League. Armstrong's new book The Zionists argues in effect that the words "Jew", "Communist" and "Zionist" all mean about the same thing.

COMMON SENSE, the bi-weekly published in New Jersey with financial support from Armstrong and similar propagandists, says: "The Zionists... have given word for the outbreak of hostilities in Korea... They are working with the enemy and will retard shipment of supplies and help the Communist forces in any way possible..."

Much of the German language press has taken a similarly bad position. For example, the Chicago Burgerzeitung devoted half of its front page to a reprint of the notorious letter sent by Herman Goering to Winston Churchill just before Goering's suicide, in which Goering insolently declares that future history will show that England and America were wrong in not having supported Hitler instead of fighting against him!

Another example is WOMEN'S VOICE, the Chicago organ of the isolationist "mothers" clubs, which says: "Bring home our boys in Korea... This war is a Jewish conspiracy."

In short, if the Korean war is not to be followed by an unprecedented flood of anti-Semitism and other dangerous agitation, we must have the means to expose and stop these evil propagandists now. <u>The need for the League's work is more urgent to-day than any time since Hitler started his pogroms</u>.

Whenever the League has had the money necessary to carry through an investigation to the point to securing public exposes and court action, we have succeeded. With your help, we will be able to deal with these merchants of evil in the same effective way that we dealt with Fritz Kuhn, The Columbians, or Joseph Kamp (now serving a sentence in prison).

You have long been a regular supporter of the Anti-Nazi League -- and because of the crisis which we now face in connection with this acutely dangerous situation, I appeal to you to send in an additional emergency contribution -- over and above anything you may have already contributed or plan to contribute this year. May we have your reply by the next mail?

Yours for a better America,

James H. Sheldon
Administrative Chairman

JHS:rt

This is my second warning and the second collection taken up by this "League" for use in "dealing with" me and others. The courageous columnist, Westbrook Pegler, said that the

Anit-Nazi League is "a furtive spying organization conducted by Isidore Lipshutz, a Belgian immigrant."[74] It is in fact a lying, spying Zionist communist criminal organization supported by Zionist communist criminals who seek to suppress the truth by bribery and otherwise.

LIARS AND TRAITORS

It is reported that this outfit has 2,000,000 members. It is an executive branch of Zionist Communists, of which the Zionist James Sheldon (whose true name is reported to be Aaron Shapiro) is the "administrative chairman," but the real head is the Belgian alien Zionist Isidore Lipshutz, who is their vice-president and treasurer.

They made a "special appeal" for money on my account on November 29, 1949, in order to "stop the hate factory" (quoting from their letter of that date.) They have not "stopped" me nor can they do so short of murder. I speak for Gerald L. K. Smith and other patriots named in the letter, in saying that each and every one of us would welcome death if necessary to save our Christian civilization and our freedom. Every one of us will be liquidated when and if the Zionists think they can safely have the job done. Our Lord and Saviour, Jesus Christ, denounced these bigoted Zionists as "liars, hypocrites and murderers," and they murdered Him. So they were then, and so they are today.

Their system is spying, lying, bribery and murder. It is the system which they employ in Russia and Poland and that they employed while they governed Germany and·Hungary. It was the plan adopted in the Nuremberg trials and in the trials of Emory Burke, William D. Pelly and others. *They seek always to*

---

[74] The Anti-Nazi League is now taking up a collection for the suppression of Mr. Pegler.

suppress truth. This explains their anti-Semitie and "Genocide" campaigns, and the above letter. It is both their religion and their policy as revealed by their Talmud and Protocols. *They are anti-Christ and anti-Christian.*

The Anti-Nazi League and the Anti-Defamation League are both communist Zionist societies with the same objectives, and composed of liars and traitors. The difference between them is that the Anti-Nazi League is financed and supported by voluntary subscriptions and Isidore Lipschutz, while the Anti-Defamation League is financed and supported by the Zionist B'nai B'rith. They both seek the destruction of our government and of Christians who interfere with their plans. They both employ spies to gather and/or manufacture evidence about Christians; it is reported that the A.D.L. has 2,000 of them.

TRY THE ZIONISTS

The American Zionists established the precedent for their own trials in the de-Nazification Nuremberg trials. They tried between two and eight million Germans *in absentia*.. Senator Langer said of these trials that they were "a sham and not justice," and that they were "aimed .at property rights." It was intended to "try the accused aggressors, convict them of having started a war, and then confiscate their property as a penalty. Thus Moscow hoped to give a death blow to the capitalistic system." He said further that "practically the entire prosecuting staff was composed of leftists, who since have been exposed .as communists and members of communist organizations."[75]

---

[75] Congressional Record, Dec. 18, 1950, page 16874.

The British established a precedent for the banishment of the Zionists in their second expulsion of the Jews. The Parliament enacted a law fixing a time limit for the exodus of the Jews. The act provided that any Jew found in England after a fixed date would be executed, which as I recall, was after six months; and the Jews migrated.

Our situation is different, but the precedent is applicable. We have approximately 15,000,000 Jews and the British had only about 30,000. The Christian Jews estimated at from 15,000 to 50,000, should be protected, and the law should apply only to *Zionist Jews* (communists). All of those remaining here after the expiration of the fixed period should be tried, and if found guilty of Zionism, executed. Membership in Zionist political organizations such as the American Jewish Congress, Anti-Defamation League, and Anti-Nazi League should be conclusive proof of guilt. The probability is that.they would migrate and that there would not be very many to try.

It is estimated that there are 20,000,000 Jews in the world and that we have about three-fourths of them. There has been a great influx during the Roosevelt and Truman administrations, and it continues despite the internal Security Act of 1950. It is reported that they are now pouring in at the rate of 2,200 a day. The immigration officials are Zionist or pro-Zionist and have been for the past twenty years.

TREASON AND TRAITORS

Treason is the worst of all crimes. It is the only crime defined by our Constitution which declares that it shall "consist in levying war against the United States or adhering to their enemies, giving them aid and comfort." Chief Justice Marshall, in the case of the United States vs. Aaron Burr, held that there must be proof of an "overt act of treason by two witnesses," for which he was hanged in effigy. The Constitution leaves it to Congress to fix the penalty. It should be death and confiscation of property. By the common law of England the penalty was "hanging followed by disemboweling and quartering," and confiscation of property.

The United States Supreme Court has held that treason is "a breach of allegiance and can only by committed by one who owes allegiance." It has also held that an alien while domiciled in a country owes a local and temporary allegiance, which continues during the period of his residence.

THE ROTHSCHILDS AND THEIR AGENTS SHOULD BE EXECUTED AND THEIR ILL-GOTTEN GAINS CONFISCATED

These arch traitors are responsible for all of our wars, including the present war, and should be made to pay for them: Their conviction and punishment will establish world peace much more effectively than their United Nations. It will also restore the solvency of our country.

The common run of Zionists should be banished to Russia, the ancient home of the Khazar Jews, or to Madagascar. Let them establish their own government and malte their own living from the soil, as we Anglo-Saxons have done.

Let us have a mass trial of all of the Zionists, as they had of the fascists in Nuremberg, Germany, and punish them according to the degree of their guilt. Every statement in my book, *"The Zionists,"* is confirmed by their record and is true. The most of them are traitors and should be executed. They seek to destroy our Constitution and to promote a welfare state. None of them are loyal to our system of government.

They are all communists or socialists. The spies and traitors that have been found in our State and other departments of government are, with few exceptions, Zionists. There are probably no exceptions, for those who appear to be gentiles may have only changed their names. *They are our enemies and the enemies of our government.*

WAKE UP!

Wake up, my fellow Americans, wake up! I beseech you to wake up. The Zionists have clandestinely imposed on us a welfare state. They operate through Wall Street bankers and the labor leaders. They plan to communize our government and to transform it into a dictatorship. The principal danger is not from Communist Russia but from Zionist Wall Street and the labor leaders; it is not from Stalin, but from Truman and Frankfurter and Acheson and Green and Murray and Reuther.

We have had two Zionist or pro-Zionist scalawag presidents -Roosevelt and Truman- and nineteen years of Zionist rule in the Executive Department of our government. The Zionists are extremely influential in both our judicial and legislative departments. They dominate our financial and economic and publicity systems. We are well on the road to their Zionist World Empire and our slavery. *Awake, my fellow Americans, awake, I beseech you.*

GEORGE W. ARMSTRONG

12.

ISOLATIONISM

The Associated Press of December 20, 1950 quoted former President Herbert Hoover as saying in a radio address:

"America's defense lines must be the Atlantic and Pacific Oceans and not the continents of Europe or Asia. Any attempt to make war on the Communist mass by land invasion through the quicksands of China, India or Western Europe would be sheer folly."

He said further that the prime responsibility of defending Europe rested on the Europeans and that "we should not land another man on their shores or lend them another dollar until they organized and equipped combat divisions of such huge numbers as would erect a sure dam against the red flood."

He proposed "arming the United States Navy and Air Force to the teeth, and to hold the two oceans with possibly one frontier on Britain and the other on Japan, Formosa and the Philippines." He said that "we have little need for large armies unless we are going to Europe or Asia." He recommended that "we give Japan her independence and aid her in arms to defend herself and stiffen the defenses of our Pacific frontier in Formosa and the Philippines."

This is the sage advice of a patriotic Christian statesman. He ignored the Atlantic Pact and the United Nations as peace agencies. We can save our government and Christian civilization by following it, and we cannot do so by following the Truman-Acheson-Frankfurter-Zionist route which is the sure road to destructfon.

Please observe carefully President Hoover's thoughtful language, to wit: "Until they have organized and equipped strong combat divisions," which they can't do without German help. They continue to destroy German factories and throw employees out of work, and they continue to refuse to accept the Germans except as enemies and inferiors. Observe his statement: "With possibly one frontier on Britain," provided of course that the British government wants protection on these terms. He is evidently suspicious, as I am, that this is another Truman-Acheson trap. The British government may not want protection against communism; three members of her cabinet are avowed communists and the others socialists.

What a contrast between this great Christian pro-American republican patriot on the one hand and the pro-Zionist Eisenhower who aspires to be commander of European troops and pro-Zionist "me too" Dewey who advocates sending 6,000,000 troops to Europe. If Congress adopts Mr. Hoover's plan we will not need a substantial addition to our Army or a sales tax or a defense mobilizer, or economic stabilizer or price and wage control, or rationing or a dictator; and we will win the war and preserve our system of government and Christian religion without the sacrifice of thousands of our young men.

President Truman said in reply that this program is "isolationism pure and simple," which is anathema to the Zionists; and so chirped Dean Acheson and John Foster Dulles of the law firm of Sullivan & Cromwell, reputed to be attorneys for J. P. Morgan & Co., and other Zionists. What if it is? It was the foreign policy of President Hoover and of every other

President of the United States except the Jewish Woodrow Wilson and Franklin D. Roosevelt and the pro-Zionist Harry Truman. It is true American policy and will save our country·from bankruptcy and communism.

Led by Congressman Smith of Wisconsin, 118 independent republican members of Congress signed a bi-partisan "Déclaration of Policy." It is a policy that every American who reveres our system of government will endorse. It is as follows:

A Declaration of Policy

"We, the undersigned, conceive that the present position of the United States is dangerous and its future tragic unless the Congress immediately undertakes a reexamination and revision of a foreign policy that in large part has been a costly failure. We submit the following as a suggested basis for our foreign policy:

1. Whatever our future military or political policy is to be, it must be determined with the full participation and approval of the Congress.
2. Make this country impregnable to attack.
3. Reduce nonessential civillan expenditures.
4. Build a strong defense system in the Western Hemisphere.
5. Establish a strong defense line in the Atlantic and Pacific. Refuse further aid of any kind to Western Europe unless persuaded that Western Europe is carrying its full share of the burden. In any case invite Britain and the British Commonwealth of Nations to participate fully in this program.
6. Conclude peace treaties with Germany, Japan, and Austria.

Those who share our views are invited to join us in a fight for survival of American constitutional government and for America itself ."[76]

The Truman-Acheson-Frankfurter program means communism with a dictator. This is obviously their purpose. They will select a pro-Zionist dictator whose powers will be expanded and never terminated. It may mean our military defeat. Probably that is also the purpose. But whether we are defeated or not, they will "spend" us into bankruptcy, which is the Lenin plan of communizing America.

The President proposes to go ahead with his program whether Germany co-operates or not. It is now clear that the people of Germany will not join us for they have said so by an overwhelming majority in plebiscites. It is reported that the people of the other European countries, including England, regard the Korean War as ours and wish to be neutral. The President asked Congress to increase our taxes and to provide 140 billion dollars for the war, and to draft a million more men to the armed services. It appears to be still *another trap*.

There are two methods of establishing communism in America with a dictatorship, and our traitors have adopted both of them, viz: (1) by conquest; and (2) by taxation. The 81st Congress increased the rate of taxation and enacted an excess profits tax, and the President proposes a still further tax increase. The Federal Reserve Board (of which McCabe, of a Morgan institution, is chairman) has frozen two billion dollars of bank reserves, which it is estimated will reduce the lending power of the banks twelve billion dollars. This is for the purpose of deflating values and impoverishing the people, and is a sure plan. It is the method by which all other

---

[76] Congressional Record, Feb. 14, 1951, page 1300.

deflations, since the creation of the iniquitous Federal Reserve System, have been brought about.

WASHINGTON'S FAREWELL ADDRESS

The father of our country, George Washington, prescribed our true foreign policy in his farewell address on September 17, 1796. Every president, and both political parties, have religiously adhered to it up to the time of the pro-Zionist internationalist, Woodrow Wilson, Franklin D. Roosevelt and Harry S.Truman.[77]

Washington, in his farewell address, said:

"Against these insidious wiles of foreign influence (I conjure you to believe me, fellow-citizens), the jealousy of a free people ought to be constantly awake: since history and experience prove that foreign influence is one of the most baneful foes of republican government...

"Real patriots, who may resist the intrigues of the favorite, are liable to become suspected and odious; while its tools and dupes usurp the applause and confidence of the people, to surrender their interest.

"The great rules of conduct for us, in regard to foreign nations, is, in extending our commercial relations, to have with them as little political connexion as possible...

"Our detached and distant situation invites and enables us to pursue a difference course. If we remain one people under

---

[77] The fundamental difference between Washington on the one band and Wilson, Roosevelt and Truman on the other, is that Washington was a sincere patriot who could not tell a lie, and they were all hypocrites who could not tell the truth.

an efficient government, the period is not far off when we may defy material injury from external annoyance; when we may take such an attitude as will cause the neutrality we may at any time resolve upon, to be scrupulously respected; when belligerent nations, under the impossibility of making acquisitions upon us, will not lightly hazard the giving us provocation; when we may choose peace or war, as our interest, guided by justice, shall counsel.

"Why forego the advantages of so peculiar a situation? *Why quit our own to stand upon foreign ground?* Why, by interweaving our destiny with that of any part of Europe, entangle our peace and prosperity in the toils of European ambition, rivalship, interest, humor, or caprice?

"It is our true policy to steer clear of permanent alliances with any part of the foreign world...

"Even our commercial policy should hold an equal and impartial hand; neither seeking nor granting exclusive favors or preferences... constantly keeping in view, that it is folly in one nation to look for disinterested favors from another; that it must pay, with a portion of its independence, for whatever it may accept under that character; that by such acceptance it may place itself in the condition of having given equivalents for nominal favors, and yet of being reproached with ingratitude for not giving more.

There can be no greater error than to expect, or calculate upon, real favors from nation to nation. It is an illusion which experience must cure, which a just pride ought to discard."

That is isolationism. It means to stay at home and mind our own business. The internationalists claim that we need the United Nations to prevent wars, and for our protection. Senator Connally, chairman of the Committee on Foreign Relations, said: "We have the United Nations back of us and it will stay." That is not true; *we* are back of them. The United Nations has been the occasion of our last three wars and it will continue to involve us in war. Instead of its protecting us we are now protecting it, and it will cease to exist when we cease to support it. We should take the necessary steps to liquidate it in an orderly manner.

www.ingramcontent.com/pod-product-compliance
Ingram Content Group Australia Pty Ltd
76 Discovery Rd, Dandenong South VIC 3175, AU
AUHW010738170925
416777AU00015BA/150